The Outrageous Idea
of Christian Teaching

The Outrageous Idea of Christian Teaching

PERRY L. GLANZER AND NATHAN F. ALLEMAN

Foreword by
GEORGE MARSDEN

Oxford University Press is a department of the University of Oxford. It furthers the University's objective of excellence in research, scholarship, and education by publishing worldwide. Oxford is a registered trade mark of Oxford University Press in the UK and certain other countries.

Published in the United States of America by Oxford University Press
198 Madison Avenue, New York, NY 10016, United States of America.

© Oxford University Press 2019

All rights reserved. No part of this publication may be reproduced, stored in a retrieval system, or transmitted, in any form or by any means, without the prior permission in writing of Oxford University Press, or as expressly permitted by law, by license, or under terms agreed with the appropriate reproduction rights organization. Inquiries concerning reproduction outside the scope of the above should be sent to the Rights Department, Oxford University Press, at the address above.

You must not circulate this work in any other form
and you must impose this same condition on any acquirer.

CIP data is on file at the Library of Congress
ISBN 978-0-19-005648-3

To all of those who embodied Christ's words a decade ago when my wife lay in bed for a year recovering from Guillain-Barré syndrome and when I lay in bed almost all of 2017 recovering from pudendal neuralgia, "I was sick and you visited me."
Thank you.
—Perry L. Glanzer

To our faculty colleagues near and far; our brothers and sisters in Christ. To our Baylor HESL and HESA students whose own journeys inspire us to growth and faithfulness.
—Nathan F. Alleman

Contents

Foreword, by George Marsden — ix
Acknowledgments — xiii

Introduction: The Challenge of Identity-Influenced Teaching — 1

1. The Fear of Teachers' Religious Identity: The Historical Origins — 17
2. How Christianity Animates a Teacher's Background Beliefs — 38
3. How Christian Teachers Transform Course Aims and Curricula — 60
4. Thinking and Acting Christianly in the Classroom — 80
5. Is There Really Baptist, Catholic, or Quaker Teaching? The Unique Contributions of Particular Theological Traditions — 103
6. Christian Teaching in the Pluralistic University — 127
7. Identity-Informed Teaching in the Pluralistic University: Important Virtues and Practices — 152
8. In Praise of Diverse Teaching Contexts — 174

When Christian Teaching Is Really Outrageous — 199

Appendix: Methodology — 207
Notes — 215
Select Bibliography — 241
Index — 247

Foreword

Anyone who identities as both a Christian and as a teacher will find *The Outrageous Idea of Christian Teaching* to be a truly valuable guide. For those who teach at Christian institutions, it will be especially useful for learning of the various ways that colleagues around the country relate their faith to their classroom practices. For most such readers this volume will provide helpful, practical suggestions for relating their faith to their teaching. For others who are Christian and thinking about how one's Christian identity ought to be expressed in the setting of the mainstream university classroom, the authors offer very careful advice on how to steer the narrow straits between hiding one's identity and imposing it on one's students.

It has been more than two decades since the appearance of *The Outrageous Idea of Christian Scholarship* (1997), to which the title of this very welcome sequel alludes. My little volume was in turn a sequel to *The Soul of the American University: From Protestant Establishment to Established Nonbelief* (1994). The impetus for writing *The Outrageous Idea of Christian Scholarship* was to answer some objections from respected academics who said that the prescriptions I offered at the end of my larger historical study were indeed outrageous. Those prescriptions were along the line of arguing that if mainstream universities were as truly pluralistic as they claimed to be, they should welcome a range of self-identified Christian and other religious perspectives along with varieties of secular viewpoints. In *The Outrageous Idea of Christian Scholarship* I attempted to show that Christian scholarship, including teaching (though admittedly not as the primary focus), was not outrageous if properly conducted.

Much has changed in American higher education since *The Soul of the American University* appeared 25 years ago. For one thing, I think the idea of "established nonbelief" that I used in my subtitle may be dated. My idea was that, much as in the nineteenth century there had been an informal Protestant establishment in mainstream American colleges and universities, by the 1970s that had largely dissipated, leaving an informal establishment of the rule that the highest forms of learning involved strictly secular viewpoints. Like the earlier Protestant establishment, the establishment of that secularist viewpoint was always informal and imperfectly enforced. But it was strong enough that its proponents could talk as though it were a self-evident consensus that traditional religious perspectives were unsuited for the highest echelons of the academic mainstream.

Today it would be hard to say that there is consensus about much of anything in mainstream American universities. Rather, it seems as though fragmentation and splintering are appropriate images for the direction things have gone.[1] Those trends were certainly already emerging in the 1970s and 1980s, but now they seem to have come to fruition. Laudable celebrations of diversity have evolved into competing tribes shaped by identity politics, grievances, and demands for protection. Even though most mainstream campuses have been spared from the worst sorts of such divisions, all have to tread lightly to avoid offenses. It seems safe to say that most American universities lack a "soul" in the sense of "a clear identity, story and purpose."[2] Almost no one seems happy about the recent state of affairs, as can easily be demonstrated by a steady stream of books and articles lamenting the state of the universities. Especially prominent have been laments over the state of the humanities. The humanities used to provide the chief source for the hope that undergraduate education, even without expressly religious teachings, might help guide at least some students toward wisdom, virtues, and civic responsibilities. Today the humanities are marginalized themselves, fragmented into competing sects and facing crises in enrollment. In a consumerist era when higher education is seen primarily as a way to improve one's vocational and economic prospects, relatively few students see mainstream universities as a place that might help them acquire a coherent philosophy of life. And while guidance toward such coherence may be found in some individual classrooms, it is not likely to be discernible in the institution as a whole.

Such fragmentation suggests that more room may be open in mainstream higher education for traditional religiously informed perspectives than may have been true in the 1970s and 1980s. How teachers might properly express perspective in mainstream classrooms is a very delicate business, and that is a matter concerning which the present volume provides some valuable guidance. In honoring various identities in today's highly pluralistic academy, religious identities often are mentioned, at least in a formal way. That recognition is aided today by growing sensitivity to the need to honor some of the scruples of Muslim students and teachers. Traditional Christians, especially white Protestants, are often more suspect, in part because they may be regarded as political conservatives and not fully open to the rights of some other minorities. Nonetheless, by now most of the intellectual grounds for trying to exclude traditional religious perspectives from the academic mainstream have proven shaky. The myths of objectivity and that advanced scientific models for thought provide the gold standard for all thought have, except in a few sectarian circles, been thoroughly exploded. By now it has been well proven that if traditional religious perspectives are presented with intellectual integrity and sensitivity to pluralistic environments, they can take their place among the perspectives represented in the academic mainstream.

Part of the reason for the improved prospects for acceptance of traditional Christian perspectives in the academic mainstream is the remarkable renaissance of an academic community of self-identified Christian scholars that has blossomed in recent decades. In the United States that renaissance is centered in the well over 100 schools of the Council for Christian Colleges and Universities. The faculties of these schools are the main sources for much of the wisdom regarding teaching found in the present volume. They also are likely to be a principal group of its readers. These faculties now form the core of one of the most impressive academic communities there is. For the past generation, highly talented young people with traditionalist Christian perspectives have been crowding into graduate programs, including at many of the best universities. The result has been that Christian colleges and universities have been able to build stellar faculties. And increasing numbers of other committed Christian professors are quietly taking places in the academic mainstream. In just about every field, traditionalist Christians can find many like-minded colleagues, including some who are well published. Traditionalist Catholics and Protestants are increasingly finding common ground. Furthermore, unlike most academic communities, this widespread community of Christian scholars is truly interdisciplinary. It is also becoming increasingly an international academic community as Christian academic institutions are developing around the globe.

Many teachers in that diverse international community of scholars who share similar faith will find the present volume useful and encouraging.

Though various biases persist today against traditional Christian perspectives, in the fragmented academy the same might be said of just about any perspective. Almost every viewpoint has its opponents who would like to shout it down. So there is good reason to believe that if

Christian teachers do their jobs well with integrity and are evidencing the virtues that are integral to the faith, such as love of neighbor, civility, humility, patience, kindness, goodness, long-suffering, and compassion, then they will be effective witnesses to their faith and contributors to the good of the human community.

George Marsden

Acknowledgments

Writing a book is certainly a community endeavor. We received aid from numerous friends, colleagues, and total strangers. Offering our appreciation to these individuals is the least we can do, although we in no way hold them accountable for any inevitable deficiencies, for which we alone are responsible. The origins of this book lie in a conversation with Paul Corts and the discussion of the idea for the survey that informed the backbone of the book. We are thankful for Paul Corts and the Council for Christian Colleges and Universities (CCCU) and their initial support for this survey. We are also grateful for the other members of the team who worked diligently on the survey, Phil Davignon and Jesse Rine.

This book would not have been possible without the willing responses of thousands of dedicated faculty members working at CCCU member institutions across the United States. Their work at colleges and universities that are generally ignored by the higher education status industry provides a quality and vitality of educational engagement often absent from institutions known for acquiring grants and athletic championships. That the work of these faculty members is deeply rooted in their Christian faith and tradition is all the more important and illuminating. This book is because of, and for, them.

At Baylor University, Jessica Robinson and Cara Cliburn Allen offered their valued assistance in terms of editing the manuscript. In particular, we are grateful to Jessica for offering numerous broad insights and editorial suggestions that influenced the shape of the final manuscript. We also received helpful suggestions from graduate student readers in one of our classes.

From Perry: I dedicate this book to our family, church community, and Baylor community members who helped our family endure two major health crises. Before my very first academic sabbatical, my wife was struck by Guillain–Barré syndrome. As she lay in bed for a year and I tried to care for a three-year-old and first grader, they all came to our rescue. Our Sunday school class brought meals for that entire year. Then, this past year when I was struck by pudendal neuralgia and could not walk or even sit for more than a half hour, our families and the Baylor community again brought meals and visits that helped sustain me while I lay in bed for a year. I am especially appreciative to all our PhD graduate students, who gave of themselves to bring meals as well as intellectual food. Thanks especially to my wife's sister, Coralee Reynar, and my best friend, Mark Mahler, who were there for me during the most difficult and painful times when I could not think straight or pray. You thought and prayed for me and comforted me. Finally, I'm thankful for the support of my wife, Rhonda, and the gift of our children, Bennett and Cody. Rhonda, your love sustained me during those dark, painful days. Thank you.

From Nathan: I would also like to dedicate this book to my coauthor Perry Glanzer. This text was formed during, and perhaps in part through, a time of incredible personal difficulty. Throughout the health crisis alluded to above, his honesty, humanity, and willingness to share his struggles with his students and colleagues was a reflection of the faithful pursuit of Christ that his life exemplifies. I am humbled and honored to be part of his personal and professional journey, here in the form of this book.

Perry L. Glanzer
Hewitt, Texas
Nathan F. Alleman
Waco, Texas
Advent 2018

Introduction

The Challenge of Identity-Influenced Teaching

The day after September 11, 2001, I (Perry) walked into my social philosophy class at RUDN University in Moscow with a heavy heart. We had been reading John Rawls's *A Theory of Justice*, a philosophical classic about how a liberal democratic state should justify its political arrangements. That day, though, I did not feel like discussing abstract philosophical questions, and I knew my Russian students at this state-funded, public university would want to discuss recent world events as well. I also recognized from our discussion about Rawls and the moral foundations of liberal democracy that I had a mixture of students with various political views in class, some of them sons and daughters of Communist Party members.

Before coming into the classroom that day, I had experienced some of the same emotions that many Americans had: sadness, grief, anger, and yes, a desire for an Old Testament, eye-for-an-eye form of justice. I am an American, after all, and in my view, terrorists had unjustly attacked American civilians. Still, I knew I needed to rein in the feelings associated with my American identity.

At that moment, however, I also knew that I could not restrain the passions this event might arouse in my students. Moreover, I knew that good teaching meant that I should not try to contain them completely. The emotions were too raw and the event too close. Still, I began the day's discussion by controlling my own painful emotions related to my American identity that might lead me to impose my voice and perspective upon students. Instead, I began class by asking a question related to the topic of justice, about which we had been talking: "Do you think America deserved the attacks yesterday?"

I found it sobering, but also oddly invigorating, to encounter a whole range of responses among my Russian students: one-third expressed deep sympathy toward America and those killed, one-third said they were unsure, and another third defended the view that America deserved the attack. I appreciated the first group's sympathy as well as the latter group's honesty. I had tried to create a space for this kind of openness by acknowledging every country's strengths and shortcomings. Overall, my desire to create a space for thinking critically about justice in countries came fundamentally from my Christian identity and its intellectual tradition. In these conversations, I often said, "Just like families, every country contains cultural vices but also has certain cultural virtues. And just like families, there are some countries you would rather live in than others." This was my attempt to encourage students to be honest about the sins and virtues of a country as well as to foster their critical thinking about justice.

So I reined in my desire to criticize the fault-finding students' apparent lack of empathy about the civilian deaths, as well as a strong desire to convert them to a position originating solely from my American identity. After the opening question, we proceeded to have the liveliest discussion we had thus far in that semester. The conversation linked some of the profound questions of justice, virtue, and identity we had been discussing on a philosophical level. The experience provided me with a powerful reminder of how one's identity influences one's thoughts and emotions when teaching about a profound historical event. It also reminded me how our non-teaching identities can enhance or interfere with important teaching opportunities.

The Controversial Conflict

In this book we focus on this key controversy regarding the practice of teaching. The core point that we address is the basic truth that teachers are not solely teachers. They may also be spouses, parents, Democrats or Republicans, Jews or Muslims, environmentalists, feminists, or members of a particular country, ethnic or racial group, or sexual identity to name some examples.

All these identities orient us morally and metaphysically. As Charles Taylor observes, "[T]o know who you are is to be oriented in moral space, a space in which questions arise about what is good or bad, what is worth doing and what is not, what has meaning and importance for you and what is trivial and secondary."[1] When a person becomes a mother or father, for example, she or he immediately inherits the moral tradition within our culture about what it means to be a good mother or father. The person may reject this tradition, but it still exists.

Furthermore, when we try to be good or excellent in any of our identities, such as being a good teacher, a good mother, a good citizen, a good environmentalist, or a good Christian, these identities and the moral traditions associated with them may come into conflict. In this respect, although our identities orient us morally within particular traditions of thought and practice, they also can cause moral problems. After all, we each have multiple identities. Many of these identities connect the individual to moral traditions linked to historical narratives and metaphysical metanarratives, from which the teacher may derive particular moral ends, virtues, rules, and practices.[2] Thus, teachers interested in pursuing the good life in every dimension of their lives must not only try to figure out what it means to be a good teacher; they must also contemplate what it means to be "good" in each of these identities (e.g., being a good spouse, parent, woman, Muslim, Democrat), then prioritize their identities when moral conflicts occur.

One of the most important life questions concerns how we prioritize, mesh, and draw boundaries among our different identities. The answer to this question lies in how we organize and mix the normative ideals associated with these identities and their associated moral traditions. There may be plenty of overlap among being a good teacher, a good feminist, and a good Muslim, but these identities may also produce conflicts. Consider how the female teacher with these three identities decides what to wear to class. Each of the three identities may provide her with particular ways of thinking about or expressing her response to this decision ("dress professionally" [teacher identity], "dress modestly" [Muslim identity], and "dress to express yourself and your voice" [feminist identity]).

We do not necessarily think teachers are unique in this regard. Individuals in any other employment or social role may seek congruence and consistency among their various roles. Still, there is something unique about being a teacher that conjoins and creates an unusual confluence of these elements. Teachers are not just performing tasks, as a dentist does; rather, their identities inform how they think about their teaching outcomes, the subject matter they present to students, their views of the students themselves, and the pedagogical choices they make. Moreover, young people will look to them as models (or examples of what to follow or not to follow) of how to be excellent not only in a particular field of study (e.g., biology, the visual arts, English literature), but also in other areas of life (e.g., marriage, citizenship, friendship). They likely do not look at their dentists, doctors, or bankers the same way.

One of the areas in which there is a wide degree of disagreement for teachers concerns the answers to the following key question: *How can or should one's other identities outside of being a teacher, along with their associated narratives, virtues, practices, and so forth, inform one's teaching?*

If one thinks that these additional identities and their moral standards can and should influence one's teaching, other questions immediately arise: When and how should these various identities be combined? Should other identities sometimes supersede one's identity as a teacher? If so, when? When should we maintain sharp boundaries between identities?

A common principle used to guide teacher conduct in the classroom, academic freedom, fails to help us answer these questions. Consider the American Association of University Professors' (AAUP) "1915 Declaration of Principles" regarding this matter:

> It is scarcely open to question that freedom of utterance is as important to the teacher as it is to the investigator. No man [or woman] can be a successful teacher unless he [or she] enjoys the respect of his [or her] students, and their confidence in his [or her] intellectual integrity. It is clear, however, that this confidence will be impaired if there is suspicion on the part of the student that the teacher is not expressing himself fully or frankly, or that college and university teachers, in general, are a repressed and intimidated class who dare not speak with that candor and courage which youth always demands in those whom it is to esteem. The average student is a discerning observer who soon takes the measure of his [or her] instructor. It is not only the character of the instruction but also the character of the instructor that counts; and if the student has reason to believe that the instructor is not true to himself [or herself], the virtue of the instruction as an educative force is incalculably diminished. There must be in the mind of the teacher no mental reservation. He [or she] must give the student the best of what he [or she] has and what he [or she] is.[3]

Although this description of enacted academic freedom suggests that the good teacher must be fully true to himself or herself, it does not answer the question of how to do that well. It also does not answer the question of how to adjudicate different identities that make up the self. What if offering the best of themselves means imparting general life wisdom that is shaped by their identities as Muslims, feminists, environmentalists, or atheists? What if it involves seeking to convert students to these identities? Alternatively, what if "giving the student the best of what [we] have and what [we are]" as faculty members means using these identities as the primary lens for teaching critical thinking? Should a Democrat then organize an English composition class around learning to analyze Fox News—a classroom experience one student described to us? Alternatively, as another student shared regarding a former professor, should a Republican spend significant periods of class time in a soil conservation class criticizing the environmental policies of a more left-leaning, Democratic administration?

Some basic ethical advice has been offered by a few past scholars. Consider Stephen Cahn's summary advice to professors in his book about the ethics of teaching: "[A] faculty member ought to guide students through a field of study, not seek to be their psychiatrist, friend, or lover."[4] Despite the clear boundary presented in this statement, the lines demarcating when one enters into these roles are not exactly clear. Moreover, others might restrict or expand these roles depending on the faculty member's situation or environment. For example, the AAUP "Statement on Professional Ethics" claims that "professors demonstrate respect for students as individuals and adhere to their proper roles as intellectual guides and counselors."[5] While both Cahn and the AAUP agree that the professor should be an intellectual guide, it is not at all clear that they agree about his or her role as "counselor." Similarly, the claim that a teacher should not be a student's friend is also a contentious matter. Although most faculty members would likely agree that friendship with a student could result in the corruption or undermining of their responsibilities to students within their specific teaching roles, it is not clear that these roles must or even should be exclusive.

This book does not claim to address all the difficult matters that arise from the dilemma of how our various identities interact with the identity of being a teacher. Instead, we focus primarily on the relationship between two particular identities—being a Christian and being a teacher—and answer the following questions: (1) *How does being a Christian change one's teaching?* and (2) *How should being a Christian change one's teaching?* While addressing the latter question, we also deal with the following related questions: What forms of expression or integration are appropriate in different university contexts? By what or by whose standards do we judge?

We think the answers to the first, empirical question are best discovered by interpretive research about how Christian professors actually claim to incorporate their Christian identity into their teaching practices. Since the answer to this question will vary by situation, the first context in which we explore answers to this question is the Christian college or university. We choose this focus because Christian teachers in a Christian context have the most freedom to explore the answer to this question in depth. These institutions also provide their faculty members with a great deal of incentive to engage in these types of conversations. In particular, we examine the answers from professors at a set of Christian institutions that claim to give primary attention to the integration of faith and learning. Once we understand the range of ways these Christian professors answer this question, we can then better explore the implications of these findings for our second, normative question in both the Christian context and the pluralistic university. It is especially in the latter context that one encounters the most polarized arguments regarding the answer to our question of whether one's Christian identity should influence one's teaching. Consequently, we think it is important to gain some understanding of the current conversation regarding identity-informed teaching in this context.

Ordering Our Identities in the Pluralistic University: The Two Sides of the Argument

Two types of arguments represent the various answers to the normative question at the heart of this book. First, although Stanley Fish does not address this matter specifically in *Save the World on Your Own Time*, his general argument clearly answers the question in two ways. If professors are teaching within faith-based contexts, Fish sees no problem with the integration of their religious identities into their teaching practices.[6] In contrast, for a pluralistic university context he sets forth a position that requires teachers to prioritize only one identity: the professional professorial identity their institutions have hired them to fulfill.

We can identify ends associated with any identity that help us evaluate what it means to achieve excellence in that specific role. Fish argues that when teaching at a pluralistic university, professors have two ends: "(1) Introduce students to bodies of knowledge and traditions of inquiry they didn't know much about before; and (2) Equip those same students with the analytical skills that will enable them to move confidently within those traditions and to engage in independent research should they choose to do so."[7] When administrators evaluate the job of a teacher, according to Fish they should do so "on the basis of academic virtue, not virtue in general."[8] Specifically, teachers should be evaluated according to the following commonly agreed upon standard that Fish describes: "Teachers should show up for their classes, prepare lesson plans, teach what has been advertised, be current in the literature in the field, promptly correct assignments and papers, hold regular office hours, and give academic (not political or moral) advice."[9] As the words in the parentheses indicate, teachers should not become advocates for political and moral beliefs and values that derive from nonacademic identities. Fish argues, "Neither the university as a collective nor its faculty as individuals should advocate personal, political, moral, or any other kind of views except academic views."[10] According to this stance, integrating one's other identities and moral commitments into one's teaching role invites extraneous moral commitments and traditions into the classroom. Fish applies his argument to all teachers, whether they are feminist, Muslim, environmentalist, or libertarian faculty members.

Fish recognizes that teachers inherit or adopt various identities over the course of their lives, although it should be noted that he characterizes these as "formative beliefs" and not identities. He insists that while these beliefs are important, we do know how to adapt ourselves to certain conventions that allow us to operate solely within one set of identities, beliefs, and behaviors. To this end, he notes, "We understand, for example, that proper behavior at the opera differs from proper behavior at a ball game, and we understand too that proper behavior at the family dinner table differs from proper behavior at a corporate lunch. . . . [W]e are perfectly capable of acting in accordance with the norms that belong to our present sphere of activity, even if our 'take' on those norms is inflected somewhat by norms we affirm elsewhere."[11] Fish goes on to point out that we also learn how to refrain from expressing religious or political opinions in certain contexts, and those who do not learn these things are often the object of ridicule and satire. Most important, Fish claims that professors are being "unprofessional"[12] when they act in this manner.

The key behavioral distinction that Fish makes between professional activity and moralizing is "academicizing" and "recommending." Recommending a particular point of view, Fish claims, "is what you do when you are a parent, or political activist, or an op-ed columnist."[13] Academicizing is what professors do. Faculty members take a topic and "*detach it from the context of its real-world urgency, where there is a vote to be taken or an agenda to be embraced, and insert it into a context of academic urgency, where there is an account to be offered or an analysis to be performed.*"[14] One can see how the importance of particular identities functions in Fish's argument. Possessing certain identities, such as that of parent or political activist, allows a person to engage in broad forms of moral argumentation or persuasion, since different overarching ends are pursued. Fish insists that professors must limit themselves to a particular type of activity that largely excludes this broad form of moral advocacy. His argument hinges on the important claim that the activities associated with these additional identities often pose a threat to the ultimate goals of teaching that must guide professors in a pluralistic university context.

For Stanley Fish, boundaries between identities and their associated practices are vitally important. In fact, Fish goes so far as to insist that the other identity roles that a faculty member inhabits can have little influence on teaching. He claims that "teaching is a job. . . . [W]hat it requires is not a superior sensibility or a purity of heart and intention—excellent teachers can be absolutely terrible human beings, and exemplary human beings can be terrible teachers—but mastery of a craft."[15] We agree with Fish that teaching is a craft that requires the same type of work to master as other crafts. Our concern, however, is whether other aspects of one's identity and the moral traditions associated with these identities matter.

It is helpful to compare Fish's view to a very different argument from Parker Palmer, a scholar who claims: "[G]ood teaching comes from good people."[16] In *The Courage to Teach*, Palmer makes this assertion because he ultimately thinks that the key to good teaching has less to do with the "tips, tricks, and techniques" of the teaching craft and more to do with the connections between being a teacher and our broader human identities.[17] He sets forth this view in his central thesis: "*Good teaching cannot be reduced to technique: good teaching comes from the identity and integrity of the teacher.*"[18] This outlook differs substantially from conventional education that "strives not to locate the self in the world, but to get it out of the way."[19]

Palmer wants to emphasize the importance of connecting one's whole self—not just one's professional self—to one's subject and one's students. In this vein, Palmer unpacks what he means a bit more:

> [I]n every class I teach, my ability to connect with my students, and to connect them with the subject, depends less on the methods I use than on the degree to which I know and trust my selfhood—and am willing

to make it available and vulnerable in the service of learning. . . . Bad teachers distance themselves from the subject they are teaching—and in the process from their students. Good teachers join self and subject and students to the fabric of life.[20]

Palmer's definitions of "selfhood" and "identity" relate to the other parts of our humanity that go beyond an individual's professional identity. In fact, Palmer defines identity broadly as "an evolving nexus where all the forces that constitute my life converge in the ministry of self: my genetic makeup, the nature of the man and woman who gave me life, the culture in which I was raised, people who have sustained me and people who have done any harm, the good and ill I've done to others, and to myself, the experience of love and suffering—and much, much more."[21]

This broad definition includes all the other parts of ourselves and our environment that encompass the various aspects of our identity. In other words, Palmer's understanding of identity includes our experiences as sons and daughters, members of particular social groups, and much more than Stanley Fish's more-limited focus on the sole professional role that teachers fulfill.

Palmer continues by describing Alan, his ideal model of what it means to be a good teacher. One of the things that makes Alan a good teacher is the way he connects his teaching to what Palmer calls the "sense of craft."[22] Palmer recalls: "Alan taught from an undivided self—an integral state of being central to good teaching. . . . In the undivided self, every major thread of one's life experiences is honored, creating a weave of such coherence and strength that it can hold students and subject as well as self. Such a self, inwardly integrated, is able to make the outward connections on which good teaching depends."[23]

While Fish insists on drawing boundaries between one's other identities and associated moral traditions and fears their corrupting influence, Palmer advocates doing the exact opposite. He maintains that good teachers know how to connect themselves and their various identities to the subject and their students. Indeed, Palmer spends little time talking about the proper boundaries teachers should draw with their students (e.g., "do not be a lover, counselor or friend"; "do not bring in outside moral traditions") and devotes much more time to providing insight into how to connect with both a subject and students. For Palmer, knowing is a relational task. Therefore, good teachers must establish intimate, loving relationships with both their subjects and students, since the "origins [sic] of knowledge is love."[24] Where and how we should place appropriate boundaries around this intimacy is not as much a concern for Parker Palmer as it is for Stanley Fish.

The Focus of This Book

Overall, we find ourselves agreeing and disagreeing with both Fish and Palmer. We think the power and popularity of each of their arguments stem from their simplicity. Yet we also think that this austerity is ultimately their weakness. The relationship between our various identities or parts of ourselves and the practice of teaching is much more complicated than these works suggest.

Consider our opening story. When I (Perry) restrained the emotions I felt due to my American identity in the classroom, why did I do it? Did I simply feel the call to be a dispassionate, objective teacher? I knew the weaknesses and ultimate futility of that approach and rejected much of what it entailed. Yet I still held back, not simply from a desire for self-protection or due to my academic socialization but because of my sense that underneath this vision still lay a valid desire to promote student learning and enact justice in the classroom. Perhaps most beginning Christian teachers *should* focus on the various moral admonitions that Fish and Cahn provide and not fret as much about how to integrate their Christian identity into their teaching. As Fish argues, simply doing their jobs would keep beginning faculty members very busy and even likely help them be good, and possibly even great, teachers.

If this argument is true for professors who are "just starting out," then why should we talk about the other, more holistic dimension that Parker raises? We also agree with Palmer that integrating one's identity is the key to becoming a great teacher. Consider again the opening story. I (Perry) held back integrating one identity (American) for reasons related to another identity (Christian). This kind of moral reasoning is not uncommon among Christian teachers.

Here the crucial point is that we contend that Christian professors must undertake the endeavor to connect and merge identities thoughtfully, ethically, and for Christians, "Christianly." A great deal of sloppy thinking exists around this topic that often reduces the options to simplistic dichotomies: discipleship or indoctrination versus true teaching. William Perry has long noted that simple dichotomies are what we should expect of early undergrads; however, we should not expect such things from professors who are supposed to be expert teachers or from the universities.[25] Yet consider the experience of Catholic literature professor Chris Anderson, who teaches in a pluralistic university setting. He observed, "The university either ignores my faith or sees it as a potential problem."[26] He notes:

> When I first read Palmer urging teachers and students to live "divided no more," to act with "integrity," no longer disguising their real identity and commitments, I said, "yes, of course," in a general way. But for a number of reasons "congruence" like this didn't seem to apply to me as a Catholic Christian in a contemporary university. In my case, congruence seemed more dangerous and problematic than for a feminist, or an environmentalist or a person of color.[27]

As this quote reveals, Anderson experienced the tension between Palmer's admonition to teach from one's whole self and Fish's guidance to draw boundaries. Not surprisingly, many educators believe that particularly when it comes to religion, we need to make sure these teachers draw strong boundaries between their identities. What makes Fish's argument somewhat refreshing is that he thinks that all teachers—the feminist, environmentalist, and Christian alike—need to think about drawing clear boundaries. Still, we want to suggest that the relationship between our teaching identity and any additional identities in a pluralistic setting requires both the courage to find congruence *and* boundary drawing between these roles. As can be readily seen, this requires a complex approach.

We believe that the basis for this approach involves recognizing three claims. First, we maintain that our identities consciously and unconsciously influence our teaching. As professors develop, they should become conscious of how their identities influence their teaching. After all, part of being a critical thinker is learning how to order the priority we place on our specific identities in particular situations. The first part of this book uses empirical examples from Christian faculty members at institutions associated with the Council for Christian Colleges and Universities (CCCU) and examples from the growing literature on this topic to help us understand the multiple and complex ways this applies in a Christian context.

Second, the role that those identities should play in our teaching depends on the identity of the institution. We believe that maximally advantageous and proper integration will look different in different environments, Christian and pluralistic alike. Navigating different institutional terrains requires understanding both the unique forms of integration and the important boundary markers required at each institutional type.

Third, what we need is a clear ethical understanding of how this integration (or lack thereof) should happen. Unfortunately, professional standards simply do not provide enough guidance or persuasive power to assist faculty members in these matters. Moreover, many people believe the moral traditions associated with their other identities should inspire and inform their teaching practices. Thus, one question that we explore and answer concerns the way teachers can and should go about integrating the moral traditions associated with their other identities with a more general ethical tradition of teaching.

We wrote this book with two audiences in mind. First, we wrote this for Christian teachers who want to learn from Christian faculty members who draw upon their Christian faith to animate their learning. We hope that this will inspire this group of readers to think more deeply about what this practice may mean in denominational, generally Christian, or more pluralistic higher education environments. Second, we wrote this book for those who are doubtful that Christianity can or even should influence teaching, particularly in a pluralistic context. We want these readers to understand the complexity of identity intersection in this particular case.

In this respect, we envision this book as a companion volume to George Marsden's influential work, *The Outrageous Idea of Christian Scholarship*. In that book, Marsden made the case that the pluralistic academy should welcome and perhaps even encourage scholarship from the perspective of particular religious traditions. Interestingly, a professor named Bruce Kuklick had a Stanley-Fish-like concern about Marsden's proposed accommodation: "It is hard to believe that Marsden actually means what he says. . . . Does he think that at his university, Notre Dame, they teach a Roman Catholic chemistry? . . . Would Calvin College actually devote itself to a Presbyterian anthropology or worry that Episcopal psychology should get a hearing? Should historians of the Reformation be primarily identified as Protestant, French or female?"[28] In contrast to Kuklick's position, Marsden held that an individual's cultural, social, and religious situated-ness fundamentally shapes how he or she interprets historical events (e.g., the Protestant Reformation,) and how he or she understands certain phenomena (e.g., human nature). To this end, Marsden noted, "In fact, conservative Presbyterians and other Reformed Christians, such as those at Calvin College, *do* have a view of human nature (and hence of anthropology in both its classic and modern senses) that distinguishes their outlook from the more optimistic views of many other Christians and secularists."[29] Marsden's vision for Christian scholarship and our vision for Christian teaching in this book certainly have much in common. Yet our argument differs from Marsden's in that it focuses on a different aspect of the professor's work: that of Christian teaching, as opposed to the scholarship that subsumes Marsden's focus.[30] Overall, we explore a slightly different set of questions: How does being a Roman Catholic influence how one *teaches* chemistry? and How does being a Presbyterian influence how one *teaches* anthropology? In other words, our focus in this book is on the ways professors' Christian identity influences how they conceptualize and enact *teaching*.

Surprisingly, even though most Christian colleges and universities are primarily teaching institutions, and faith-based institutions spend a considerable amount of time and energy promoting the integration of faith and learning, much of the writing about faith animating learning is focused on Christian scholarship. As David Smith and James K. A. Smith, the authors of *Teaching and Christian Practices*, remarked. "It seems remarkably difficult for Christian scholars to focus on the classroom for very long."[31] They also pointed out that in the whole area of scholarship devoted to faith and learning, "it seems that 'learning' is most often meant [as] primarily the kind of learning that makes faculty learned, rather than learning understood as the pedagogical experiences of students."[32] Even the broader subject of spirituality and teaching has received little attention. Elizabeth J. Tisdell has claimed, "With a few exceptions, only minimal consideration has been given to how spirituality can inform teaching."[33] Only in the past decade have additional works about this subject trickled out, and these works have largely drawn upon the individual experiences of specific teachers.[34]

This book helps expand this literature and the argument that faith does make a difference in terms of how faculty teach, and it provides concrete examples of how they do so. Regarding this latter point, another distinctive feature of this book is that, unlike the few works addressing the Christian teacher and teaching, it relies on extensive empirical research from thousands of Christian professors. We draw upon the data from a broad national survey to unpack specific examples of Christian teaching from a wide range of disciplines.

Of course we must first answer a foundational question: What do we mean by the words *teacher* and *teaching*? A teacher is someone who engages in teaching. We define teaching as involving all the background thinking and practical work related to conducting a class in a traditional educational setting. Thus, our focus includes but is not limited to particular classroom strategies and practices. We also address how teachers perceive their students' identities, understand their own motivations, formulate and create a syllabus, choose the curriculum, grade, interact with students outside of class, interact with the institutional expectations they encounter, and other compelling aspects of a faculty member's teaching responsibilities. As this definition reveals, this book takes a view of teaching that is *broader* than other volumes addressing Christian teaching that focus primarily on pedagogy or classroom practices.[35]

The Roadmap of the Book

In chapter 1 we begin by outlining the origins of the tension that is purported to exist between being a teacher and a Christian, or more explicitly, we explore the moral tradition of teaching and the Christian moral tradition. The idea that teachers should somehow *not* integrate their religious identity is a rather recent development in the life of the university. It is helpful to know the historical origins behind this view and the reasons for its emergence. Furthermore, as represented by Palmer, the current counterargument for reintegrating one's identity into his or her teaching role draws upon older ideals, but it also differs in important ways. The first chapter explores both the similarities and differences between the older arguments and newer arguments for integrating one's whole identity with one's teaching.

Chapters 2 through 4 explore the question of what difference being a Christian might make for being a teacher. Although many scholars have previously explored this question from theoretical perspectives or from personal experiences, most discussions about the difference Christianity might make for teaching have not relied on empirical findings. These chapters fill this significant scholarly gap by reporting the results of our own study of how over 2,300 Christian teachers at 49 Christian colleges and universities within the CCCU view the influence of their Christian tradition on their teaching. These chapters first attempt to gain a sophisticated phenomenological understanding of teachers' perceptions. Using this understanding, we then evaluate the normative implications for Christian teachers in Christian contexts. Chapter 2 covers our findings concerning the background role that teachers' Christian identity and related convictions play. Chapter 3 discusses how Christian teachers believe their identity shapes their approach to their objectives and choice of curriculum content. Chapter 4 examines what Christian identity means for actual classroom practice regarding pedagogy, ethics, and modeling. In addition to discussing our findings in these chapters, we also include short vignettes from teachers that demonstrate our points in greater detail and from a broader group of traditions.

Chapter 5 explores the related question of what role particular theological identities may play in teaching. Christian teachers are usually not simply *Christian*; they are also Baptist, Catholic, Reformed, Quaker, Wesleyan, and so forth. This chapter explores the explicit role these particular denominational identities play in the practice of teaching and examines the tensions that might be created for teachers when undertaking this task in a context that is perhaps more generally Christian or is not consistent with one's particular identity (e.g., a Catholic or Anglican teaching in a Baptist or evangelical context).

With a more sophisticated empirical understanding of how teaching is informed by one's Christian identity, chapters 6 and 7 investigate the most difficult question: *What should be the ethical guidelines for mixing one's Christian identity with one's teaching in a pluralistic university?* In the current, postmodern era, we allow and perhaps even expect faculty members to integrate their various identities into their teaching practices. One might, for example, teach as a feminist, environmentalist, or Marxist. With this in mind, what role can and should Christian teaching play in the pluralistic university? Chapter 6 explores how a professor might teach from a Christian perspective while also considering the ends or overall purposes of the pluralistic academy. The seventh chapter then takes up this question regarding the more specific matters of classroom curriculum and pedagogy.

Finally, chapter 8 explores the importance of a just educational system for nurturing different kinds of identity-informed teaching within specific types of university environments. It makes the case for why we need a pluralistic system of education to respect the various facets of identity-informed teaching.

1
The Fear of Teachers' Religious Identity
The Historical Origins

> In a religiously pluralistic culture, peace is achieved by eliminating what is divisive from public institutions, and religion was clearly divisive.
> —Warren Nord, describing the history of American education[1]

The belief that teachers should limit the influence of their nonprofessional identities, especially their Christian identities, while practicing their craft is a recent invention. It has arisen only in the last 150 years. Indeed, professors who taught during the first 600 years of the university's existence would have considered this suggestion astounding, since the Judeo-Christian metanarrative formed the heart of the Western world's intellectual story.[2] In contrast, today many assume that professional identities should be separated from religious identities. How this change occurred is a fascinating story. This chapter provides a brief overview of how the new ideal of "the good teacher" as someone who reduces the influence of any religious identity emerged.

The Early European Tradition

Although the Christian church fractured into Orthodox and Roman Catholic branches in the eleventh century (officially in 1054), all of the original European universities were founded under the Roman Catholic arm of the Church.[3] By 1500, the 70 existing European universities still officially espoused only one religious identity, that of Catholicism.[4] As a result, virtually every professor identified as Catholic, and in most cases universities required that their faculty be members of the priesthood.[5] Despite this uniformity regarding a broad religious identity, a plurality of religious identities existed among Catholic clergy due to the existence of a variety of religious orders. Yet although Benedictines, Dominicans, Augustinians, Franciscans, and teachers who did not identify with religious orders taught in universities, they were virtually all Catholic.

For the first 300 years of the university's existence, a common Catholic theological narrative also nurtured a shared moral tradition for these faculty members and shaped the moral expectations the university had of its teachers.[6] For example, university leaders expected professors to demonstrate certain religious virtues. The ideal medieval professor "was meant to be humble before God, the source of all knowledge, and before the providential order of the creation, which the hierarchical arrangement of disciplines merely reproduced."[7] Virtues that were emphasized included "impartiality, goodwill towards his colleagues and his pupils, [and] keenness in work."[8] Certainly university leaders did not expect teachers to leave their religious identity at the door of the classroom; rather, they expected the teachers to bring their Catholic identity to bear on a wide range of classroom content, pedagogy, and ethics.

This shared moral and theological commonality does not mean religious debates and differences did not exist. The presence of different orders led to religious disputes, and debates (*disputatio*) existed as a central feature of the university.[9] These debates supplied the pedagogical means by which to sharpen one's view of God and God's world. Since the educational system fostered religious debate, it comes as less of a surprise that three of the most well-known protesters against particular Catholic Church doctrines and practices—John Wycliffe, John Hus, and Martin Luther—taught in universities.[10]

The Protestant Reformation that Wycliffe, Hus, and Luther helped to initiate did not change the expectation that university professors would fuse their Christian and teaching identities. The sixteenth-century Protestant Reformation, however, did eventually alter the overarching, unified theological narrative that had guided many universities and their professors. When Lutheran, Reformed, and Anglican universities slowly and painfully came into being, the sectarian university was born. Teachers at these universities eventually had to identify as Lutherans, Calvinists, or Anglicans.

Another important consequence of the Protestant Reformation was the growth of expanded political authority over Protestant universities. This authority increased because political entities no longer had to contend with the centralized Roman Catholic Church for influence and power. As a result, political authorities decreased faculty freedom and exerted more control over faculty teaching practices, sometimes even mandating the texts used in class.[11] Of course this governmental control also extended to faculty members' religious identities and beliefs. As one scholar noted of teachers at this time, "[F]rom the sixteenth century onward, the [political] authorities superintended the religious position of students and professors."[12] For example, the English Crown required all professors and students at English universities to be Anglican. This same pattern of political enforcement of religious identity applied to most Lutheran, Calvinist, and Catholic universities in continental Europe during this time.[13]

The political authorities later not only weakened professors' academic freedom, but also eventually undermined the religious identity of both Protestant and Catholic universities. When Pope Clement XIV disbanded the Jesuits under political pressure in 1773, he left more than two dozen European universities founded or overseen by the Jesuits without a clear religious identity.[14] Political leaders and their followers willingly stepped into this educational void and transformed Jesuit educational institutions in their territories into national educational institutions that marginalized both theology and the Church in daily university life and teaching.[15]

Furthermore, the rise of secular political movements during the Enlightenment (1715–1789) and the French Revolution (1789–1799), continued to expand the political control of the universities in the name of secular reason. Since the leaders of these movements rejected Christianity and ecclesial authority, they maintained that a secular nation-state should control universities to further the promotion of liberty. They also claimed that church-related universities restricted free thought, created division, and did not always produce the types of graduates that met the needs of a secular nation-state.[16]

Ironically, Enlightenment thinkers and revolutionaries who claimed to advance secular reason actually helped bring about the destruction of two-fifths of Europe's universities. For instance, the Enlightenment-inspired French Revolution led to the destruction of all the Catholic universities in France. The Napoleonic conquests that followed also devastated Europe's university system.[17] Between 1789 and 1815, 60 of Europe's 143 universities ceased to exist, leaving only 83 universities.[18] Europe would not reach the same number of universities again until the late nineteenth century.

Within the remaining universities, continued nationalization helped to transform the core identity of European professors from Protestant or Catholic faculty to political employees. Peter Vandermeersch summarizes the transformation that the prioritization of political identity brought about in professors during this time:

> State commissioners were sent to the university to verify the professional orthodoxy and diligence; chancellors appointed by the crown . . . involved themselves in the day-to-day control of the academic and religious life of both senior and junior members of the universities; the subjects to be taught were imposed by the government; the publications of the professors were submitted to a governmental *approbatio*; the professor became a civil servant whose *licentia docendi* [license to teach] was controlled and whose *libertates, immunitates et honores* [liberties, immunities, and honors] were both guaranteed and limited by the civil authorities.[19]

Overall, the new European nation-states functioned as a substitute for the Catholic and Protestant Churches in the life of the university. Whereas previously early scholars had viewed university education as discovering and imparting God's wisdom to restore the image of God in humans, the new European universities increasingly focused on shaping good citizens and discovering new knowledge to advance the nation's power. Yet whereas European professors became primarily employees of the state during the late eighteenth and early nineteenth centuries, American professors experienced a different kind of relationship with the government and a unique kind of freedom.

Similarities and Differences between the American and European Experiences

The new American experiment produced a system that both modeled parts of the European higher education system and experimented with new forms. As in Europe after the Reformation, religious competition in the New World spurred the growth of educational institutions. Yet this growth proved more diverse, particularly in the American colonies. Although the Catholic Church founded more than 30 universities in Latin America and Canada between 1551 and 1791,[20] it was Protestants who undertook the most significant institution building in the American colonies. Starting with the founding of Harvard by Congregationalists in 1636, six different traditions established eight colleges in the American colonies (the other seven are William and Mary, founded by Anglicans in 1693; Yale, founded by Congregationalists in 1701; Princeton or the College of New Jersey, founded by Presbyterians in 1746; Columbia, founded by Anglicans in 1754; Brown, founded by Baptists in 1764; Rutgers, founded by the Dutch Reformed denomination in 1766; and Dartmouth, founded by Congregationalists in 1769).[21] Although Catholics established Georgetown in 1789, their entry into American higher education was more gradual than that of their Protestant counterparts. Overall, the United States of America encompassed the most diverse set of religious institutions of higher education in the world. Nowhere else on the globe could one find Anglican, Baptist, Catholic, Congregational, Presbyterian and later Lutheran, Methodist, Presbyterian, and Quaker colleges in one country.

The American colonies also differed from Europe in that religious pluralism extended to the entire population and even to some colonial governments such as Rhode Island, Pennsylvania, New York, and New Jersey. In addition, the church played a more important role in the control and support of colleges than did colonial governments, particularly at Yale and Dartmouth.[22] In fact, one scholar claimed about early colonial colleges: "In every case, the colonial governments refused to assume primary responsibility for the control and support of the institutions established in their midst."[23] In this respect, the American situation demonstrated a considerable difference from university life in Europe.

These two realities produced tension regarding the identity of these early colonial colleges and their faculty. Though today virtually all of the early colonial colleges are categorized as private universities or colleges, in the early colonies no such distinction between public and private existed.[24] Civic leaders and the populace at large understood the colleges to be serving the whole colony, similar to a public university today, even though particular religious denominations sponsored the colleges.[25] Consequently, in response to the growing pluralism in the early colonies, the institution that most accommodated religious pluralism, the Rhode Island College (later Brown University), in its charter of 1764 made one of the first demands upon college teachers to limit the influence of their religious identity on their teaching and to privatize certain religious discussions:

> And it is hereby ordained and declared, that in this College no undue methods or arts be practiced to allure and proselytize one another or to insinuate the peculiar principles of any one or other of the denominations

into the youth in general.... And that the public teaching shall, in general, respect the sciences; and that the sectarian differences of opinions shall not make any part of the public and classical instruction; although all religious controversies may be studied freely, examined, and explained by the President, Professors, and Tutors in a personal, separate, and distinct manner to the youth of any or each denomination.[26]

This groundbreaking charter sets forth a wholly new vision for religious teaching in college, one that had never existed in Europe. In the name of respecting religious pluralism, it sought to limit the teacher's academic freedom regarding religious content in the classroom. It also privatized certain academic religious discussions.

In addition, some religious and political leaders within these colonies began to express frustration with local denominational colleges that did not change their standards to accommodate the increasing religious diversity. Due to these pressures, denominational colleges began to make accommodations to those outside their denominations. Princeton addressed this problem by allowing all types of Protestant students to attend, but the trustees still required all faculty to be Presbyterian.[27] When leaders in New York discussed founding King's College (Columbia) as an Anglican institution, Presbyterians revolted against this notion. One of the Presbyterian leaders, William Livingston, argued that what he preferred was an institution that "cannot, with any reasonable propriety, be monopolized by any religious sect."[28] According to his idea of a colonial college in a religiously pluralistic environment, each institution would be "entirely political, and calculated for the benefit of society, without any intention to teach religion, which is the province of the pulpit."[29] Livingston did not want political authorities to enforce an overarching, particular confession (as in Europe). His guiding assumption was that a "political" college would focus on the common good, whereas a denominational college would only serve the church to which it was connected.

In the end, the King's College leaders insisted upon having an Anglican president and a generally Protestant faculty, as well as on the teaching of "the great principles of Christianity and morality in which true Christians of each denomination are generally agreed."[30] Rhode Island College (later Brown University), Rutgers, and Dartmouth would also apply the same approach. Overall, the early colonial colleges experienced a great deal of political pressure to accommodate America's growing religious pluralism by expanding their religious requirements for both faculty and students. As a result, nowhere else could one find institutions with such diverse sets of Protestant faculty.

The role that political powers played in enforcing religious identity stipulations proved to be distinct in the formation of the new nation of the United States. Since the federal government would not support a particular Christian confession (an approach that each of the original states also eventually adopted, the last being Massachusetts in 1833), the religious identity requirements of professors were left primarily to the university (not to national political authorities).[31] This institutional independence from governmental regulation regarding the religious beliefs and identity of faculty was not present anywhere in Europe.

What is striking, however, is how deeply America's political architects feared this situation. They worried that the religious sectarianism that this freedom produced would threaten the country's unity. For example, the first six presidents of the United States supported creating a national university that would bind America together.[32] George Washington explained his reasoning for this creation: "Amongst the motives to such an Institution, the assimilation of the principles, opinions, and manners of our Country Men, but the common education of a portion of our Youth from every quarter well deserves attention. The more homogenous our citizens can be made in these particulars the greater will be our prospect of permanent union."[33] Although today's American universities champion diversity, the founders of the nation were actually intent on encouraging a certain degree of ideological commonality grounded in a common American identity.

Even the most liberal of American thinkers shared this concern, particularly with regard to diverse theological identities. When writing about establishing an institution of higher education in Virginia, Thomas Jefferson and James Madison wondered openly about the danger of "sectarianism" and sectarian professors. James Madison described their thinking: "A University with sectarian professorships, becomes, of course, a Sectarian Monopoly: with professorships of rival sects, it would be an Arena of Theological Gladiators. Without any such professorships, it may incur for a time at least, the imputation of irreligious tendencies, if not designs. The last difficulty was thought more manageable than either of the others."[34] This approach to the structuring of one of the first state universities, the University of Virginia, contrasted sharply with the solution to religious pluralism that Jefferson and Madison proposed in political life. Both in Virginia and in the US Bill of Rights, they suggested a public life closer to the "Arena of Theological Gladiators" Madison mentioned. Yet although German universities tested the option of allowing rival religious confessions to exist in one theology department,[35] Jefferson and Madison dreaded the adoption of this approach in the more pluralistic context of American higher education.

Instead, they proposed a university that would teach common religious and moral knowledge. For example, in a report from the Rockfish Gap Commission on the Proposed University of Virginia, chaired by Thomas Jefferson, the committee stated: "In conformity with the principles of our constitution, which places all sects of religion on an equal footing . . . we have proposed no professor of Divinity; and tho[ugh] rather, as the proofs of the being of a God, the creator, preserver, and supreme ruler of the universe, the author of all relations of morality, and of the laws and obligations those infer, will be within the province of the professor of ethics."[36]

Jefferson and his colleagues obtained state funding, not for a secular university, but for a theistic/deistic state university that would teach in a moral philosophy course the basic moral and religious beliefs upon which most American would agree. They also sought to avoid robust intellectual discussions about theology and the possible moral differences that emerged from different theological identities and traditions by eliminating the position of professor of theology. This approach was hardly neutral; George Marsden described Jefferson's rationale for state-supported deism: "From his perspective liberal religious views appeared objective and scientific and only traditional ones appeared sectarian. Hence, he saw nothing wrong with using the state to enthrone his objective scientific views."[37] Jefferson was blind to his own biased efforts to obtain state funding for an educational institution that would reify his deistic identity and shun theological differences.

American State Universities and the Myth of the "Common" Teacher

Jefferson's type of thinking fostered the emerging myth of the "common" teacher. Just as the myth of the common school helped America deal with religious pluralism,[38] the ideal of the common teacher also helped the early United States contend with the increasing religious pluralism in America. In the newer public institutions founded by state governments, teachers were expected to inculcate common moral and religious knowledge and ideas. The nurturing of students' other sectarian identities was to be completed at home or by churches (e.g., the emerging Sunday school movement) and was not a practice that was encouraged in these public educational contexts.

The myth of the common teacher fits with America's early "melting pot" metaphor. While this ideal helps promote political unity, the obvious problem is that the whole concept of an early American college lacking an explicit, guiding religious tradition is a myth. What existed within the early American state-funded college system was either a form of established deism/Unitarianism (such as Jefferson's University of Virginia) or established Protestantism (applicable to most of the institutions). For instance, in 1841, when regents for the University of Michigan described the ideal faculty member, they wanted to avoid "the morbid prejudices of sectarians" and "the sectarian of the atheistical or infidel party or faction."[39] They claimed that the university should be built on a general belief in what is held common among Christians, since "the great mass of the population profess an attachment to Christianity and, as a people, avow themselves to be Christian."[40] Thus, the ideal professors were:

> men to be found in all different Christian sects of sufficiently expanded views, and liberal spirit, and enlightened minds, devoid of the spirit of bigotry and narrow prejudices of sect and of party, that can be selected and deputed to such a work, whose public spirit and philanthropy and whose love of country and attachments to the interests of their State and its entire population, will always furnish the best and only true guarantee against the evils of sectarianism.[41]

Since most Americans were Protestant Christians, professors needed to be generally Christian but not overly committed to any particular Christian tradition or denominational identity. As seen in this quote, educational leaders did not downplay particular sectarian identities for religious reasons. Similar to the early founders, they justified the de-emphasis on political grounds. The "common teacher" in a public institution who de-emphasized his or her sectarian identity was really being a good American.[42]

Despite the establishment of state institutions such as the University of Virginia and the University of Michigan, particular Christian denominations were still largely responsible for the establishment and expansion of American higher education following the Revolutionary War

(1775–1783).⁴³ Unlike in Europe, the growth of colleges and the religious competition spurred by this freedom and diversity continued into the nineteenth century in America. Although only 29 permanent Protestant colleges existed before 1830, 133 were created between the years 1830 and 1861.⁴⁴ This growth included a variety of denominations that did not have universities in Europe, including Baptists, Methodists, and Quakers. Altogether, 165 of the 182 colleges in America began under the control of Christian denominations.⁴⁵

After the Civil War (1861–1865), however, the educational leaders of the new universities wanted to emphasize and prioritize the important political commonality that would prove foundational to maintaining a robust American identity. For example, in Daniel Coit Gilman's inauguration speech at Johns Hopkins University in 1876, he claimed the emerging research university should strive for "freedom from tendencies toward ecclesiastical or sectional controversies."⁴⁶ Gilman specified that to avoid these types of controversies, when hiring faculty members he wanted professors with attitudes toward religion and politics that "preclude the uncalled-for expression of these differences which are likely to impair the usefulness of the University."⁴⁷ Gilman represented what past figures had tried to achieve, since he thought faculty who sought to integrate their denominational teaching into the university would inhibit its flourishing.

Although Johns Hopkins University was not a state institution, Gilman located its unity in its national identity. D. G. Hart summarizes Gilman's justification for the modern research university, arguing that it "arose from a desire to serve and shape the recently reunified nation. This nation-serving character of the university movement meant that all higher education worthy of distinction was public, not in the sense that funding came from the state, but in the sense that it served public or national ends."⁴⁸ During that same inaugural event, Harvard's president Charles Eliot illustrated this outlook when he claimed that "a university cannot be built on a sect, unless, indeed it be a sect which includes the whole of the educated portion of the nation."⁴⁹ We should note, though, that although national identity supplied the source of unity for the university and professors, the leaders of these universities still expected their professors to be Protestant Christians and expected this religious identity to be the primary support for their moral lives.⁵⁰ In other words, university administrators still expected professors to merge their Christian identity with their teaching identity, albeit in a general way. They also wanted to make sure professors thought of themselves as Americans first, who avoided prioritizing a specific denominational identity of Baptist, Presbyterian, or Methodist.

Although focusing on national or public identity to promote unity was common among early research university leaders, most such universities were private (e.g., Johns Hopkins University, Stanford University, University of Chicago, Harvard University). As a result, research university professors did not become political servants as they did in Europe. Instead, in America a new and overarching American identity ideal emerged in the mid-nineteenth century to guide research faculty members: that of the professional, objective professor.

The Professional, Objective Professor

Professors first formed academic professional organizations in the mid-1800s in the discipline of the sciences. The first use of the word "scientist" appeared in 1840, and the first professional scientific society was founded the same year. These two events marked the beginning of "professional self-consciousness."[51] Since these academic societies published journals and held annual meetings at which faculty members discussed their research findings, their primary focus was scholarship, not teaching. Potential scholars entered into the profession and its conversations by convincing their peers of their expertise in the discipline. As Thomas Haskell describes, "[A]ll had to submit to the potential tyranny of the majority of the competent."[52] Sociologically-speaking, these professional associations allowed professors to build independent groups of authorities and peers apart from the state, the university, or religious denominations. For example, in Europe professional societies provided a counterculture and authority to state control,[53] while in America these societies helped professors gain freedom from the democratic masses, religious denominations, or the colleges themselves.[54]

This development fostered important changes within the identity of professors. Whereas scholarship had not always been a significant part of a professor's job, academic leaders and professors themselves increasingly expected faculty to engage in specialized research as the fundamental expression of their vocational identity. In other words, a good professor now must be a good scientist. The good scientist held up Francis Bacon's ideal of the objective, detached observer as the ideal from which one should approach the search for knowledge.[55] Rooted in the scientific ideal of standpoint objectivity, this perspective held that the standards and methods associated with one's professional identity (e.g., historian, biologist, psychologist) and the knowledge one acquires by applying those standards and methods should not be influenced by one's other particular identities (e.g., Catholic, Hispanic, working class, woman). At that time, this primarily meant one's religious identity. George Marsden terms this approach "methodological secularization"[56] and notes that although professors at America's first research universities applied it as did European universities. As Robert Anderson writes of European university professors, "By the 1870s, most scholars thought that religion was a matter of private belief, and that objective truth was attainable by the application of agreed scientific methods."[57] Thus, to be a good professional scientist meant one attempts to study nature, society, history, and so forth by separating one's professional work from the influence of personal identities and the narratives, beliefs, practices, and traditions associated with them. One should seek *objective* knowledge.[58]

The ideal of a good scholar had important implications for the ideal of a good teacher, especially when considering the relationship of the teaching identity with other identities. The German professor Max Weber exemplified this approach. Weber outlined his case for the good scientific professor in a speech he gave in 1918 at the University of Munich, later published as an essay, variously translated into English as "Science as a Profession," "Science as a Vocation," or "The Vocation of Science." It is important to note that the German word translated as "science," Wissenschaft, includes all the fields of academic study.[59] With a touch of humor, Weber started by sharing what many find true in the university: "According to German tradition, the universities shall do justice to the demands both of research and of instruction. Whether the abilities for both are found together in a man is a matter of absolute chance. Hence, academic life is a mad hazard."[60]

Weber argued that we must realize science does not offer the answer to many questions, including "the 'way to true being', the 'way to true art', the 'way to true nature', the 'way to true God', [and] the 'way to true happiness.'"[61] If this is the case, then what does science offer? For Weber, the good, scientific researcher pursues the discovery of objective facts and the relationships between them that help us progress toward greater objective knowledge.

According to Weber, good teachers should *not* allow their research or teaching to be tainted by ethical or political position-taking. He presented the following example of a person acting in his or her political identity versus professional identity as a professor: "For opinions on practical political issues and the scientific analysis of political structures and party positions are two different things. If in a public meeting one talks of democracy, then one makes no secret of one's personal attitudes; indeed, to take sides clearly is one's damned duty and obligation in this context."[62] In contrast, "the true teacher will guard against imposing any attitude on the student from the lectern, whether explicitly or through suggestion."[63] What is the moral basis for this normative argument? Weber admitted that "one cannot demonstrate to anyone scientifically what his duty as an academic teacher is."[64] In other words, Weber freely confessed that his ideal of a good teacher is a normative one, a matter of value, not derived from facts established by science.

To defend his position, Weber pointed to two practical results. First, he argued that the teacher's moral duty is to serve his or her students. One serves his or her students by providing them with objective knowledge and scientific expertise, not by teaching about one's personal political or ethical perspectives. Furthermore, the ultimate goal of the scientific vocation for Weber was the search for truth. He argued, "I am willing to demonstrate from the works of our historians that, whenever a man of science brings in his own value-judgment, a full understanding of the facts *ceases*."[65] In sum, similar to the way professors who bring their other identities to bear upon their professional academic tasks corrupt the ends of science, professors who teach a captive audience of students corrupt true learning when they attempt to use their professional status and power to convince students of their personal convictions.

Second, an important corollary of this ideal of the objective, professional professor is that teachers should no longer be expected to serve as moral guides who can help students live the good life. In relation to teaching, Weber rejected the idea that professors should seek to provide broad forms of moral inspiration for life to students or serve society by presenting themselves as moral leaders. "The error of that part of our youth," Weber argued, "is that they seek in the professor something other than what stands before them—a *leader*, not a *teacher*. But our place at the lecture is solely that of a *teacher*."[66] The reason, Weber claimed, involved professors' lack of qualifications to be moral leaders: "Fellow students! With these demands on our qualities of leadership you come to our lectures and you fail to say to yourselves beforehand that out of the hundred professors at least ninety-nine not only do not and should not claim to be football coaches in the field of life; they cannot even claim to be 'leaders' in matters of conduct."[67]

For Weber, scientific academics should focus less on broad forms of service or teaching that impart moral instruction and should pay more attention to their specific, scholarly quest and the specific form of teaching associated with and required from it. In Weber's words, the science or social science professor's job "today is a 'vocation' conducted through specialist disciplines to serve the cause of reflection on the self and knowledge of relationships between facts, not a gift of grace from seers and prophets dispensing sacred values and revelations."[68] Ultimately, Weber contended, "the prophet and demagogue do not belong at the lectern."[69] Weber articulated clearly the modern idea of the objective, professional professor.

Weber's ideal of the objective, value-neutral teacher was not without its early critics. Weber himself acknowledged regarding his vision of the good professor, particularly his belief that professors should refrain from expressing their values, that "some highly-esteemed colleagues are of the opinion that it is not possible to carry through this self-restraint and that, even if it were possible, it would be a whim to avoid declaring oneself."[70] Although these colleagues questioned the feasibility of this type of restraint, others criticized the self-deception that the "objectivity ideal" would foster. Nearly thirty years later, Walter Moberly would argue:

> Whether neutrality is desirable or not . . . [w]hen probed it is found to be a sham. It turns out to cover an uncritical acceptance of the common assumptions of the day or those of some particular social or professional stratum. In other words, so-called academic objectivity is a fraud; the fraud is nonetheless disastrous and reprehensible because [its] perpetrators are commonly also its victims and deceive themselves as successfully as they deceive others.[71]

Despite critiques such as these, Weber's vision largely won the day. Parker Palmer provides a recent description of the academic culture Weber helped to establish in the university:

> Though the Academy claims to value multiple modes of knowing, it honors only one—an "objective" way of knowing that takes us into the

"real" world by taking us "out of ourselves." In this culture, objective facts are regarded as pure, while subjective feelings are suspect and sullied. In this culture, the self is not a source to be tapped but a danger to be suppressed, not a potential to be fulfilled but an obstacle to be overcome. In this culture, pathology of speech disconnected from self is regarded, and rewarded, as a virtue.[72]

One can find numerous confessions of teachers originally trained in this tradition. One teacher said of her early teaching, "I rarely brought my own experiences into class and virtually never mentioned anything I would have considered 'personal.'"[73] George Marsden, writing in 1997, provided another example of this outlook. He told the story of a religion professor at a private university who "believed it was inappropriate for anyone who practiced a particular religion to teach about that religion. To do so, he thought, would be to transgress standards of scientific detachment required for the proper study of religion."[74] Weber would have been proud.

The Postmodern Critique of the Objectivity Ideal

In the postmodern age, critiques of the ideal of the objective teacher have proliferated. Critics tend to focus on two points. First, like Weber's colleagues, more professors increasingly proclaim the impossibility of his approach. Their disagreement stems less from the inability of professors to refrain from promoting their values and more from the overarching belief in the impossibility of finding an objective account of knowledge uncorrupted by our individual social locations and various identities. Warren Nord helpfully summarizes this emerging postmodern outlook:

> We are all constrained by the particularities of our cultures and subcultures; we inevitably interpret the world in terms of our own time and language, our own class, race, and gender. There is no way of stepping outside our cultural skins, outside the traditions and social locations that shape our ways of making sense of the world, to discover what is objectively true or reasonable. Rather, "truth," "reason," and "objectivity" are always internal to a cultural tradition, language-game, a narrative, an ideology, [and] a worldview.[75]

Put another way, we all inherit and adopt various identities (e.g., race, class, gender, religion) that shape the lenses through which we perceive and interpret the larger world around us. Acknowledging this truth means that we must give up on Max Weber's objective ideal of teaching. Chris Anderson, a Christian professor who teaches in a state university, relates his frustration with the Weberian teaching ideal: "In a classroom at a state university . . . I must teach as 'objectively' as possible, *which of course I never do. No teacher can.* Objectivity isn't possible or desirable, in the teaching of the Bible or in the teaching of any other subject."[76]

Anderson's point about objectivity not even being desirable points to a second major objection raised against Weber's "objective teacher ideal." This complaint concerns its desirability. Some of the most powerful critiques of Weber's outlook have emerged from members of ethnic and gender minority groups, who emphasize how white, male teachers who taught "objectively" actually undermined the advancement of learning. The African American feminist bell hooks provided a helpful example and a stark contrast to Weber's approach. In *Teaching to Transgress*, she began not by separating herself from the subject discussed but by telling the story of how she perceived teachers throughout her life. She also spoke highly of her teachers in the all-black school she attended as a youth, who poured themselves into teaching. In contrast to Weber's objective teacher who separates fact and value, bell hooks described her former teachers as on a moral mission: "We learned early that our devotion to learning, to a life of the mind, was a counter-hegemonic act, a fundamental way to resist every strategy of white racist colonization."[77]

Moreover, to aid in achieving this end, instead of separating themselves from knowledge or students, her teachers connected themselves to their students and the subject in the most intimate of ways: "[M]y teachers made sure they 'knew' us. They knew our parents, our economic status, where we worshipped, what our homes were like, and how we were treated in the family."[78] In contrast, hooks found Weber's ideas in action when she entered the realm of education dominated by whites: "Knowledge was suddenly about information only. It had no relation to how one lived, behaved. It was no longer connected to antiracist struggle. Bussed to white schools, we soon learned that obedience, and not a zealous will to learn, was what was expected of us."[79] This method of education, which remained highly disconnected from her identity as an African American, almost undermined her zeal for learning. After surviving this disempowering experience, she found university life reflected a similar outlook. Here, a supposedly objective approach to knowledge actually hid a particular white agenda, which involved an expectation that students, particularly black students who might be interested in empowerment, would conform to the larger ideals of the predominantly white university. In the book, hooks claimed, "During college, the primary lesson was reinforced: we were to learn obedience."[80]

She also found that when she experienced the *supposedly* objective teacher, this ideal undermined the teaching process and left her bored and uninspired. It also led to a host of consequences that were the exact opposite of what she had experienced with her other, inspiring teachers. In contrast to her elementary teachers, who knew her in her identities outside of solely her student role, "the objectification of the teacher . . . reinforces the dualistic separation of public and private, encouraging teachers and students to see no connection between life practices, habits of being, and the roles of professors."[81] Of course, this approach entails leaving the other identities of a teacher, whether good or bad, at the door as well:

> This meant that whether academics were drug addicts, alcoholics, batterers, or sexual abusers, the only important aspect of our identity was whether or not our minds function, whether we were able to do our jobs in the classroom. The self was presumably emptied out the moment the threshold was crossed, leaving in place only an objective mind—free of experiences and biases. There was fear that the conditions of that self would interfere with the teaching process.[82]

Instead, bell hooks yearned for teachers who would connect their entire selves in a more Palmer-like manner to the teaching process. She wanted what she had experienced from her early teachers.

The argument hooks made focuses on two key points also made by other minority scholars.[83] First, objective teachers fail to inspire learning. Second, those teachers who claim to be objective actually advance agendas and views of knowledge colored by their own socially constructed and situated identities, which shapes the knowledge professors choose to teach in class and how they present it. In contrast, the critics from traditionally underrepresented groups believe a teacher can and *should* bring his or her other identities into the classroom in positive ways. Similar to hooks, they see identity connections as not only necessarily influencing one's classroom practices but also contributing to and addressing corruptions within the teaching profession. As a result, the teacher with a moral mission grounded in his or her identity is the ideal of the good teacher.

Postmodernism and the Identity Conflict

These contentions provide some helpful background to the arguments between Stanley Fish and Parker Palmer discussed in the introduction. Interestingly, neither scholar praises the model of the objective teacher as understood according to older modern ideals (e.g., those of Max Weber and the Enlightenment rationalists). As a result, both Fish and Palmer take different approaches to this discussion.

In many ways, Parker Palmer takes a position similar to that of bell hooks. He believes we should abandon *both* the ideal of the objective professor who pursues objective knowledge *and* the ideal of the professional professor who separates herself from her other identities. Palmer echoes bell hooks: "The oppression of cultural minorities by a white, middle-class, male version of 'truth' comes in part from the domineering mentality of objectivism. Once the objectivist has 'the facts', no listening is required, no other points of view are needed. The facts, after all, are the facts. All that remains is to bring others into conformity with objective 'truth.'"[84] He also contends that Weber's ideal of the objective teacher produces a damaging form of personal alienation in faculty members. These ideals encourage them to alienate themselves from their students and from their own hearts. Palmer summarizes the effects of separating ourselves from our other identities thus: "We lose heart, in part, because teaching is a daily exercise in vulnerability. . . . To reduce our vulnerability, we disconnect from students, from subjects, and even from ourselves."[85] Ultimately, he thinks the model of the objective teacher distorts the way in which we actually come to know a subject. The result is that the ideal of the objective teacher who passes along objective knowledge undermines the ultimate goal of learning that teachers hope to reach and provide for their students.

In contrast to Palmer's argument, Stanley Fish is not ready to abandon important elements of the ideal of the objective teacher, and for that matter, he appears to resist giving up on the word "objective." Fish claims that whether we should embrace "objectivity" "depends on what you mean by 'objective'. If you mean a standard of validity and value that is independent of any historically emergent and therefore revisable system of thought and practice, then it is true that many postmodernists would deny that any such standard is or could ever be available."[86]

It would appear that Fish counts himself among these "many postmodernists," since he later asserts "that whatever universal values in independent truths there may be (and I believe in both), they are not acknowledged by everyone and no mechanism exists that would result in their universal acceptance.[87] If so, Fish's outlook strongly resembles that articulated by Stanley Hauerwas:

> [T]he idea of objectivity, which is mistakenly assumed to be exemplified in the sciences and an elusive goal for the humanities, is a deeply flawed notion. In the name of objectivity the assumption has been underwritten that knowledge is only good insofar as that which is known is freed from any tradition of inquiry. Yet the sciences work well exactly because they exemplify a traditioned mode of inquiry which, moreover, requires the student to be capable of participating in such a tradition.[88]

It is this professional scientific tradition to which Stanley Hauerwas refers that Fish believes can help provide some sort of communal standard. Despite the unavailability of a standard independent of any tradition, Fish argues that there are still ways by which we can evaluate teachers. He hopes to ground faculty members' boundary-drawing efforts by appealing to the identity of a teacher as a certain kind of professional. Every professional has certain standards by which one is judged good or bad. Fish argues:

> But, if by "objective" one means a standard of validity and value that is backed up by the tried-and-true procedures and protocols of a well-developed practice or discipline—history, physics, economics, psychology, etc.—then such standards are all around us, we make use of them all the time without any metaphysical anxiety.... [O]bjectivity is just another name for trying to get something right in a particular area of inquiry.[89]

Thus, instead of promoting the ideal of a value-free or objective professor, Fish looks to the historically-established and agreed-upon professional standards for obtaining knowledge as our source of truth. As a result, Fish claims professors can find in these professional criteria well-developed, "objective" standards for obtaining excellence in each academic discipline.

Fish has much in common with Max Weber. Though he does not share a similar epistemology, Fish still contends that something similar to Weber's professional-scientific model of teaching should be retained. As a result, he claims, "It seems, then, that the unavailability of an absolutely objective vantage point, of a god's-eye view, doesn't take anything away from us."[90] Fish's "professional professors" must focus on adhering to the standards and end goals of their profession and not allow their teaching to be corrupted by other identities and the values associated with them. For Fish, this means that professors should only teach ethics when the ethics taught are those associated with the academic identity of the professor (i.e., what it means to be a good biologist, historian, or sociologist).

Overall, postmodernism not only helpfully highlights the importance of identities outside the teaching role for influencing teaching but also sheds light on how we prioritize our identities, draw boundaries between them, and eventually fight about their relationships. In other words, we must not only understand the relevance of feminist, Marxist, or Islamic scholarship, but we must also understand how these identities may shape teaching. After all, our identities and associated narratives influence how a person understands the overarching purpose of education (e.g., preparation for a career, humanization, formation of future citizens, promotion of student development—depending on one's definition of humanization, citizens, or development). These varying ends influence one's view of the appropriate content of the curriculum (e.g., common knowledge, different identity stories), which has an impact on one's teaching methods and ultimately influences the proper structure of the education system. The conflict between Fish's and Palmer's outlooks is not a modern-postmodern one. Instead, it relates to identity boundaries.[91]

Christian Colleges and Universities and the Christian Teacher

During the same period that teachers began casting aside the influence of their other nonprofessional identities, many historical Christian colleges and universities also went through the process of casting aside their religious identity.[92] Other Christian institutions, however, made efforts to enhance and strengthen their Christian identity.[93] Much of the scholarly discussion about these efforts has focused on structural matters or professors' scholarly views, with the result being that empirical studies of how religious believers might teach differently remain lacking.[94]

The lack of such exploration is surprising considering that hundreds of Catholic and Protestant colleges and universities still exist.[95] Although the vast majority of these institutions are no longer counted among the leading institutions, such as the Harvard, Yale, and Princeton of the past, many of the professors in these institutions still take seriously their Catholic and Protestant identities in their central endeavor: teaching. In fact, many of the more recent Protestant institutions have joined in an effort to emphasize what has been called the integration of faith and learning, or what we prefer to call faith animating learning.[96] In the next four chapters, we attempt to address this deficiency by investigating the positive methods by which this group of Christian teachers bring their religious identities into the classroom. By exploring the variety of ways these Christian professors undertake this endeavor, we hope to demonstrate the complexity of this enterprise and provide an empirical basis for exploring questions about the role of identity-shaped teaching in various kinds of universities.

2

How Christianity Animates a Teacher's Background Beliefs

> I am called to love both my subject and my students and to speak the truth in love to my students.
>
> —Christian professor and academic dean

What difference does a professor's Christian identity make in teaching? We think the best way to answer this question is simply to ask experts who would know: Christian professors at Christian colleges and universities that devote attention to how a faith identity animates learning. What George Marsden said about Christian academic communities and scholarship can also apply to Christian teaching: "In such communities there is a constant alertness to Christian perspectives and what difference they may or may not make."[1] They also give attention to the practices of Christian teaching in all its dimensions, especially since almost all of these institutions are primarily teaching institutions. Scholars find that alertness and attention to deliberate forms of practice are necessary for excellence.[2] Moreover, as anyone familiar with obtaining excellence in a practice knows, experts tend to understand things differently than novices. Just as a seasoned golf pro can analyze a developing golfer's swing and see all the problems or marks of excellence, or a great musician can hear the subtle flaws or beauty of an emerging musician, a scholar can analyze data and see significant differences. In contrast, the novice will fail to see subtle or important nuances.

To date, few scholars have addressed the general topic of how a Christian teacher's *identity* influences *teaching* in higher education.[3] In fact, David I. Smith and James K. A. Smith claim that in the midst of the recent robust conversation about Christian *scholarship*, "the central task of *teaching* almost completely dropped off the scholarly radar."[4]

Indeed, broad, empirical surveys examining the extent to which faculty serving in faith-based institutions embrace and express their Christian or specific denominational identity in their teaching (as opposed to in their scholarship) are completely absent from the scholarly conversation about the value of a religious identity within American higher education.[5] While there are some rich individual statements,[6] scholars have not undertaken a national study of this matter until now.

Surveying Christian Teachers

To address this gap in the scholarship, we conducted a survey in which we asked more than 2,300 professors at 49 Council for Christian Colleges and Universities (CCCU) institutions in North America about the relationship between their Christian tradition and their teaching.[7] Surveying Christian professors at these Christian colleges and universities helped us understand the myriad ways Christian professors incorporate their identity in a supportive context. In these Protestant institutions, professors place a special emphasis on integrating faith with teaching.[8] Moreover, students think they do an excellent job. In our own survey of 6737 students at 34 of these institutions, close to 90 percent of students stated they were "very satisfied" or "satisfied" with the "faculty's integration of faith and learning."[9]

The strength of our approach lies in the fact that we surveyed the nation's experts—professors whose primary task is to teach Christianly in an academic environment that gives them full academic freedom to do so. Drawing upon their knowledge and practice then helps us to address the question of what Christian teaching should or could look like in a more pluralistic setting (the topic of chapters 6 and 7).

In our survey, we asked participants to state the broad theological tradition with which they identify. Survey respondents selected from a menu of faith tradition options that included Anabaptist, Anglican, Baptist, Catholic, Eastern Orthodox, Evangelical, Pentecostal/Charismatic, Reformed, Wesleyan, and Other (see table 2.1 for the results).[10] Since our sample came from Protestant institutions, the sample largely included professors who identified with a Protestant tradition. Consequently, one limitation of our approach is that we did not survey professors in Catholic or Eastern Orthodox institutions (although there are Catholic and Eastern Orthodox professors at the Protestant institutions we surveyed). Thus, in order to supplement these findings throughout the book we also draw upon examples from Catholic and Eastern Orthodox teachers in the limited literature on this subject.

Table 2.1 Broad Theological Traditions of Faculty Respondents (n = 2,307)

Broad Theological Tradition	Percent of Respondents
Baptist	19.5
Evangelical	19.0
Wesleyan	17.6
Reformed	12.4
Pentecostal/Charismatic	7.6
Anabaptist	6.5
Other	4.6
Anglican	4.6
Catholic	4.4
Lutheran	2.9
Eastern Orthodox	0.8

We think it is important to recognize that choosing a theological tradition versus understanding it as an inheritance is, as Lincoln A. Mullen states, "distinctly (though not uniquely) American."[11] He observes that one study of 40 countries found only 4 countries that had a conversion rate of individuals from the particular religious identity of their birth of more than 10 percent and two of them were North American: Canada, Chile, New Zealand, and the United States.[12] In addition, a 2009 Pew study found that 46 percent of Americans had changed the religious or nonreligious tradition of their birth. These choices are likely to have been undertaken with at least some significant thought.[13]

We then asked the respondents whether this theological tradition influenced the following areas of their teaching: (1) Course Objectives; (2) Foundations, Worldview, or Narrative Guiding the Course; (3) Motivations for or Attitude toward the Class; (4) Ethical Approach to the Course; and (5) Teaching Methods. As can be seen from these options, we understood "teaching" in our survey to involve all of the background thinking and practical work related to conducting a class. The resulting faculty responses to this question, by percentage, are shown in table 2.2. Over three-quarters of the teachers understood their particular Christian identity to be an influencing factor in their motivations, guiding foundations, worldview or narrative, and ethical approach to the class. In contrast, less than half of survey respondents believed their faith tradition was relevant to the formation of course objectives and/or their teaching methods.

Table 2.2 Influence of Theological Tradition (Percent of Respondents) (n = 2,307)

Does your theological tradition influence the following areas of your teaching?	Yes	Don't Know	No
Course objectives	48	9	43
Foundations, worldview, or narrative guiding the course	79	5	16
Motivations for or attitude toward the class	78	6	16
Ethical approach to the class	84	4	12
Teaching methods	40	20	40

We initially set out to discover what difference particular Christian traditions (e.g., Baptist, Wesleyan, Reformed, Catholic) made to the participants' teaching. Therefore, the teachers who indicated "no" in table 2.2 may still think Christianity in general did shape their teaching, since we asked them to think in terms of their specific intellectual and theological traditions within the broader identity of Christianity. So why then do we think our research can answer both what difference Christianity makes *and* what difference a particular Christian tradition makes? For each question, we also gave respondents an opportunity to provide qualitative examples from their experience.[14] In the qualitative area, we found that 60 percent of professors included answers that exemplified what difference Christianity in general makes in their teaching, and the other 40 percent of answers related to the difference their particular Christian tradition made. In other words, it is clear from the qualitative answers we received that many professors either simply understood the phrase "theological tradition" to mean their general Christian identity and the broad Christian theological tradition, or they wrote down differences they thought their tradition made, but that are really differences Christianity in general makes. A few professors even recognized the possibility of offering these different answers in their responses. For example, the following respondent distinguished both the general influence of Christianity and the particular influence of a theological tradition on his teaching:

> My broader Christian tradition leads me to view my students as "divine image bearers" who are worthy of my best efforts, patience, and faith in their ability to grasp and employ effectively what I am teaching them "for

Christ and his kingdom." My evangelical piety causes me to not only teach but also seek to mentor, pray for, and spiritually nurture my students.

Another professor made a similar sort of distinction:

> I don't think my specific Southern Baptist heritage per se affects my ethics . . . but definitely my Christian heritage does. I try to approach my course and my students in a Christ-like manner that would be honoring to God. In other words, I can't think of anything specifically that is "Baptist" (in comparison to other Christian denominations) that would cause me to act differently than other evangelical denominations.

Overall, as the next three chapters reveal, our research helped us discover answers to both what difference one's general Christian identity makes and what difference a particular denominational identity makes to the respondents' teaching.

In this chapter and the next two, we focus specifically on the responses we classified as generally Christian. We placed responses in this group if respondents did not mention a particular Christian tradition in their answers and if the types of emphasis the professors mentioned were in agreement with most Christian traditions.

Generally, we found Christianity animated these professors' teaching in six different ways (see table 2.3),[15] almost all of which are also aspects mentioned in the literature that discusses distinctive Christian scholarship.[16] We

Table 2.3 Ways Christian Identity Animates Teaching

The Teacher	The Student	The Discipline
The overall metanarrative or worldview		
Motivation		
Identity beyond teacher, student, and subject		
	Ends of teaching	
Class content		Class content
Pedagogy		

classified three of these activities as undertaken solely by the teacher, one focused only on students; one focused on teacher and the subject taught; and the other two involved the teacher, the student, and the subject. Teachers from all faith traditions mentioned in our survey engaged in these activities, to varying degrees. In this chapter we examine the first three components depicted in table 2.3, which are important background beliefs regarding the central character of the professor; the setting; and the larger story shaping how the professors interpret the world, their own thinking about teaching, their students, and their discipline.

One's Metanarrative or Worldview

Thinking about teaching requires that one orient oneself in a narrative context. In fact, we contend that there is no such thing as critical thinking apart from a particular standpoint, identity, and narrative. One needs an identity and standpoint from which to reason. As Charles Taylor observes, "Our identity is what allows us to define what is important to us and what is not."[17] Indeed, identifying as a Christian often serves as a kind of shorthand for a whole tradition of theological and moral thinking formed by a unique understanding of the characters and setting in the universe as well as the larger story in which we find ourselves. It should be no surprise, then, that someone who claims that God exists, acts in human history, and reveals these realities to us considers these realities important in approaching the practice of teaching. This is true no matter what the subject.

For most teachers we surveyed, identifying as Christian linked them to a metanarrative derived primarily from the Bible that Christians have developed over time within their communities. They used this metanarrative to engage in what we call *Christian critical thinking*. Since we argue that every person must reason within a larger metanarrative about the world that establishes the major setting, characters, and story, we think most forms of the term *critical thinking* should be preceded by an adjective.[18] In other words, worldview- or narrative-informed thinking is not unique to Christians. Scholars articulate this starting point in many ways. Some talk about it as a worldview or paradigm.[19] Some suggest that a narrative provides an understanding of the key characters as well as the overall story one uses to make sense of the world and the ends of education.[20] In the academy, scholars ranging from philosophers to scientists also engage in this narrative- or worldview-dependent reasoning.

In the survey responses we received, the nature of the relationship between Christian identity and course-shaping perspectives that teachers expressed often followed a particular pattern. Teachers first articulated a primary theological belief rooted in their Christian identity and its associated story, then drew an implicit or explicit connection to their teaching. For example, one education professor shared this: "God has gifted each of us to join in His work in the world. Because I am a professor in teacher education that translates into the understanding that I am equipping teacher candidates who will effectively represent Christ in what, where, whom and how they teach." As this example demonstrates, a respondent's theological perspective was often a statement about God or God's actions in the world. In other words, the professor made God and God's story the starting place of his view about teaching (e.g., "My learning outcomes derive from my view of God and who He is in my life."). Of course, teachers did not always express this outlook in a uniform fashion. Three particular ways of articulating these foundations emerged as a result of our analysis.

First, some professors focused on a multifaceted understanding of God's story with humanity using broad, theological themes (e.g., "The framework of historic Christianity is the ultimate story: God, Creation, Fall, Redemption, Judgment, and Restoration, Final Estate."). Like the teachers quoted in the following list, professors often mentioned how they began with this type of narrative framework and then applied it to their discipline:

- "We are made in the image of God, but are also radically depraved, finite, fallible and fallen. Science without religion, true religion, to guide it, can be a force for evil."
- "Believing in the narrative of creation, fall, and redemption shapes our approach to literature."
- "I teach incorporating an aesthetic shaped by Christian doctrines such as creation, fall, incarnation, and redemption."

Although this particular way of summarizing the Christian drama by focusing on the particular themes of creation, fall, redemption, and restoration (the last of which is curiously missing from these quotes) is quite common among the Reformed Christian tradition,[21] we found it employed by scholars from almost all traditions.

Second, other teachers took a similar theological approach, but they mentioned only one specific aspect of God's character or one part of God's story with humanity that influenced or shaped their thinking about teaching. For instance, with regard to God's character, professors referred to a variety of characteristics, such as:

- God's sovereignty (e.g., "The sovereignty of God guides all that I do, including my understanding of how faith and politics interface. I can't teach political philosophy or legal theory apart from that view.");
- God's creative power (e.g., "All of our work and thoughts are done before the face of God. All things should be done unto Him who is the Creator of all we study and the gifts we have to study this creation."); or
- God's grace and love (e.g., "I approach the class with an attitude that we all deserve grace. As free receivers of God's grace and love, I offer the same to my students.").

With reference to God's story with humanity, teachers linked their injunctions to the specific content of their disciplines. A number of professors, particularly those in the sciences, emphasized some aspect of what theologians call the "doctrine of creation." One professor in the sciences shared this: "Understanding God created everything means that nature is real, good, orderly, and contingent, all of which affects how we think about science." Others, however, emphasized a different part of the Christian story. For instance, a modern language teacher provided a theological exposition of how to think about languages in light of God's view of languages as revealed at the end of the Christian narrative:

> The narrative into which I fit my work is this: My work is predicated on at least two assumptions: (1) languages are important to God, so important that in the apocalyptic vision of people gathered around the throne praising God and celebrating God's salvation (Rev. 7:9–10), languages (plural) remain: the acclamations of the throng are multi-lingual; (2) diverse creatures, and by implication a diverse humanity, can abide in peace and harmony within the holy realm of God (Isa. 11:6–9). Because, in the ultimate scheme of the universe, languages are important and peaceful diversity is the direction in which God is moving the world, I engage in the work of teaching and learning languages and using language education for promoting intercultural understanding and peacebuilding.

In this case, the end of the Christian story was especially important for shaping how this professor understood the ultimate importance of diverse languages.

Finally, other professors wrote less about broad or particular theological themes and focused more on the source of knowing from which these particular theological beliefs derive, the Bible itself (e.g., "My goal is to teach biblically."). For these professors, the Christian scriptures provided the foundation or starting point for their worldview and therefore directly shaped how they thought about teaching. The following examples demonstrate the centrality of the Bible to this type of thinking for professors from various disciplines:

- "A Christian worldview guides the course in almost every way—through the inclusion of Bible verses to provide a context in which to understand the material." (psychology professor)
- "I teach my courses on the clear foundation of belief that the Bible is the inspired word of God and that we have no hope apart from the gospel; the Bible is to be believed and lived; God is to be honored and obeyed. Jesus is to be pre-emminent in all things; etc." (philosophy professor)
- "I always take a Bible-believing, Christian perspective when thinking through my courses and include Bible references and examples to help clarify points and objectives." (education professor)
- "As a born-again believer, I believe that the Bible is the basis for decisions and guidance in forming the way I treat others and the view I have of the world." (business professor)

As these comments indicate, these teachers understood God's special revelation found in the Bible to be the key source and perspectival lens through which they viewed all of learning.

Of course professors might combine two or three of these approaches—what we termed theological narrative, theological themes, and biblical emphasis. For instance, a literature professor indicated how she brought particular theological themes from the Bible into her class discussions: "Because I believe the Bible is truth, my writing courses include discussions of what the Bible says about language and creativity. We are image-bearers, and our creative work can/should glorify God." In other cases, teachers incorporated this kind of perspective more implicitly. One art professor talked about how he tried to frame the story of the classroom in light of a particular biblical theme:

> Doing one's best work is not merely a matter of seeking a superior grade, it is an act of obedience to the Maker who gave my students the privilege of seeking an education, and is a privilege to be handled no less than the "talent" left in the hands of the good steward. "Running the good race, serving the master as unto Christ himself," and other Biblical imperatives inform the reasons for classroom ethics.

In this example, the professor identified a theologically-informed perspective ("obedience to the Maker"), connected it to an educational issue (educational stewardship), and supported his view with various scriptural passages.

Overall, our survey answers revealed the unsurprising reality that Christian teachers reason about teaching in light of God and God's story with humanity. Moreover, due to its complexity and richness, teachers creatively draw upon this story in a variety of ways that prove far from uniform. In the examples they provided, our respondents drew upon the general Christian metanarrative or specific parts of the narrative to shape their perspective on their teaching practices.

Motivation

God motivates Christian teachers. This finding should not be surprising, and scholars certainly recognize God's role.[22] What proves to be illuminating, however, are the variety of ways teachers in our study expressed the nature of this motivational relationship. The professors we surveyed focused on three aspects of their relationship with God that inspired them: (1) the need to glorify or worship God, (2) their response to God's presence or call, and (3) their response to God's character.

Throughout the Christian scriptures, the first response to recognizing God's presence for individuals often involved worship focused on glorifying God. In addition, the Christian church often considered this response the central orientation of the Christian. The Westminster Shorter Catechism famously described the chief end of humans as "to glorify God and to enjoy him forever."[23] Not surprisingly, numerous Christian educators in our survey articulated this end as well. One science professor simply explained, "Christians can do science to the glory of God and the benefit of our neighbor."

This focus has two linguistic forms. Most usually stated this motivation in a rather straightforward manner (e.g., "I approach my teaching from a Christian framework of glorifying God in my approach, attitude, and teaching strategies."). In a few cases, professors drew a connection between their desire to glorify God and their work ethic or effort (e.g., "I believe that the Bible teaches a strong work ethic in order to glorify God—therefore, I approach my classes in a way that would bring honor to God."; "All things to the best of your ability, and all things to the Glory of God."). Although somewhat similar to those who talked about bringing glory to God, other teachers contended that their work comprised a form of worship of God. This perspective included statements such as the following:

- "All I do is an act of worship."
- "Study is a form of worship and giving honor to God."
- "I believe that my teaching is an act of worship so I try to do my best in class each day."
- "In the classroom, I feel a strong obligation to present my work as an offering to Christ."
- "I equally desire that every aspect of my work as a prof (thinking, doing, being) be a form of worship—loving God back."

Some professors also wanted to make clear that this attitude of worship in class meant one could not split education into two spheres, with one addressing the sacred and the other the secular. These teachers explained that everything is sacred and therefore everything, including teaching, involves worship. For instance, one professor wrote, "Our work and worship are of one cloth; there cannot be a dualistic sacred/secular split. All that we do 24/7 is a living out of our belief." For these professors, the concept of glorifying or worshiping God involved more than what occurs in a church or university chapel service. Participants believed engaging in the professorial vocation with a certain kind of God-directed motive is itself a form of worship. Worship occurs in front of a class and at one's desk, not merely in a sanctuary.

Regarding the second aspect of their relationship with God that inspired them, Christian teachers talked about ways that a relationship with

God transformed how they thought about the teaching profession in light of God's presence or actions. This transformation happened in a variety of ways. One group of professors simply understood themselves as, first and foremost, working for God and not merely an earthly boss. Consequently, they perceived this kind of working relationship as increasing their efforts at striving for excellence (e.g., "I truly believe that instructors at Christian universities have an enormous obligation to God, Himself."). This outlook is somewhat similar to that of individuals who perceived that teaching for God's glory influenced their approach to work. In this case, believing one works for God produces a greater sense of responsibility due to the heightened status of the relational source of motivation.

Moreover, a number of teachers suggested that God is the one who initiates this sacred responsibility. Indeed, a common way God's actions transformed the teaching profession for professors from a variety of disciplines had to do with the concept of God's calling. In most cases, the calling was stated rather straightforwardly:

- "Teaching is a calling I have from God, which is precious. I am eager to be a godly influence on my students." (arts professor)
- "God has called me to teach. Those He has called he also equips for service. God uses me as His tool to mold his children to be the servants He has called them to be." (education professor)
- "I am called to serve God first and foremost and I believe, then, that as a teacher I am called to serve the body in the same way in my classroom." (communications professor)

In this understanding, teaching is not something that these educators chose for themselves or something from which they primarily derive meaning and pleasure. They do not teach simply because it feels good when they see students learn or because they have some particular passion for a certain subject (although we do not doubt that these two elements may inform their experience). Teaching is something God invited and equipped them to do.

As was sometimes the case with the themes we found, these two motivational themes (glorifying/worshiping God and responding to God's call) were not mutually exclusive. For example, one mathematics professor combined the concept of calling with the theme of glorifying God: "My motivation comes from my calling and giftedness from the Lord. I am fulfilling His call, and I want to use my gifts for His purpose and glory." Or as another physical sciences professor summarized his motivations using two of these themes: "Study of creation as worship, developing young scientists as a calling."

When these two themes were taken together, we found Christian educators understood God as changing the nature of work itself to worship, changing one's ultimate place of responsibility for that work, and changing the source of motivation for one's work. In other words, the external reality of God and God's interactive relationship with humanity changed their internal motivations for working in the teaching profession. For other teachers, however, this narrative is not the full story.

A third group of teachers focused less on the ways God's presence or actions changed their view of the teaching profession and concentrated more explicitly on the way particular aspects of God's character, as revealed through the biblical narratives, motivated them. Three particular aspects stood out among those mentioned by professors: grace, love, and truth. The following quote from a nursing professor provides the most extensive reflection on the theme of grace:

> God has done amazing and gracious acts and transformation in my life. His gracious acceptance of and validation of me and His design in me makes me a faculty of graciousness. I have high expectations b/c I believe that if God calls students to a line of study (nursing in my case) that He will also provide all that is needed to meet the inevitable and character-building qualities encountered in the journey/process. So, I can expect a lot [because] I know He delivers and provides a lot. But, the process, the journey is long, winding, different for each person, and grace for that process/journey needs to be part of the support and undergirding and coming-along-side that is a part of the provision God lends for the process/journey to progress and be endured (at times).

Although grace served as a motivation for professors' work, they also saw it extended to the whole of their lives. As a communications professor noted, "I operate out of grace-based theology that recognizes my sinful nature and dependence on God for forgiveness, salvation, and sanctification. This influences everything I am and everything I do."

A similar type of motivation stemmed from a teacher's understanding of God's love. A philosophy professor stated: "Because the love of Christ constrains me, I work day and night to teach my classes and disciple individuals." Similar to the concept of grace, this understanding of agape love served as a motivational factor. Another education professor spelled this point out clearly: "I am motivated by the belief that every student is loved by God and has a significant reason for living. This causes me to care deeply for my students and take my teaching seriously." Yet teachers also indicated that their motivation often related less to a specific way of approaching class policies and more to a particular focus on embracing all students or demonstrating particular virtues to students. For instance, as one business professor shared, "God loves all people and wishes everyone to be saved; therefore, I try to show concern and love to all my students."

Finally, a number of professors used the phrases "God's truth" or "All truth is God's truth" to connect God to their professional endeavors. Similar to expanding the concept of worship, this outlook allowed them to move beyond narrow conceptions of Christianity's role in the educational enterprise:

- "I believe that all truth is God's truth and that makes me excited to pursue truth in history."
- "All truth is God's truth—created by Him, formed by Him. Our study of this world is, in essence, a study of things that He created, things that reflect Him."
- "I believe that all truth is God's truth and that we are called to live in the tension of being finite human creatures who use the best scientific method and the best Biblical study to come to a more integrated and holistic understanding of every topic we study. God calls us to know God and to know God's creation."

Again, these kinds of emphases on God's character are not at all mutually exclusive from the other two broad motives.

If one combines the previously discussed ideas, a broad theological narrative about God's role in motivating professors emerges. God calls individuals to teach and therefore endows them with a particular identity. God has called them to serve their students and the academic community. Indeed, God is a teacher's ultimate supervisor, and one remains responsible to God in the stewardship of this responsibility. In addition, God provides teachers with gifts, including love, grace, and mercy, that compel them to act. God's grace and love also motivate them toward empathy, understanding, perspective taking, truth speaking, equipping, and other ends. The larger purpose of the proper exercise of this calling is God's glory, and the nature of this work is itself worship.

More Than Teachers, Students, and Subjects

The Christian story also changes one's vision of the whole teaching enterprise by transforming one's view of students, other teachers, subject, and self. Christian teachers do not simply view their students according to one identity (student) or according to other identities that might receive greater attention in the academy today, such as gender, race, sexual identity, or socioeconomic status. This additional emphasis takes four different forms.

First and foremost, Christian teachers talk about viewing students as being made in God's image and then unpack the implications of that identity. For example, one business professor stated, "Each student is an image bearer of God and deserves respect and my very best efforts." The implications drawn from this identity would vary according to teacher and discipline. Some would focus on God's love or creativity, while others might emphasize the need to respect those made in God's image. One art teacher commented, "Made in the very image of God, I teach that we cannot help but reenact creation, as we do that of God which has been implanted in us by the Great Creator, as we embody God's image and being."

Not surprisingly, we found references to humans being made in God's image throughout the responses from teachers in a variety of disciplines, who also drew a variety of conclusions about the particular aspect of God's image that applied:

- "My worldview is influenced by my belief that God made all things good; we are made in His image in our creativity." (English professor)
- "A belief that I have been born again by grace through Jesus Christ to reflect the image and goodness of God in a broken world and I have been endowed with intelligence, talents, and opportunities with an obligation to develop those to the fullest extent so that I may be a blessing to others guides the way I interact with my students and faculty." (psychology professor)
- "I believe every student is created in the image of God with intrinsic value and worth; each has a God given purpose in life." (education professor)

- "We are created in God's image, to know him, serve him and love each other with forgiveness and mercy." (arts professor)

As the last quote indicates, the idea that humans are created in God's image is not simply an appeal to a vague form of spiritual union or connection.[24] It is also not a simple Jeffersonian appeal to equality such as one finds in the Declaration of Independence. Although being created in God's image does support this ideal of equal worth and value, it also has many other implications. It provides an ideal for ultimate human development: to be fully developed as a human being is to demonstrate the character qualities revealed by God (e.g., love, wisdom, forgiveness, creativity). Teachers hope to develop that image. As one business professor noted, "Each learner is created in the image of God; I seek that image in my teaching."

Second, Christian teachers also talk about their students in familial ways that could be foreign to nontheistic teachers. One psychology professor in our survey stated, "Each one is a beloved child of God, even when they don't meet course requirements." In other words, the teachers see both their students and themselves as part of God's family. As one teacher mentioned, "Each student is in the same position before God as I am. We are all children of God." Still, another professor combined both a reference to the image of God and two different familial references. Both transformed her love toward them: "I see my students as created in the image of God and loved extravagantly by Him. I love them as brothers and sisters in Christ or sons and daughters in Christ."

This outlook also has important implications for how Christian teachers understand authority and power in the classroom (for an example, see box 2.1). It elevates students to a level equal to or even with the teacher. One psychology professor ordered these identities in her response: "Christian brother/sisters as primary relationship; Christian scholar mentor as secondary relationship." In this respect, by understanding a student's identity within the Christian story, professors transform the teacher-student relationship into a more equitable and familial one. As a mathematics teacher shared, his Christian faith tradition led him to this outlook: "Belief in the importance of lived theology affects how I view my students as God's beloved sons and daughters and my attitudes toward them."

Third, Christian teachers also view their students and their subject in another way that transforms the teacher-student-subject relationship. They often mentioned that their "students are gifts from God." In addition, others

Box 2.1 Seeing Students as More Than Students

In Carolyn Call's essay "The Rough Trail to Authentic Pedagogy: Incorporating Hospitality, Fellowship, and Testimony into the Classroom," she provides a helpful extended illustration of seeing one's students as more than just students.[32] Call, a professor at Saint Mary's College, narrates her attempt to incorporate the three practices of hospitality, fellowship, and testimony into her adolescent psychology class. Of this experiment, she writes:

> This was easily the most difficult class I have ever taught. . . . [M]y personal reaction to the class was more often tears than . . . laughter. It was a deeply humbling process. Until I taught this class, I didn't realize just how emotionally removed I had been from my previous students and how comfortable this was for me as an instructor.

What had removed Call from her students was her past professional style of acting solely as a professor and treating her students as simply students. She became emotionally reconnected to her class through her meditation upon what it means to extend hospitality. She recognized that "the dynamic of hospitality includes becoming aware of a particular identity of self (disciple, believer, child of God), recognizing the stranger before us (as Christ or as the image of God), and then providing for the other. Receiving guests is an honor and a gift from God."

Applying this perspective proved particularly challenging when she had to deal with a student she called Kathy, a junior art major, who "was easily one of the most opinionated, disruptive, and socially unaware students I have ever had." It did not help that her written work was atrocious. At the beginning of one class, Call observed Kathy making fun of another faculty member with other friends: "I mean he just stands up there, like 'Duh—I'm so boring.'" Kathy and her friends then went on to recite numerous examples of this teacher's behavior that they found amusing. Call felt deep emotional pain upon hearing this critique and wanted to scream at Kathy and her friends for being so disrespectful.

> Instead, I took a deep breath and prayed in silence: "I love these people. I love these people. God help me to love these people.". . . The mental and emotional energy it required of me to turn to these students in love was tremendous. Yet in that moment I knew, in a way I had never experienced previously, what it means to teach as a Christian. It has everything to do with how I perceive my students, starting at the very beginning of the semester. My perception has to be colored by trying to perceive them as Christ would have: surely flawed in many way, yet worthy of love and respect, attention and focus.
>
> Call noted later in conclusion that she ultimately learned to see her students "as children of God and as loved by God, regardless of how I felt about them at any given moment."

claimed that students *have* gifts from God. To speak of students as gifts or as possessing gifts means there must be a Giver. A communications professor wrote: "I encourage students to understand that we serve a God who communicates, and He uses speech (and communication technology) to help us change the world. We are obligated to use the gift of communication wisely and well." Clearly, for the professor who spoke about God's gifts, the students' parents or impersonal fate did not supply those gifts.

This perception about *students as gifts with gifts* extends the identity of teachers and their responsibility with students. Because God entrusts teachers with the gift of students with gifts, professors perceived themselves as stewards entrusted with their students' care and development. As one philosophy/theology professor wrote, "I am a steward of God's classroom and His students. I must do my best to prepare the best lesson possible for His classroom. I must be on a stewardship for which I am responsible, not just to the college and their parents, but to God."

This view also extended to the teachers' disciplines. Christian professors also viewed their subject or specialty as a gift that needed stewardship. A literature professor shared this with us: "Because I believe that all people are made in the image of God and that language is a gift from God, we are to treat other people and language with the respect and admiration we would give a gift." This outlook reflects the view that just as God takes care of his whole creation, humans are to be God's embodied representatives on earth and stewards of all of God's creation, including the creations that humans make.[25] For Christian professors, academic disciplines are an extended human dimension of God's creation. Humans continue to build up storehouses of knowledge that need to be stewarded.[26] Some professors added an additional way of conceptualizing stewardship. One biology professor simply said, "I believe that I should be a worthy steward of our planet and its inhabitants." In other words, all of creation needs to be stewarded.

If we are to summarize this theme, it is that teachers receive multiple gifts from God—their students and their gifts as well as the gift of their discipline, and if we want to go further, all of creation. All of these gifts are to be stewarded, and teachers recognize that they will need to teach their students how to steward all these gifts.[27]

Fourth and finally, teachers also viewed students within the overarching Christian story and not merely in one theological theme. In other words, they understood students to be created in God's image and children of God but also as sinful and in need of deliverance. For example, an economics professor demonstrated this multifaceted outlook: "I assume that humanity is fallen and in need of redemption. Also, I see people primarily not as consumers, but as producers or creators, as created in God's image." Science professors offered the same view not only of students but also of their fellow professionals: "Science is done by scientists—agents who are finite, fallible and fallen."

When thinking about how to view their students in a classroom setting, some professors also sought to place their students and their particular teaching practices in this story. For example, one arts professor noted:

> I believe that we are all fallen sinners, but that we can all be redeemed. Those that come to saving faith in Christ are gifted to serve Him. All of us need to be held accountable to give a good and honest effort to tasks that are presented to us. As faculty members, we need to see the potential in each student and do all that we can to help our students grow in faith as well as in our academic discipline and in the ability to use their gifts more fully for Christ's service.

Interestingly, this overall perspective reflects what one finds in sophisticated works such as Mike Higton's *A Theology of Higher Education*. Similar to the teachers in our study, Higton baptizes learning so that it emerges as a practice of discipleship. He contends that learning is a gift "received on the path of discipleship."[28] Along this path of learning, students experience a continual "breaking and remaking" of the sense that one has made of God, oneself, and the world, similar to what one experiences through active participation in Christ's crucifixion and resurrection.

Overall, we find these statements about how to best understand the core identity of teachers and students to be striking, especially when compared to the AAUP's *Statement on Professional Ethics*, mentioned in the introduction. This professional statement talks about the responsibilities of professors in light of five identities: as scholars of a discipline, teachers, colleagues, members of an academic institution, and citizens. In the teacher relationship, professors serve in their "proper roles as intellectual guides and counselors."[29] Although the statement insists professors should respect students, the AAUP statement does not link the basis for this respect to any particular view of our common humanity.

In contrast, Christianity adds additional dimensions and depths through which one can think about the teacher-student relationship that supply a supporting set of reasons for demonstrating respect and even love for students. Students are made in the image of God and are children of God; therefore, they deserve respect and love. Furthermore, while Stephen Cahn makes the ethical claim that a faculty member should not be a student's friend,[30] these Christian teachers who participated in our survey claim they want to see their Christian students as brothers and sisters in Christ and as gifts from God who need to be stewarded wisely. This kind of identity transformation can make a radical difference in how one lives out one's calling to teach. It certainly means that when it comes to their students, Christian faculty operate with different anthropological assumptions.

A Christian Analysis

We do not believe that our findings represent the fullness of a normative Christian approach to teaching in these areas. After all, the breadth and diversity of responses that is a strength of our approach also contains a limitation we freely acknowledge: an accumulation of hundreds of pithy responses, even when considered together, cannot possibly represent the richness or fullness of the Christian tradition, or for that matter, a professor's full theological perspective.

We do think a robust Christian vision should include and combine these different strands, but we also believe additions from Christian theology, dialogue with other actors in the university, and contemporary scholarship can enhance this vision. With regard to Christian theology, some of the themes we observed, when considered alone, could represent a simplistic theology in danger of reducing scripture or theological sayings to platitudes applied randomly to one's professional desires and outlook. At times, earnest singular responses could appear to bend to the temptation to spiritualize every aspect of life through the use of religious language, sometimes called "Christianese," that might cloak rather than reveal meaningful personal and professional struggles that might require a more sophisticated theology. For instance, without additional nuance from a healthy Trinitarian theology and attention to the whole Christian story, stated truths about the goodness or sovereignty of God may too easily overlook other theological themes about Christ's suffering presence within the pain and brokenness of the world and the implications of this theme for the motivations of Christian teachers.[31]

Similarly, a fuller Christian theology leads us to contend that Christian teachers must always consider the power dynamics inherent in teacher-student relationships even when understanding and viewing students as part of God's family and as brothers and sisters in Christ. What exactly the nature of that relationship might entail requires dialogue with students. The invocation of spiritual justification by fallen humans in power can serve to oppress if the last word of interpretation is reserved for those in power.

Finally, the themes we found can be enhanced by the perspectives of contemporary scholarship. For example, what exactly does it mean that one is a recipient of God's gift and grace and that we are sinners? Our own encounter with critical theory has helped both of us to recognize that our current academic gifts and teaching callings may also be enabled by unearned abilities, circumstances, and identities (e.g., being American, our access to education, our supportive parents, being male, being white). Furthermore, some of these advantages may be less God's gifts than advantages derived from unjust systems of social privilege. In our own lives, recognition of various social advantages helps us be more fully aware of the gifts and grace we have been given (e.g., loving and supportive parents, a country with an advanced education system), as well as of the need to address certain systematic injustices pertaining to race, gender, or class. Thus, we recognize that the initial findings we set forth could also use additional theological development.

Conclusion

To see oneself and one's students in light of an overarching cosmic drama with God as the central character of the story transforms these Christian teachers' vision of themselves, their discipline, and their students. They do not work for themselves, the government, or some otherworldly entity. They work for God and God's glory because of who God is, what God has done, and what God continues to do in the world. This transforms their motivation and their view of their students. They are not simply teachers. They are much, much more. They are called by a gracious, loving, and truthful God to transform the lives of their brothers and sisters in Christ who are made in the image of God.

We do not at all wish to imply, however, that because these Christian teachers draw upon these motivations, views of their students and subject, and other background beliefs that they are automatically superior teachers. Each of us has known Christian teachers who make these connections but who could not connect with students or advance their learning. In fact, we would ask Christian teachers: *What good is it if you believe these things, but fail to be a good classroom teacher?* In the next two chapters, we explore the connections that teachers make between their Christian identity and their actions in the classroom.

3

How Christian Teachers Transform Course Aims and Curricula

> It is our privilege as well as our duty to lead our students to "become beholders" of the God who not only created our world but remains always present, always active, and always loving within it.
> —Eric Cunningham[1]

Eric Cunningham, a professor of history at Gonzaga University, begins his history class in an unusual way. In an essay subtitled "Transforming Self and World through the Study of World History," he writes, "The first thing I tell [students] is that the study of history is holy, hermetic work, and I warn them that if they are not willing to experience a significant personal transformation during my class they should drop immediately and enroll in another, less existentially demanding section."[2] Cunningham's introduction indicates immediately how his Christian identity transforms his understanding of history. Not surprisingly, as a historian, to justify his outlook he refers back to the roots of the Jesuit tradition that sponsors his institution: "The 1599 *Ratio Studiorum* states it is 'one of the leading ministries' of the Society of Jesus to teach to students 'all the disciplines . . . in such a way that they are aroused to a knowledge and love of our Maker and Redeemer.'"[3] For Cunningham, stewarding this privilege is something that must be taken very seriously by every Christian teacher and scholar. He makes it clear from the start that his teaching goals are not merely "secular." After all, he writes, "If our teaching mission is to become nothing more than the presentation of content and teaching our own tests, the state university is just as effective, and a good deal more affordable."[4]

Cunningham's objective is not simply to find God working through every historical event. Instead, he attempts to view the whole discipline of history within a larger sacred paradigm. He maintains that one of the key weaknesses of a purely secular history is that "world history books come up short when it comes to explaining what the purpose of history may be."[5] In particular, historians often assume certain conventional narrative models, even when these models are unsatisfactory. For instance, he believes that these conventional models do not help explain the particular crisis we now face after modern, secular approaches to history have been found wanting.

To demonstrate the crisis, Cunningham points to the postmodern preoccupation with eschatology and dystopian futures. One can easily find this preoccupation in popular books and movies that constantly envision how life will look after modern civilization ends. Most of these visions are unimaginative, dark, and dreary. He claims that "our modern civilization is out of ideas."[6] As a result,

> we intuit that modern civilization is ending, but we do not know what comes next, and we cannot envision it. This is the historical trap that we have set for ourselves by buying into the false notion that material progress is a never-ending enterprise. Because we are no longer beholders of the transcendent transhistorical, we are stuck with dystopic visions of world disaster and diminished human prospects.[7]

In other words, the current secular view of history is in crisis. In the period before the modern one, history gained meaning through the view that God is working in the world. This view gradually gave way to "an exclusively secular worldview based on modern 'faith' and endless material progress."[8] Yet if we can no longer have faith in material progress "in the modern world, history has, in a real sense, become meaningless."[9] Jean Francois Lyotard's famous book on the postmodern condition received attention because it revealed the nakedness of modernity's claims. It demonstrated

> that the dominant narrative of progress was itself as vulnerable to replacement as the earlier providential model had been. The historiographical problem with this outlook, which Lyotard also foresaw, was that without some informing narrative, providential or progressive, the historical process had nowhere to "go." . . . What was once the most forward-looking and optimistic civilization and human experience has become a global cult of doubt and despair.[10]

Thus, he wants students not merely to evaluate the content of history but to understand that the overarching narrative by which they understand history must also be critically evaluated. He notes of historical interpretation, "We are trapped in the wrong story and we need to rewrite it. The various meltdowns of modernity are simply what we get when we individually and collectively buy into the false myth of historical materialism and attempt to live in the counterfeit culture that this worldview inevitably engenders."[11]

Students do not always know the background beliefs of a teacher, but as in Cunningham's case, they usually discern or learn quickly how a teacher's worldview influences the ends and curriculum of a course. The next two chapters identify these more overt expressions by exploring how Christian teachers believe Christianity influences the *why*, *what*, and *how* of teaching. Overall, teachers in our survey articulated and differentiated between two major perspectives on how Christianity changed the ends, content, and methods of their courses. We call these the spiritual addition and Christian transformation approaches. Spiritual addition professors, as the name implies, understood their Christian identity primarily as inspiring the addition of certain objectives, content, and methods to their classroom. Christian transformation professors, similar to Cunningham, drew upon the Christian tradition to reconceptualize or re-enact major parts of their objectives, content, and methods in ways that are more radical. In this chapter, we illustrate these differences and classify the specific ends and curricular views that the professors in our study claimed were influenced by their Christian identity.

The Ends of Classroom Teaching

In the modern age before the end of the Cold War, many professors believed the ends of particular history, chemistry, or sociology classes should be the same, no matter where one taught. Some contemporary professors may still hold this view. In our postmodern age, however, most educators understand that professors in different university contexts will teach the same course in different, and sometimes radically different, ways. Not surprisingly, the majority of Christian professors in our survey claimed their particular Christian identity led them to conceptualize the outcomes of their teaching differently.

Teachers variously communicated these ends as objectives, goals, expectations, hopes, or aspirations. In other words, they did not simply discuss course objectives listed on a syllabus and instead took a more expansive view. One professor articulated this outlook as follows: "It's not an objective I would state in the syllabus, since it's not one that can be assessed, but I tell students in courses that my primary objective is that they encounter Jesus Christ and grow as his disciples in love of God and neighbor."

Spiritual addition professors' Christian faith led them to identify ways in which they expanded their objectives. In addition, they often used the language of "spirituality" to refer to a dimension different from "secular" learning.[12] For instance, one teacher shared, "I aspire to see my students growing spiritually as well as intellectually." Teachers emphasized this approach most often in professional fields such as nursing or education, where a set of secular professional standards and objectives already exist, but the professor added or emphasized an additional "spiritual" component, as one professor illustrates: "For a nursing pediatrics course: identify psychological, spiritual, ethical, and cultural variables that impact the delivery of education and care to members of the child-rearing family. This is done with the understanding that the spiritual dimensions are a fundamental component of nursing care." Respondents like this professor attempted to counter the view sometimes promulgated through naturalistic reductionism, which ignores an important dimension of humanity.[13]

Of course we also found this approach in other disciplines such as literature and history. For instance, a literature professor noted, "I try to have at least one objective in each course specifically tied to Christian faith, for example, in African American literature we analyze how the Biblical text and Christian faith were used both to justify slavery and work for its abolition." Again, typical of the spiritual addition approach, this professor understood the Christian faith to *relate* to one objective, while the rest of the objectives were not considered to be related to it.

The second type of teachers, Christian transformation educators, were like Eric Cunningham. They set forth ends that reconceptualized the entire educational process as something sacred or related to God. James Sweeny summarizes this view as the ontology of grace or "the understanding of a created order which is graced or penetrated by the active presence of God."[14] As a result, "[t]he ontology of grace is . . . a perception that changes everything."[15] The following comments illustrate this outlook: "Because I want all students to follow the way of the Lord, I work hard to show them that nothing is neutral. All of life is religious."; "Believing that the whole world belongs to God and will ultimately give allegiance to God . . . I want students to see that God wants all the areas of culture to be redeemed."

Consequently, Christian transformation teachers understood Christianity as altering their overall course objectives as opposed to simply adding an additional end or two to address spiritual matters. They apprehended every aspect of a subject as being shaped by Christian theology and ethics. Following are two examples, one from a Protestant teacher and one from a Catholic professor (not from our study):

- "Since I believe that all of life is a reflection of our biblical worldview, all course objectives are molded by an eye to what is normative and obedient in a given subject area."
- "The goal is to expose students to the realities of the world through the lens of Catholic social teaching, inculcating in them a deep sense of solidarity."[16]

Such educators often taught more in the arts and sciences than in the professions, as the following examples from our study demonstrate:

- "My Christian worldview serves as a foundation for integration of faith and psychology that is woven into all of my classes."
- "We do all our work as service to Christ. So, my students must learn certain facts about the physical sciences, but also must learn how to apply them, for God's glory, and our neighbor's benefit."
- "All of our life interacts with our faith. So in a history class, I might have an objective related to how history reveals the relationship between humanity and God."
- "Appreciate the beauty of mathematics as an extension of the Creator."

Since these professors were not dealing with introducing students to a set of standards already established by a professional society, they had more freedom to reconceptualize the ends of teaching in light of Christian theological perspectives.

Still, we should note that *some* educators teaching in professional fields also took a more transformative approach regarding their expected ends. For example, one health care educator offered, "I believe in a strong personal ethic towards the delivery of health care in the example of Jesus serving others. I expect that students will provide patient care with dignity, respect, honesty and humility without forcing personal beliefs onto the patients." In this case, the objective covered a broad range of virtues that could apply throughout one's nursing practice.

Both the spiritual addition and Christian transformation approaches involved identifying unique objectives that spring forth from the Christian tradition. Our study revealed that teachers from a variety of Christian traditions embraced four types of objectives.

1. Helping students recover a holistic understanding of God's intention for human persons
2. Developing a deeper relationship with Christ
3. Learning to understand and apply a Christian worldview or specific theological doctrine
4. Developing ethical thinking and behavior

Professors who provided examples of the first two objectives focused on a particular aspect of the Triune God. Professors who articulated the first objective emphasized God and God's intentions for humans, which involved drawing out the implications of a Christian understanding of the human person that would help their students achieve more holistic development. Reflections like these were common from the professors in this category: "I seek wholeness in restoring the image of God in students over information acquisition."; "Seeing students as made in the image of God places higher value on them in my eyes and [a] desire to help influence [or] contribute to their development . . . my objectives are not just task or learning oriented but may include character, or compassion, etc."

Professors who espoused the second objective articulated their overall transformational goal as involving a relationship with Christ. Generally, these responses focused

- on some form of personal encounter (e.g., "I am driven by the desire to help students become better disciples of Jesus."),
- internal change and growth (e.g., I want "to help students better understand the saving grace of Jesus and to grow closer to him."), or
- personal development resulting in associated behaviors (e.g., "Fundamentally I want students to embrace the sacrifice of Christ and have that play out in their best thinking and their daily lives in ways that bless them and draw others to Christ.").

The third way of articulating Christian-informed objectives was the most pervasive. It involved two types of approaches. In many cases, professors used references to "worldview" to articulate the influence of Christianity on their course objectives (e.g., "Course objectives include discussions on what it means to practice as a nurse from a Christian Worldview."). Worldview language has a long history among Protestant colleges and universities.[17] The objectives articulated using worldview language usually took a couple of different forms. Some respondents simply sought for students to think about worldviews in general (e.g., "I desire for students to be able to understand the worldview that is behind the context of a literary text."). More often, however, professors sought to make sure their students encountered and thought about their own worldview in light of a Christian or biblical worldview. The following quotes from two professors provide an apt illustration:

- "Teaching science-based courses. . . . My theology helps me approach this topic from a Christian worldview and helps me to shape objectives in a way that helps the students consider their worldview while considering a biblical view."
- "One course objective I listed in my syllabus was: integrate a biblical worldview of health care and science with concepts related to human physiology."

We found one of the attractive elements of worldview language is that it focuses on helping students understand and critically apply a broad theological way of thinking to the subject matter that could be shared by all Christians.

Besides worldview language, professors often articulated Christian objectives that required students to understand and/or apply a particular theological doctrine that could be held by all or virtually all Christian traditions. Often this approach involved emphasizing some aspect of the doctrine of creation.[18] One professor shared: "One of my course objectives is to present educational psychology from a Christian perspective and require students to reflect upon traditional and current research in this area from a Christian perspective. . . . In this course, we view children and youth as the Imago Dei, created by a Creator and beholden to Him." When summarizing the overall hopes or outcomes for this course, this professor continued, "My end goal is that students know the content as well or better as students from a secular institution and can see it through the lens of Scripture." As can be seen from this quote, professors often used similar terms such as "Christian worldview," "Christian perspective," or "biblical perspective" interchangeably to describe what they hoped students would learn.

The fourth type of objective focused on a particular ethical outcome (e.g., "Jesus loved and ministered to the outcast and lowly."). Christianity, like most historical, religious, and philosophical traditions, provides a larger story that makes sense of and justifies ethical views. In particular, this story and its interpretations, such as "Jesus loved and ministered to the lowly and outcast," helps determine particular ethical teachings that teachers consider important, as the faculty member mentioned previously stated, "My students must see the lowly person as Jesus would see them. Love, care, minister to that person not ignore or walk around on the other side."

While similar ethical teachings may be found in other traditions, they may not be prioritized or conceptualized in the same manner. For instance, when one of us interviewed over a hundred post-communist teachers throughout post-Soviet Russia and Ukraine, numerous teachers noted that while communist ethics shared many similarities with the Christian ethics they were now learning, it did not teach about forgiveness. In contrast to communist ethics, these teachers found that forgiveness is a central theme and virtue in Christianity.[19]

Not surprisingly, we found that professors understood their theological tradition and beliefs as factors that shaped the ethical objectives they set for their students. Hundreds of professors pointed to specific virtues they expected from students or sought to cultivate in them:

- "I teach economics, which means I teach about stewardship over everything entrusted to us."
- "I teach history . . . I try to teach in such a way to develop empathy for our historical figures among the students. I try to help them see that our historical forbearers were image bearers just as we, and they deserve our courtesy and respect."
- "This [art] department espouses values that include being disciplined in your work, using your gifts and talents in a way that serves others and God, hospitality towards others, collaboration with others and the pursuit of spirituality."

One particular virtue that the first of these examples illustrates is the common ethical objective of stewardship. Professors wanted their students to learn how to steward. The stewardship could be of their minds (e.g., "Everything we have comes from God. This includes our intellect. The principal of being good stewards with our minds . . . plays a significant role in my course objectives."), their overall gifts (e.g., "I encourage my students to be good stewards of their gifts."), a disciplinary area (e.g., "discussion around stewardship and our responsibilities as Christians in leadership"), finances (e.g., "emphasis placed on financial stewardship when teaching personal finance to juniors and seniors"), or even the whole world (e.g., "emphasis upon stewardship of God's world").

We should also note that although our request for examples from professors sometimes elicited short responses that fit into only one of our categories, other responses included objectives that included additional categories or combined two or more of our categories. Professors commonly wanted students not only to develop a Christian worldview relevant to their discipline but also to apply these perspectives to their coursework and develop certain virtues as a result. To illustrate, we share here a final example from a qualitative interview one of us did with a Christian transformation professor.

Example: Why Learn German?

David Smith, a professor of education and former professor of German at Calvin College and the director of the Kuyers Institute for Christian Teaching and Learning, has made it his scholarly mission to help Christians understand how a reflective Christianity can transform one's teaching. In the following interview one of us did with him, Smith discusses how he has sought to change his students' understanding of why someone should learn a language.[20]

David Smith: Foreign language in the world at large has often been conceived in fairly self-centered, utilitarian terms. Why do I learn a foreign language? So I can earn more money? So that my country can get more economic advantages so that we can become more economically competitive? So that I can get smarter and go to grad school? These motivations for learning another language do not necessarily focus on the importance of the people who speak that language as people themselves. . . . One of the things I started doing in our core classes, where the students have to be in the foreign language class, is every week I have them read a scriptural text in German. We do a little bit of language work with it, and then I discuss it with them for five minutes in Friday's class. The point is not just that we read the Bible; the texts deal with hospitality to the stranger, cultural diversity, the power of language, and those kinds of issues. Through all of those texts, I try to build coherently over a semester. I want to give them a sense of theological coherence and not just little snippets. I've built a case for saying to them that a fundamental part of being human, a fundamental part of loving your neighbor as yourself, is to love the foreigner as yourself, to love the people that are culturally different from you.

I ask them outright, in class, "Do you want to spend the rest of your life living out the all-too-common attitude that says if anybody else in the world has got anything to say to me they've got to learn to say it the way I hear, because I'm not going to lift a finger to learn to hear the way they speak? And because they probably don't have anything that I need to hear anyway?" . . .

We've actually done a little bit of small scale research on how their views change. For instance, we did a survey of our incoming freshmen. One of the things we asked them was, "Are there Christian reasons for learning foreign language?" And they often said no, about half of them. A big chunk of them, 40 percent, said, overseas mission or evangelism. . . . The next question was, "Why are you in a foreign language class?" Less than 1 percent said for foreign missions. You've got a huge disparity between the official rhetoric and their own experiences of learning. . . . So, it's pretty pointless for them. Either there isn't a Christian reason or there's a Christian reason that is irrelevant to their aims and goals in life and their experience.

At the end of the semester, after we'd been doing the [hospitality to the stranger] study, we found that there had been a big shift through the semester in their ability to articulate different Christian reasons for studying other languages and cultures in terms of loving your neighbor, in terms of understanding other people, and so on. I even had one or two dramatic instances, like I had one guy who came into my office at the start of the semester and he said, "I want to be straight with you, I don't think I should be in this class. I don't agree with there being a foreign language requirement at a Christian college, I think it's a waste of my time. I'm not very good at it, I've got no use for it in my future life. I really think you're just wasting my time and money." He was quite pleasant about it. He said, "I'm not going to cause you trouble, I'm going to do the work, I just felt I needed to say that at the start of the course." So, I thanked him for his insight and as class got underway we started going through these texts.

About five weeks into the semester he came to my office. We'd just been reading stuff out of the Pentateuch about hospitality to the stranger and so on. He said, "These texts we've been reading in class, they're wild. Is there anything else I can read about this?" So, I gave him a copy of our book [*The Gift of the Stranger: Faith, Hospitality and Foreign Language Learning*], and he came back two days later and bought another copy for his high school teacher, and then I didn't see him for a few weeks. A week before the end of the semester he came back to me. He had to write an argumentative essay for his 101-Composition class on any topic he chose. He wanted to know if he could interview me because he had chosen to write on why every freshman at a Christian college should be made to learn a foreign language. Sometimes it's quite a dramatic worldview change, just through that simple process of instructing them in some ethical background for why they're doing what they're doing.

I don't stand up in class and say, "You're in a foreign language class because it will make you smarter or because you'll earn more money or because it's part of core curriculum you've got to do it." Instead I say, "This is part of the formation of your ethical identity as a human being. Many of you are culturally insulated. The world is inhabited by other people that God made that are just as important as you are. That's part of the rationale for why we are doing this right now." And then the next step, I start saying that to them, the reason for our foreign language program is hospitality to the stranger. . . .

The reason we have foreign languages on our Christian curriculum is not just so we can earn more money, although that might be part of it. I say to my students,

> If you come out of my German class and use my German for business purposes, which I hope some of you will, but you use your German to rip off Germans more effectively to just get better and better deals at their expense, then you've failed. You're not one of my graduates. Because that's not what you are learning German for in my class. You are learning German, so you can learn to bless strangers. And when you use German in a German business context I hope you're going to learn to understand German culture and love German people enough that you're going to be trying to do deals that benefit both parties. That will be an outcome of your having been in this foreign language program.

Curricular Sense-Making, Construction, and Content Building

We also found an important difference between spiritual addition and Christian transformation professors regarding curricular sense-making, construction, and content building.

Spiritual Addition Teachers

Spiritual addition teachers, as one would expect, simply added Christian material to classroom content or curriculum to make their classes more "Christian" in nature. They discussed three types of additions to their curriculum due to their Christian identity.[21] The first type of addition pertained to the inclusion of specific Christian scripture passages to support points (e.g., "I may utilize passages of Scripture to illustrate points."; "I incorporate Biblical scripture into writing prompts and lessons."; "[I] always include Biblical examples to support content."). The second form of addition involved simply adding Christian material to the content of the course, as one professor mentioned: "I sometimes draw examples from the music literature of specifically Christian works and discuss what I know of the circumstances of the composition, the composer's faith, work and situation. I discuss musical techniques/tools/tendencies that have known theological references." In these cases, professors assume a divide between the regular secular curriculum and the spiritual components.

Finally, the most predominant addition involved inserting ethical material. For instance, one professor wrote, "I choose texts that emphasize ethical issues." In some cases, professors combined the inclusion of ethical material with the teaching found in the Bible (e.g., "In nursing, it is logical to bring in the teachings of Christ regarding the value of human life."; "When discussing ethical business practices, I bring in the biblical teachings of Christ.").

As the most commonly mentioned approach in our study, the ethical addition to course content deserves further exploration. The literature on moral education in higher education has found that the substance of the ethical material added to a class or program often involves emphasis on three different aspects: virtue, social justice, or community service.[22] Christian professors in our survey mentioned an intentional inclusion of each of these strands.

The most common emphasis that our professors cited was the inclusion of a particular virtue. These virtues pertained to positive character strengths, representing two types we label "redemptive virtues" and "common virtues." In the Bible, the theme of the imitation of Christ is prominent. Biblical scholars note that within the Christian scriptures the imitation of Christ is particularly commanded with regard to various virtues he demonstrated (e.g., sacrificial love, humility, servanthood or service, forgiveness or grace).[23] We call these redemptive virtues because they require one to move beyond equal treatment and take a lower position that gives up power or that responds in a virtuous way to offenses or enemies.

As illustrated by the absence of forgiveness in the Soviet communist ethical tradition mentioned previously, these redemptive virtues are more likely to be excluded or downplayed in other moral traditions (e.g., Aristotle thought humility was a vice).[24] Indeed, one finds this reality among the character education tradition in the United States. Among the list of virtues found in those character education laws in the United States that mention 64 different virtues, not one includes humility, servanthood, or peacemaking as a virtue to be emulated.[25] Furthermore, only one state lists forgiveness, and only one lists service. In addition, not one list mentions the theological virtues of faith, hope, and love as especially important or worthy of being emulated.

In contrast, redemptive virtues such as humility (e.g., "Our theological tradition promotes humility."), love of enemies ("I teach love of enemies."), and peacebuilding (e.g., "I encourage peacebuilding concepts in student learning objectives.") were some of the key virtues added by Christian professors. The rationale for these difficult virtues came from placing oneself in the Christian story and associating with Christ's model or example.

The second set of virtues teachers mentioned are often found in character education programs in a variety of public schools and universities, and include respect, kindness, care, and honesty.[26] We call these the common virtues, although the theological rationale for emphasizing them may not exactly be common. One professor's response illustrates this nuance: "I have one course where we discuss ethics of human subjects in research. My theological tradition is 'care for one's neighbor,' especially those who may not be able to care for themselves. We discuss the biblical tradition of how one cares for one's neighbor and relate that to designing human subjects research." This professor made this connection explicit by noting the need for respecting "a patient's right to make an educated decision about the benefits and risks of the study and to protect the patients from being misused." While protecting vulnerable research subjects is a common moral imperative, this professor drew upon a biblical rationale for justifying it.

Within this category of common virtues, educators most often mentioned honesty because it relates to academic standards (e.g., "We frequently discuss how to be people of integrity. We discuss how ethics impacts research, classroom behavior, moral dilemmas on the job, and daily life."). For other faculty members, honesty, integrity, and trust were foci as elements of future professional behavior, as one professor explained: "One assignment I give for seniors is to write an essay: What am I willing to lose my job for? Thinking about living with integrity and care primes us to consider different options when ethical challenges come our way." This emphasis on honesty is not surprising in light of the fact that a key set of ends for most classes includes learning and the pursuit of truth, which are compromised by academic dishonesty.

While virtues were the most common form of ethical content added to a course, some teachers also mentioned the other two strands of course additions, social justice ("choice to make 'Social Justice' the course theme for the writing class") and service ("Service-learning is part of my courses."). As the following examples illustrate, the three strands of virtue, social justice, and service could be combined:

- "[Our Christian tradition] places a high value on servanthood and service learning. This leads me to find ways for class members to serve the community by establishing a home school teaching class in my education methods courses."
- "My goal for each semester is to encourage the students to examine their positions regarding the social injustices occurring in the world and their personal response to those injustices. I believe that the Old Testament prophets and Christ teach a responsibility of one to another. However, I would like to point out that the Jewish and Catholic faiths teach this as well, and I feel very strongly that it is not useful to attach that idea solely to Christianity. We discuss this in class as well."

As the teacher last quoted indicated, these latter themes may not be mentioned as much in our survey responses simply because teachers did not view this theme as something distinct to their particular Christian tradition or even the Christian tradition as a whole. General moral virtues and general moral principles are also emphasized in secular literature and practices pertaining to moral development in higher education.[27] The contrast becomes most apparent when considering the redemptive virtues. In the examples from professors in our survey that went beyond redemptive virtues, the Christian distinction emerged only when combined with a particular scriptural or theological reference (e.g., "Character Education course includes a goal on the fruit of the spirit and character").

Christian Transformation Professors

Christian transformation professors also incorporated ethical components into their curriculum, as well as other more specific Christian theology. The major difference between these professors and the Spiritual addition educators is that they perceived their Christian identity, and thus the Christian theological and ethical components, as influencing their curricular sense-making, construction, and content. Since Christian transformation professors understood all of life to relate to sacred and spiritual matters, they did not separate out some parts of a curriculum as being more spiritual or religious than others (e.g., "There is no distinction between 'sacred' and 'secular' knowledge.").

Consequently, Christian transformation professors did not write about adding extra Christian content; instead, they discussed how they added theological perspectives to their whole discipline, course, or particular subject under discussion. Here is an example:

> [Christianity] not only influences course objectives but entire courses. . . . For example, in a Finance class, I start out by trying to help my students see how religious orientation, creational structure, and the various ways that people have developed the creation affect what happens in business and finance. I then challenge them to think about how finance needs to be "reformed" to become what God expects of his people.

The professor designs the course to help students view the whole discipline or subject of study through a Christian theological lens. In another case, the professor simply discussed placing the whole course's subject matter within a collective theological conceptualization that guides his collective purpose: "We believe that God made us to be dialogic creatures with the ability to communicate; therefore, we take the approach that communication studies are important." Finally, another professor identified a holistic outlook that represents the Christian transformationist approach, informing us of his concern that his students "see the 'big picture' of how my discipline fits into the scheme of God's plan for redeeming the creation."

The Christian transformation professors also took particular parts of a course and then discussed them using a wider Christian perspective. A chemistry professor described this approach: "A major topic in general chemistry is energy relationships in chemical reactions. Burning of fossil fuels for energy is a chemical process. These ideas lead to a discussion of our God-given roles as stewards of creation and a conversation about God-glorifying ways to use energy resources, both fossil and renewable." In this case, the professor brings the subject matter back to one of the key student identities discussed in chapter 2. In the Christian story, we are stewards of God's creation.

Since these small snippets and quotes may not give one a full sense of how the Christian transformation professor might go about changing a course, we have included a vignette that continues the interview with David Smith previously cited.

Why Learn German? The Curricular Transformation

Some may not think Christianity relates directly to teaching German beyond its cultural relevance to German history and culture. In contrast, David Smith takes the purpose we quoted previously and relates how this purpose transforms his curriculum.

David Smith: If I start saying . . . to my students [that] the purpose of our foreign language program is hospitality to the stranger, and then my course materials are all about checking into hotels and about buying meals in restaurants and how to cash your travelers checks or abstract grammar exercises, than I am going to end up performing a contradiction between what I say the aims are [and] what the content of my curriculum is. Take the first two weeks of my 201 class. The syllabus says review of the present perfect tense. It's the tense the Germans use to talk orally about past events. My standard textbook . . . gives a bunch of example sentences that are mostly set in a business office context. You then do a set of ten-question exercises where you have to manipulate various past tense sentences, which are all set either in financial contexts or in vacation contexts: "Hans and Sabrina have gone on vacation. They paid a lot for their hotel. Eric has bought a new car." That's what you get. You can learn German that way, students come out after two weeks, they can do the present perfect tense. So, you meet some of your goals. You meet the kind of goals that are tested on standardized tests and so on. But at the same time, you're also portraying a picture of German culture that's extremely shallow and two-dimensional. Germans might be pretty consumerist but that's not the whole truth about German culture. You're assuming that the whole purpose of language learning is basically for economic and leisure purposes and there isn't any kind of ethical context to it.

So, what I do instead is I take the life story of a lady called Adaline Kelbert, who is not famous.[28] You would never have heard of her. She was a ninety-three-year-old German housewife, a friend of a friend. Lived in Hamburg. Because she was a friend of a friend we managed to get family photos, take recordings of her telling her story. We made transcripts, so we've got a whole bunch of material.

She was born in 1903 in the Ukraine. Her family owned a farm, but WWI came along in 1914. They became refugees because the war came through and they wandered about 2,000 kilometers across the future Soviet Union. They ended up living with a Tartar family in a two-room log cabin for nine months. Then they found a German-speaking Mennonite village nearby and found accommodations there and some work and then eventually made their way back to their hometown after WWI. They got their farm back.

Then Adaline married, and she and her husband took over the farm. Of course, the Russian Revolution had happened, and the authorities turned up and the land was confiscated and so they became displaced again. They ended up living in another village, working on a collective farm. WWII came and then Germans invaded and came through their village and then retreated and took all the German speakers away with them. Her husband and two sons were conscripted to fight in the German army and she was put on a train for Hamburg. After the war she managed to find her husband and one son, and they settled down in Hamburg and lived there for the rest of their lives. So just a normal central European twentieth-century life story.

I had a two-week teaching unit. The first week we basically spent getting to know her story. I start the first day, I have a PowerPoint presentation with all the family photos. You can do lots of simple oral work with that. I just put a photo up, I'll say, talk to your partner, describe what you see in the photo as much as you can. And then we talk about it together as a class. We do lots of speaking practice. We gradually narrate the story and get to know Adaline Kelbert and her husband. We then start to read transcripts of more detailed sections of the story. We listen to her telling parts of the story and have students narrate parts of the story to each other. We do lots of language work out of that.

Even just in that part of it, there are hooks in there where I can also do some things that are not in the standard textbook. For example, when she stayed with this Tartar family in a two-room log cabin, no furniture. Family of five, they didn't speak each other's language. At that point, I say to my students, "Let's do some pair work, let's so some role play. Imagine this scenario. First of all, how many rooms does your parents' house have?" They say "eight, twelve, fourteen, fifteen, etc." Okay, "I want to imagine this scenario, a family of five turn up on your doorstep. They are from a different ethnic group, and they don't speak your language. They clearly need to stay for longer than a couple of weeks. I want you to role play the conversation that happens between you and your parents." Again, now at this point I'm getting more than the present perfect tense. What I hope I'm getting is some spiritual challenge. These Tartars weren't Christians, but they practiced hospitality to strangers.

There's another point when they move to the Mennonite village where she says, "We lived well there. There was milk and there was bread. We had work and they gave us a house in which to live. They spoke German in the church." She's so excited and she goes on about this. I ask students, "What five things do you need to live well? List them." Adaline Kelbert says you need bread, you need milk, you need work, you need a roof over your head, and you need a church that speaks your language. So, using a story like that gives me hooks to sort of hook into the moral imagination of my students.

The second week, having worked on Adaline Kelbert's biography, I then give them a set of questions and they have to go out into the community and find someone who's over 70 years old. On campus there's a retirement village right across the road and they have to interview someone for an hour in English about their life story, using an interview outline. Then they have to bring that back. They have to report orally in German in class to each other and then turn it into a piece of biographical writing about their American interviewee based on the interview, and then we get cultural comparisons with Adaline Kelbert's life story. They get to do a piece of extended writing using her story as a model. Now, by the end of two weeks they can do the present perfect tense pretty much as well as if I'd used the standard grammar text. But I've gained a lot of other things as well, including consistency since I've been telling my students our curriculum is for learning to be hospitable to strangers. I brought the stranger into class, and I had them listen to her life story.

Conclusion

How are we to explain the differences between the spiritual addition and Christian transformation professors? One possible explanation comes from Douglas Jacobsen and Rhonda Jacobsen's book *Christian Faith and Scholarship*, in which they observe that the differences between how Christian professors approach scholarship could come from what Richard Foster identities as different traditions of spiritual practice. The traditions of spiritual practice Foster describes tend to transcend church affiliation and theological traditions; they are

1. the contemplative tradition, which focuses on a relationship with God developed through prayer;
2. the holiness tradition, which focuses on the development of Christian character;
3. the charismatic tradition, which focuses on spiritual power;
4. the social justice tradition, which focuses on social and political transformation;
5. the evangelical tradition, which focuses on conversion and theological orthodoxy; and
6. the incarnational tradition, which focuses on integrating faith into all of life.

One might argue, regarding these spiritual traditions and scholarship, that each influences Christian teaching in unique ways.[29] Spiritual addition professors tend to draw on the first five categories, while Christian transformation professors tend to focus on the incarnational tradition. There may be some truth to this view, but we think making such a sharp contrast misses one of the essential points we found, which can be seen most clearly in our extended examples. Spiritual transformation teachers, we contend, draw upon almost all of these traditions to transform the whole of their objectives, curriculum, and as we shall see in the next chapter, pedagogy. They do not neglect issues such as spiritual practices, character development, or social justice, but they incorporate them into their objectives, curriculum, and pedagogy in a more seamless way.

4

Thinking and Acting Christianly in the Classroom

> Behaviors taken alone are rarely distinctive except as they become moments in stories. . . . Pedagogical practices will appear most distinctively Christian when set amid confessed Christian faith, though they may express a Christian posture in the world even when we are silent about our motivations. The goal is not to find some technique that Christians can copyright. The goal is to shape a set of practices that are consistent as we can manage with the story of all things made new as the kingdoms of this world become the kingdom of our God and of his Christ.
>
> —David I. Smith, *On Christian Teaching*[1]

God and economics apparently do not go together. When philosopher Warren Nord examined 40 of his own university's economic texts at the University of North Carolina, he found that only one mentioned religion at all—a passing historical reference.[2] He also reviewed 6,700 pages of 14 high school textbooks about economics and discovered only 3 pages that dealt with religion. Virtually all of that material was about the era before 1550.[3] Moreover, he discovered that authors simply asserted the economic values set forth, such as efficiency, freedom, and growth, or justified them on the grounds that they helped achieve national goals or are common values one can just assume. The authors never connected the values to any larger moral tradition or metanarrative beyond utilitarian individualism.

Peter Alonzi, a professor of economics at Dominican University, does not rely on texts to transform his course. Instead, he shares a simple pedagogical strategy for helping students think about economics Christianly. He calls it "Pauses." He explains this concept simply, "There are times in my economics course when pausing to behold allows me to share with students my sense of the presence of God in economics."[4]

Like spiritual addition professors, Alonzi begins the course with a prayer, but it is a prayer that directly relates to the overall metanarrative that he uses to surround and transform the course. The simple prayer is: "Thank you for the sun that warms us, the air that inspires us, the rain that refreshes us, and the earth that feeds us and is our home. No human has made these, they are Your gift to us."[5] What some might see as a simple spiritual exercise, he understands as establishing an important presupposition that guides the course's overarching paradigm. He sets before students this thought: "While taking resources for granted is a convenient assumption, it is most important to remember that natural resources are not just there. They are gifts. So at the very beginning of the course we pause. We call natural resources by their true name—gift—when we say thank you to the creator."[6]

From this beginning, Alonzi then moves into presenting the common economic models related to issues of supply, demand, and pricing. Early on, he pauses once again to ask students to think critically about one of the elements of economic models: the able adults who make economic decisions in the common model. He asks this question about the economic model: "Who is left out of the model, and who is responsible for those left out?" He wants students to consider an important ethical matter. "For it is in facing this question we hear the invitational test and measure of any society: how it treats its less fortunate. We sense the truth offered in Luke 12:48. 'When a man had had a great deal given him, a great deal will be demanded of him.' We begin to sense the common good, and with that, the presence of God."[7]

After another pause, Alonzi asks students to consider another question, pertaining to a Christian perspective on utility maximization: "What is at the center of the person's preference ordering?" Students often claim that selfishness stands at the center. He also observes of students' answers, "God is squeezed out, unneeded and unmentioned. And most devastatingly, we don't know that we don't know that God has been squeezed out."[8] He then makes students aware of how modern economic theory has squeezed God out of the picture and offers a different view of the economic person with God in the picture: "Rather, the 'Economic Person' is one who knows he or she is a creature merging at birth from the source and remerging at death with the source. This Economic Person, in his or her temporal parenthesis of 30 or 60 or 90 years, is a temporary caretaker, a steward of the resources entrusted by the source, the Love."[9]

When it comes to the technical lesson related to profit maximization, Alonzi once again pauses. He says students often make a critical mistake here. They think that since profit is total revenue less total cost, profit maximization means that one should merely make profits as big as possible. Alonzi points out, "But without pausing, the student might corrupt profit maximization into the mere miserly accumulation of more. Students miss God's presence. They miss God's call for business people to be effective stewards of the resources entrusted to humanity by God."[10]

In all of these pauses, Alonzi tries to communicate the importance of placing economics within a larger metanarrative. He concludes, "Without neglecting or turning from the concepts and principles of economics—indeed, while engaging them rigorously—we realize the presence of God right in the middle [of] the course. We realize God's presence because we pause to behold. If we fail [to] pause, the class skitters along the surface, confuses the part for the whole, and misses the opportunity to realize God's presence."[11] Alonzi's pauses are a rather simple pedagogical practice, but they transform the whole nature of his course.

So far we have discussed the background beliefs of teachers and how they choose outcomes and the curriculum, but now we come to what many actually define as teaching—pedagogy. In this chapter we address how Christianity can change teachers' pedagogical practices, classroom ethics, and modeling.

Pedagogical Practices

One of the complaints about pedagogy at Christian colleges and universities articulated by David Smith and James K. A. Smith is that "the typical pedagogical practices of the modern university often remain largely unrevised as the default medium within which attempts to think, speak, and educate Christianly are conducted."[12] Our quantitative survey would appear to affirm that claim for a majority of the faculty surveyed. Only 40 percent of faculty indicated that their pedagogical practices were shaped by their theological tradition. Twenty percent were unsure—more than twice those who reported being unsure in any of the other categories. Part of the reason for this problem may be the fact that only 4.6 percent of published scholarly journal articles on faith-learning integration deal with pedagogy.[13]

How Christianity influences pedagogy has not been an important scholarly emphasis. David Smith also contends that other factors such as the current rewards system, training, and habits of mind regarding teaching in higher education reinforce this situation.[14]

The 40 percent of faculty who affirmed this connection, however, provided us with a variety of ways in which their faith tradition influences their pedagogy. Once again, we noticed a difference between spiritual addition and Christian transformation professors. The spiritual addition professors mentioned that they added a particular spiritual practice such as devotional Bible reading or prayer to, or shared the personal story of their own Christian conversion with, their classes. The following examples are representative of this outlook:

- "I begin each class with a meditation. The meditation is begun by a Bible connection. There is always a time of joys and concerns for students to share needs in their personal lives."
- "I start each class with scripture reading and prayer."
- "[I] have shared my testimony in class [about] life experiences that God has helped get me through."

Professors did not mention these practices solely as in-class additions, they also claimed they engaged in these practices outside of class (e.g., "I pray privately for the class and intercede for my campus and my students."). In the end though, educators understood these activities as additions to the regular teaching activities of the class.

In contrast, spiritual transformation educators focused on three pedagogical approaches. First, they looked at the area of pedagogy differently. As one teacher noted, "Teaching methods are influenced by belief in teaching as a gift from God, to support students in their role of gaining knowledge to develop their gifts from God." Similar to the whole idea of viewing students or subject matter as a gift, this teacher understood pedagogy as a gift to be stewarded for others. She derived this perspective from seeking to think and live in light of the overall Christian story.

Second, while these educators used Bible reading or prayer while teaching, they did not simply add these practices to the start of class. As Alonzi's prayer at the beginning of his economics class illustrated, spiritual transformation teachers tried to integrate these practices into class in ways that connected with the content and students. For example, instead of placing prayer at the beginning of class, some professors incorporated prayer into the class when it related to the particular topic (e.g., "For example, in current events based classes, we might stop in the middle of a news story or current issue, identify some of the affected parties, and have three or four students pray for what we are learning about."). They took a similar approach with the use of the Bible. They might also include a certain kind of content or assignment for biblical reasons, even if it actually involved learning how not to rely on the Bible. A professor shared the following example:

> In Business Ethics, the reason I insist that students need to be able to make a case for asking a non-Christian colleague in a secular business setting to do the right thing by using a secular argument rather than "Bible-thumping" is that, based upon Rom 1:18ff; 2:14, all persons have a moral awareness. Hence, secular ethics, at best, focuses on some aspect of this God-given moral awareness all persons have or had until they repressed it (Rom 1).

In these cases, faculty did not necessarily see the addition of these practices as something disconnected from course objectives or their students. In fact, some teachers articulated scripture's vital importance to the overall class objective. One teacher claimed: "I am interested in students finishing a course with an increased sense of/encounter/with the God of truth, rather than merely understanding theological propositions. Consequently, I encourage prayer and devotional activities along with theological discourse in an integrated fashion."

We want to note, however, that with both types of professors, the Christian practices that were mentioned tended to focus on prayer and inclusion of the Bible. As a result, we did not find what two recent Christian authors have suggested Christian teaching needs: the incorporation of a wider range of Christian practices into teaching that are also nurtured in the church, practices such as hospitality or fellowship (see box 4.1).[15]

Third, Christian transformation professors articulated their perspectives on *why* a particular teaching practice should be incorporated into their teaching in light of their Christian outlook or narrative. Since a teacher must justify a particular method in some way, teachers drew upon their Christian identity and its associated narrative to justify the importance

Box 4.1 Experiments with Christian Practices in the Classroom[25]

The illustration in chapter 2 of Carolyn Call's experience with shared practice in the classroom mentioned the transformative effect of showing hospitality. She also incorporated another Christian practice into her teaching: fellowship. Christian fellowship she understood as more than "hanging out." Rather, "[i]ts end or purpose is to build community and strengthen the mortar of relationships between persons. . . . Fellowship also serves to build a narrative identity for a community." Pedagogically, she sought to nurture fellowship by employing three methods: (1) an opening "call out" exercise, (2) a mid-class break with food, and (3) and closing "joys and concerns" time. She explained, "My hope was that these would act in concert and help to create a loose mortar of care between these students."

The opening "call out" exercise involved asking students to go around the class and choose a word or phrase to describe from where they were coming. Pedagogically, she found this exercise helped her obtain a pulse of the class, often ignited discussion later in class, and helped her students to settle into the class and focus. Sharing food during the break proved to be a winner among students, but it also led to deeper conversations and asking others questions. It also produced a relational warmth among students. She commented, "The power of this interaction was clear when I reviewed the student evaluations at the close of the semester: they indicated that students found the sharing of food to be the central element of a shared sense of community."

The final sharing of joys and concerns, however, did not result in simple happy feelings and rosy emotions. For this part, Call simply asked students to share joys and concerns, about which she asked those who pray to do so. This resulted in a wide variety of sharing of humorous and serious requests. It also led to a deep vulnerability among students about the issues plaguing their personal lives. As a result of this exercise, Call found something in her heart:

> As much as I love my students and want the very best for them, I was surprised to realize that I did not want too much knowledge about

> them. I found it too heavy to bear. This realization gave me pause and has led me to re-evaluate some of my own motivations behind my teaching.
>
> She concluded, "Engaging with the practices in my own life and then bringing them into the classroom stretched my understanding of the moral aims of teaching and reminded me of our deep responsibility for the spiritual and intellectual lives of our students."

of particular pedagogical practices. Following are some of the activities educators mentioned:

- **Group learning:** "God made the human brain to be interactive and form patterns. I do not believe that it can do this well if I stand and lecture all the time. Therefore, my theological tradition has influenced my teaching by becoming much more student-centered rather than teacher-centered. I provide much more choice and group learning, projects, and learning activities in class rather than lecture."
- **Student reflections:** "I have always appreciated that my theological tradition has not given me black-and-white answers, but has allowed many answers to be "gray." . . . I don't tend to give black-and-white answers to my students. But I will give a lot of feedback—an alternate view, a different way to view their life or the subject matter. I tend to give a number of journaling assignments in my faith integration components. This is the opportunity I use to see how they think and what they think and to engage in conversation with them."
- **Service learning:** "In many courses, we conduct service-learning projects serving the poor and homeless. How we take care of the poor and suffering is absolutely key to Jesus' teachings."
- **Use of primary sources:** "I believe especially in the power of the written word—the Scriptures, foremost, but also writings of church leaders and the holy witnesses who make up our heritage. I encourage students with book lists and additional reading and writing and use primary sources so they can hear the voices of the church speak into their lives today."

- **Openness to challenging questions:** "I am willing for students to ask challenging questions and to follow truth wherever it leads, in the confidence that all truth is God's truth and all truth discoveries will ultimately lead back to God."

There is nothing uniquely Christian about the specific methods being used. In fact, the professors are largely incorporating many of the progressive, student-centered teaching practices prized within the contemporary university. Yet their support of these methods is related to their Christian identity. Interestingly, in her study of faculty spirituality, Jennifer Lindholm found that "faculty members who themselves are spiritually inclined are more likely (largely irrespective of disciplinary affiliation and personal demographic characteristics) to use student-centered teaching methods."[16] We found Christian professors use these student-centered methods for specifically Christian reasons. What is uniquely Christian is the justificatory reasoning supporting the method chosen by the professor.[17] They sought to make their pedagogical practices consistent with the Christian metanarrative.

The transformation of pedagogical practices discussed by these teachers also included outside the class activities, such as the following:

- **Approaches to student grading:** "I do not let their theological tradition or their reluctance to accept other traditions influence my grading of their progress in the French language."
- **Discipline:** "Discipline should be restorative and provide students with opportunities for redemption."
- **Design of assignments:** "I choose to assign papers for students that are not carefully tailored to avoid plagiarism. They are free to choose a subject of their choice. By being in a Christian community I choose to trust the integrity of my students."
- **Reading methods:** "[I]sometimes help them learn how to properly question a text.... The key is thinking truth and letting the texts examine you just as much as you examine the texts. You must know the original intent of the authors of a text to really get its meaning and meaning is what is most important. After all, Jesus as the logos is the meaning, the touchstone for understanding properly both God and man."
- **Relating to students outside of class:** "I treat students with respect. I interact with them with concern for their spiritual life and growth."

As a set, these practices and pedagogical approaches highlight teachers' deep concerns for how students are formed, both through the overall processes of education and through practices consistent with their view of the story of all things.

To provide an extended example of this approach, we once again turn to David Smith, who has made it his primary mission to help Christian teachers think in Christian ways about their pedagogy. In his recent book on the subject, he gives a vignette of how he opens his German class. He first arranges the chairs in groups of four. Next, he explains:

> I ask the students to pair off within their groups. I tell them that each person will have two minutes to share as much as they can about themselves in German to their partner. I specify that this is to be a slightly odd conversation—not the usual give-and-take, but one person speaking in the other listing for a full two minutes, with the roles then switched. . . .
>
> After the four minutes, I stepped in with fresh instructions. I asked the pairs to combine back into groups of four and tell them that they now have one minute each to introduce the partner to the group, beginning German, based on what they learned from their first conversation.[18]

Smith later contrasts this opening to an experience of students who took an analytic philosophy class four decades ago from Robert Dearden at the Institute of Education in London. Dearden dove into his first argument and discussion, and a student interrupted:

> "Excuse me," she intervened, nervously but with some determination, "but do you think we might begin by introducing ourselves, so that we know a little about each other? Otherwise we are just, well . . ."
>
> Just sources of argument?" [o]ffered Dearden.
>
> "Yes."
>
> "Well, that's exactly what you are here— sources of argument. It does not matter who you are or where you come from. What matters is the quality of your argument. If you want to know more about each other . . . you can meet in the pub afterwards."[19]

In making this comparison, Smith makes the point that even minor classroom decisions are guided by ethical perspectives formed by a larger worldview.

His choices were shaped by an understanding that students are not primarily "minds, achievers, customers, or challenges, but . . . images of God called to faithful living and to love of God and neighbor."[20] In other words, Smith affirms the common theme we found among our transformationist teachers. They understood Christian-informed pedagogy to mean not that Christians have some special methods only they use, but rather that they choose and justify their pedagogy using thinking shaped by the Christian narrative. As Smith relates regarding this opening vignette, "Christians are not the only ones who value community or seek to honor students. Yet Christians do so for Christian reasons, and Christian reasoning was involved in my choices to focus on listening, respect, name learning, safety, community and the like."[21]

Ethics

One of the things I remember most about my (Perry's) favorite professor at Rice University was the class in which he cried. I had taken two semesters of American intellectual history from Professor Haskell. He taught in a dispassionate way almost that whole time, but he also had a wonderful way of engaging the class in the most profound intellectual questions and themes shaping the nation's history. Toward the end of the second semester, we covered the civil rights movement. As Professor Haskell related the stories of some of the civil rights martyrs and the treatment of civil rights protesters, he started to weep and exclaimed loudly through his tears, "These are fellow human beings!" In that single instance of emotion, Professor Haskell became not merely a professor, but a fellow human being sharing and mourning the moral tragedy and sorrows of humanity.

Beyond this singular outcry, however, I usually did not know Professor Haskell's moral outlook. Professors at Christian universities were more overt in how they expressed their ethical views. When providing examples of how their Christian identity influenced pedagogy, teachers often used virtue language to describe how they applied a particular practice or justified their choice for using certain practices. In other words, the teachers did not merely discuss teaching students about these virtues (which were discussed in the content section) but emphasized the need to demonstrate them in their classroom practice ("an attitude of service and hospitality towards all students").

While in some cases teachers simply identified virtues and their use (e.g., "Justice should be tempered with grace."), in many others teachers tied them to some of the identities and/or larger theological narratives we described previously. For example, consider the following examples from professors, each of whom refers to different aspects of the Triune God:

- "As fellow image bearers, we are called to relate to each other as mutual servants of our God, and thus we should support and respect each other and the work that we do. So we are responsible to God and to each other for how we do our work, and how we support, communicate with, and correct each other."
- "In class, I introduce myself, in part, as a believer in and actor within grace. I firmly believe in the gospel as the good news of grace in Jesus Christ, unlimitedly demonstrated by God to us. Our own failures and limitations of grace that render our relationships broken also allow us to be called by God's grace as responsible agents of reconciliation through grace to the world around us—in our classrooms, in our families, in our whole lives."
- "Responsiveness to the Holy Spirit rather than rely on professional society ethics code books."

The first professor uses two particular identities—image bearer and mutual servants of our God—to provide a shorthand narrative reference for the justification for supporting and respecting others and showing responsibility to God in one's work. The second professor draws upon God's grace as a motivation for her own demonstration of grace in the classroom (and her effort to have the story of God's grace shape students' motivations). The final professor finds ethical authority and aid outside of the professional field in the Holy Spirit.

While these examples involved the general application of virtue, in many cases professors specifically identified how the application of virtue changes their classroom pedagogy. The particular academic or professional practices varied widely (e.g., course discussion, test taking, writing, discipline), as one professor exemplifies:

> Ethics is one of many important ways that one brings faith to bear on the educational enterprise. An ethical classroom experience goes beyond fair treatment and honesty. In an ethical classroom students are not pitted against each other as winners and losers; the class is set up to build bonds

of trust and support. Forgiveness, one more chance, and respect describe the teacher's response to students who struggle to learn.

Similar to this teacher, other respondents mentioned several particular virtues or groupings of virtues that fit into our redemptive and common virtue categories.

With regard to common virtues, over one hundred teachers focused explicitly on demonstrating respect. As mentioned in the previous chapter, the basis of this respect almost always derived from the particular theological belief that all students are made in God's image (e.g., "Because all people are created in the image of God, they must be respected in all communication."; "Because I believe that all people are made in the image of God and that language is a gift from God we are to treat other people and language with the respect and admiration we would give a gift."). For many Christian professors, this theologically-derived respect was foundational to their classroom pedagogy.

Similarly, professors in our survey often evoked the common virtues of fairness and justice in their descriptions of student assessment, evaluation, and treatment parity. As one professor noted, "All students, no matter their cultural or spiritual differences, are treated the same with reference to their personal beliefs or convictions. They are all treated equally." Similarly, another professor related justice to grading and assessment in the name of increased understanding: "I believe in the importance of justice in grading and providing students with feedback that provides them guidance on how to improve their scholarship."

Respondents regularly linked fairness and justice to the importance of redemptive virtues such as grace, mercy, and forgiveness. The virtues served as an additional modifying factor (e.g., "On occasion I extend surprising grace: [I] let a student make up a missed exam but give them no advance notice of the make-up opportunity.") or as a balancing factor in their behavior or ethical thinking (e.g., "Because God is redemptive, I seek to enforce justice tempered with mercy. Thus if I catch students cheating I flunk them, but if they confess cheating, I only give them a zero on the assignment."). In addition, for a number of these professors, mercy, grace, and humility were important points of theological emphasis that shaped their approach to classroom practice generally. This approach was summarized by a professor who desired to be Christ-like by being, "honest, truthful, patient, loving, caring, and steadfast in all that [one] do[es]" or another who used practices such as "cultural humility" to "come 'along-side' students and share power for their learning" in ways that "may not necessarily agree with [the teacher's] perceived need[s]" or teaching preferences.

Similar to grace, mercy, and forgiveness, some faculty respondents employed a general ethos of Christ's love and compassion generally as expressions of professional empathy, understood as a grounding orientation to life and teaching. The following examples demonstrate teachers' expressions of care for the individual students' well-being:

- "I love my students as individuals, am committed to exploring the reality of truth with them, and demonstrating patience toward them by encouraging them to ask 'big' questions about life and faith."
- "I love my students and care for them as individuals. I want them to make godly choices. My desire is to see them grow spiritually as well as intellectually. I seek to be and to create servant leaders."

Again, teachers often linked this virtue to some particular aspect of educational or professional practice and saw this as part of their pedagogy.

As suggested in the redemptive virtue examples, a subset of faculty respondents explained their ethical approach through the juxtaposition of what might be called "hard" or "common" virtues or principles (defined as firm, constant standards applied to all) and redemptive (defined as person-specific) virtues. In many cases, respondents applied this approach to their responses to student work and behavior, including grading, cheating, and learning. One teacher shared, "My belief system is one of grace, guidance and discipline. I exercise grace through trials (classroom mistakes/unethical behavior) but I do so in the form of discipline that is given in a way to help guide the student not to make future mistakes." Similarly, another faculty member emphasized a clear standard that she based on her scriptural interpretation, yet explained that this standard is delivered with grace: "My expectations, based on scripture, are that of honesty and integrity. I deal with students, who are not ethical, in firm, but gracious ways with an emphasis on consequences of our choices."

Modeling

By far the most frequently mentioned pedagogical method Christian teachers noted was modeling (see box 4.2 for a curricular example). These

Box 4.2 The Ethical Outcome of a German Class

Ethical illumination is not the first outcome one expects when asking what a student has learned in German class. However, David Smith describes a striking ethical outcome that he found after doing the unit on Frau Kelbert described in chapter 3.

David Smith: I'll have all my students send me an email just on, "What did you learn in the last two weeks?" And I'll get emails back saying things like "I hope I'm like Frau Kelbert when I'm 93 because I really admire her." Now to me that achieves another of my objectives, because it's hard to be prejudiced against Germans if Germans are your heroes. So one of my personal goals for my four semesters of core German study is that by the end of those four semesters, first of all every student in my class would have heard a German person say something that changes their life morally and spiritually. They've heard that from German lips. But it will be different things for each student. . . .

But also that they will have encountered real Germans and come to admire them. In the wider discussion of foreign language education for hundreds of years there's been this vague hope that by having foreign language learning you make people less prejudiced. There's very little evidence that that is the case. In fact what can happen in short and averagely taught foreign language programs is that people reinforce their prejudices. You learn . . . a little bit of language, not enough to communicate, and perhaps something about festivals. If foreign language learning is supposed to reduce prejudice, grammar drills and a few culture facts are not going to do that.

I figure maybe biographical narrative might contribute something. . . . So in one sense it's very consistent with our heritage here at Calvin College because the famous line here from Calvinist theologian Abraham Kuyper is, "There is not a square inch in the whole domain of our human existence over which Christ, who is Sovereign over all, does not cry, Mine!" . . . every square inch, including pedagogy, including foreign language learning, including German grammar instruction. You've got to figure out how this can become redemptive.

teachers shared Parker Palmer's perspective: "I teach more than a body of knowledge or a set of skills. I teach a mode of relationship between the knower and the known, a way of being in the world."[22] For example, one teacher provided an extensive explanation of this common practice: "I think that students learn by example and repetition. I think that they are influenced by mentors and therefore, I try to a good role model. Lead by example, if you will. I think it is a tremendous responsibility to be a role model to these students, more so than just providing them with coursework or factual information." While one might expect this obvious pedagogical approach from any teacher, the Christian teachers expressed it uniquely (e.g., "I model the expectation of working unto the Lord."). This uniqueness took three forms.

First, a few professors mentioned the importance of modeling particular practices related to their spiritual lives, such as prayer or being a witness for Christ. One professor explained, "I try to model reliance on prayer and obeying the Holy Spirit when making decisions in class," while others explained the importance of prayer (e.g., "I model a close walk with God through my prayers before class."). Another faculty member expressed a desire for the students to "live faithfully and speak winsomely so that others may come to know Christ." To this end, the faculty member tries "to model for students this type of life in all my interactions, including within the classroom." In most cases. however, the modeling related to two other matters.

The second and more prominent form of modeling teachers emphasized involved the need to model the virtues they expected students to have:

> One of my course objectives and attitudes that I hope to model in the classroom is developing the intellectual virtues of humility, courage, wonder, understanding and wisdom. The humility to recognize my fallibilism and hence the need to carefully listen to those whose assertions differ from my own. The courage to subject my own beliefs and those of others to critical scrutiny in my pursuit of godly wisdom and truth. A wondrous receptivity to new truths and strange persons that come my way. The requisite understanding to grasp how various things hang together and the wisdom to conduct myself in accordance with what I trust that God has entrusted me with.

While some professors merely listed the particular virtues that they hoped to model, faculty respondents often connected their reason for emphasizing the importance of modeling to the Christian tradition. ("Ethics is rooted in Christianity. Therefore, I ought to be a moral example to my class.") The most common way teachers expressed this outlook involved imitating or modeling Christ, which usually meant exhibiting particular virtues Christ demonstrated (e.g., "servant leadership"; "treating my students with love in my heart"; seeing it as the teacher's personal responsibility "to model God's love to my student while encouraging and helping them to master the content of my courses"). One faculty member even went so far as to say, "I attempt to model my personal ethics after my understanding of Jesus' life. In that case, I expect that students will relate to each other based on the principles Jesus followed when relating to everyone, including the marginalized."

As a result of this emphasis, certain types of virtues, or what we call the "redemptive virtues," which require one to take a position of less power or give up the ability to exercise a particular power, were considered especially important. These virtues included humility (mentioned by the philosophy professor in the previous paragraph), servanthood ("I am to model the behavior of a servant-leader."), and grace and mercy ("I try to model grace, mercy, and holiness in my behavior and interactions with students."). Certainly holiness is a unique virtue usually not listed among virtues identified by positive psychologists or state character-education laws.[23]

The third form of modeling teachers mentioned involved demonstrating what it means to be *good* or *excellent* in a specific professional context (e.g., "I set the model for them to follow with the patients in how they are treated."). Of course, what it means to be a good professional also involved demonstrating particular virtues. The teachers in our study, however, emphasized the application of the virtues in this professional context, usually focusing on what it means to be a good Christian scholar or teacher. The following examples illuminate this approach:

- "I aim to bring both elements of the descriptor 'Christian scholar' to bear in my classroom work by modelling and expecting Christ-centered, intellectually rigorous engagement with literature. As well, I try to model and encourage the practice of humble, patient reading—not to mention humble, patient interpersonal relations—described earlier in this self-study."
- "If I expect students to be kind, welcoming to all their classmates, honest, patient with me and their classmates, attentive, respectful, well-prepared, enthusiastic, disciplined in their work, and otherwise

> engaged in the class, then I must manifest those same characteristics in our time together. My grading will be clear and fair, I will return papers and other written work reasonably quickly, I will provide proper oral feedback on class presentations, etc.... [M]y actions will (hopefully) be the actions and conduct of a good Christian steward in the class."

In the last example, we observed a common tendency we noticed in other answers: the importance of modeling for this teacher arose from an understanding of identity springing from the Christian narrative (e.g., stewardship).

Furthermore, in a number of these cases, teachers emphasized how Christ served as a model regarding not only teaching methods but also other professional practices. The following example provides the application of this perspective to the broader professional vocation of teaching, removing it from the isolated perspective on pedagogical practices:

> I teach journalism and public relations courses. Ethics, honesty and truth are integral principles for professionals in these fields. Determining what is true, what is ethical is not just an exercise in cognitive acrobatics but modeling ourselves after He who is Truth. My students tell stories/craft messages to impact a particular audience. The most powerful example I know of is reminding students that God had/has a message for humanity that we, the audience, need to receive, hear and act upon. How did God craft that message to meet the audience's needs and prove the credibility of the message? By sending Jesus, who is the Word, is God and is human—Jesus is the content, the person and the medium—totally integrated for powerful, effective outcomes when we act.

Overall, we suggest that modeling is the ultimate incarnational expression of Christian teaching, in that one imitates Christ by incarnating the highest life ideals revealed by God (see box 4.3).

Combining All the Elements

While the brief qualitative responses provide only short, clear examples of a particular strand of emphasis, we want to be clear once again that we doubt most Christian professors employ just one of these approaches. In

Box 4.3 Ethics and Modeling

In an essay entitled, "Stumbling toward Grace," Ann Green, a professor of English and graduate director of the Writing Studies Program at St. Joseph's University, shares how she applies a particular Christian practice to her classroom.[26] "When other members of my family, not Catholic, ask about my personal relationship with Jesus Christ, I think about communion. My relationship with God is based in communion; not only in the literal sense of the host but also in the communal, the community." She finds in the model of Christian communion something she can also take to her classroom: "If I am engaged in the Jesuit mantra of finding God in all things, the place where I find God in my daily work is in my students and my relationships with them and in the community we create in the writing classroom."

Green describes herself as a feminist Catholic and therefore finds herself drawn to critical pedagogy. Yet, due to her experience of Christian communion, she finds Elizabeth Ellsworth's critique of critical pedagogy compelling. Ellsworth "argues that there must be time for knowing people outside of the classroom in order to develop trust when talking about difficult and challenging subjects like racism."

To build this kind of trust, Green requires all students to take part in an out-of-classroom experience that simply involves being in fellowship together. Of course, students make lots of excuses about not wanting to come, and she expresses her raw frustration with the hassle of dealing with students' resistance to this simple community-building activity, "Why I think, do I want to spend time with students? 'I am busy, too,' I mutter under my breath. I'd rather spend time playing Angry Birds than spend time answering e-mails about this."

One of the keys to the endeavor, she maintains, is that she has the students take charge of planning the event. She notes, "Pedagogically, if they design the activity, they own it. Spiritually, if this is all about a journey toward Grace, no one can be on the sidelines. We all must participate in the trip." She describes one such class experience in which the class decided to get together for a potluck and watch a movie. She noted, "Nothing at all memorable happened. . . . I think we broke bread together, we came closer to grace."

How did this simple act of community, modeled on the communion she experiences in her church community, change the class? She observes that before the potluck, "Vicki already had a series of absences that put her in danger of failing the class. Mary struggled to do her schoolwork while balancing her job, her internship, and caring for her sister's other child. The class has been a very quiet one." Green then reports some small changes, "After the potluck, other students in the class asked about Mary's nephew, and Vicki came to class. When we read Edwidge Danticat's *The Dewbreaker* about torture in Haiti and immigration to the United States, Alice, a very quiet person, the child of Haitian immigrants, spoke about some of the Creole in the text." Certainly, one could chalk all of these changes up to other factors. As Green observes, "Nothing miraculous happened, it may be Vicki would have come to class, Mary would've shared about her nephew, and Alice would've offered her insights without a potluck." Yet although Green considers another explanatory framework, she concludes regarding this explanation, "[B]ut I don't think so. I think we broke bread together, and became closer to grace."

This kind of education, which considers the whole person, builds trust, and allows for greater vulnerability, leads to a certain quality of learning that Green hopes extends to life: "If we create spaces where students can integrate the spiritual, intellectual, and emotional aspects of their lives by breaking bread together, we can foster in them the kind of 'whole person' we too would like to encounter when we seek medical care, and we send our children to elementary school, and when we too need charity." Green herself exemplifies this kind of whole person when she deals with students. She relates, "[L]ater on that semester, and Mary's nephew was sick. She cried in my office, I took Mary across campus to the local sandwich shop and bought her a pizza because she had not been eating anything. When you know your students, *cura personalis* extends to the corporal works of mercy, too, I guess. They are more apparent to me than the spiritual ones, so I [try] to meet those needs when I can."

Green is explicitly aware of the type of model she is trying to portray to students: "By building relationships with the students in the writing classroom, I'm trying to model a process that applies for both writing and social justice work. If I want to teach justly, the way the class is structured

> must be based in the process of engagement that recognizes the personal and establishes the communal, and the way that writing is assigned, too, must move from the personal toward the communal." Green engages in all of these activities with the larger Christian story, particularly God's gracious gifts in mind. She notes that "ideally, classrooms can be communities where we share grace.... Developing relationships and building community is a way of inciting the transcendent and creating a space for the possibility of grace."

fact, the lengthier and more sophisticated responses mentioned a combination of some of the strands we just described. Often these combinations involved setting forth a particular Christian identity, unpacking its narrative implications, and then moving to its importance for teaching objectives, content, and/or methods. For example, one professor described how the Christian narrative influenced her curricular perspective, ethics, and modeling:

> I believe that all students (people) are created in the image of God and need a Savior. I approach my students and subject matter through a biblical worldview, respect each person as a creation of God, provide an example for my students to emulate, and show them that we all fall short of perfection.

This combination of different types of emphasis took many different forms. Another professor provided a helpful example of how a Christian transformation educator sets forth a brief understanding of important theological views regarding identity, ethics, and Christian practices and then applies those elements to the particular practice of dealing with a student who plagiarized an assignment:

> My understanding of the importance of truth, human sinfulness, the need for confession, and forgiveness shapes how I have responded to a student who has cheated. For example, when I have discovered a student who has copied a classmate's paper, I will ask both students for a private meeting. In the context of that meeting, I will show the student the evidence for the act, and ask for his/her explanation. Typically, a student will confess

right away. Occasionally, a student may make excuses, and I gently but firmly encourage them to acknowledge their error. When they have done so, I explain the consequences for their act, but also offer forgiveness and a plan for the future to avoid such acts. If the student has used another's paper without their permission, I encourage him/her to seek the forgiveness of the classmate. In a few cases, I have also worked with the victim of plagiarism to help him/her work through the sense of betrayal and anger towards a fellow student.

We contend that combining several strands in this way creates a stronger Christian understanding and presence in the classroom. Ideally, Christian teachers would draw upon the Christian narrative to shape their view of students, objectives, curriculum, pedagogy, and grading, and they would seek to apply a variety of the themes we discovered.

Conclusion

So how does Christianity change a professor's teaching? As chapters 2–4 indicate, the answer for these Christian teachers is multifaceted and complex. First, it involved elevating God and God's story. Teachers perform for God on God's stage and for reasons that link to the larger story that God creates and weaves together. To this end, they view their task as more than helping advance a profession, providing students with capacities, or creating citizens (ends that are common to non-Christian teachers and more pluralistic settings). They understand themselves and their students as God's image bearers, needing to show particular types of virtue both within and outside the classroom in order to experience human flourishing.

In the classroom, professors tend to take either a spiritual addition or Christian transformation approach to their teaching purposes, content, and methods. As the name implies, for the former group this involves adding some biblical, theological, or scriptural objectives, content, or methods to what might be understood as the "usual fare." For the latter group, this approach changes everything about the class, especially the lens and story by which one examines course purposes, content, and methods.

Overall, both groups add objectives that involve the holistic recovery of God's intention for human persons, the development of a deeper relationship with God, the integration of a Christian worldview, and the formation of ethical thinking and behavior. They also apply broad interpretive views or particular curricular choices to the curriculum that reflect the broad Christian tradition. Finally, they add Christian practices to their courses and justify their methods, ethical teaching, and modeling using the Christian narrative.

To tie together all the strands we found in our qualitative coding process, we have summarized them in table 4.1.[24] The activities of the teacher appear on the left side of the chart and the objectives for the students are on the right.

While we based this typology on descriptive data, we think it has some normative implications for the Christian colleges and universities we surveyed and perhaps other types of Christian colleges and universities that we did not (the large number of Catholic institutions). Faculty development courses at Christian colleges could help faculty become increasingly conscious of these nine strands and consider how to apply them all to their teaching. We find that sometimes faculty think they are failing to integrate faith and learning when in reality they simply are not conscious of the different ways their teaching is shaped by their Christian faith.

Christian educators, we suggest, should include and synthesize many of the different strands that emerged from our descriptive study into their teaching. By adopting this practice, the Christian nature of their teaching would not rest on one or two strands that may easily become weak and tattered when left to themselves. Instead, Christian professors ought to weave together a thick cord of several strands to provide a strong and robust line of help to students seeking the wisdom of faith-shaped course objectives in the classroom. Since these various categorical inclinations can be found

Table 4.1 Ways of Integrating One's Christian Identity and Tradition

Activities of the Teacher	Objectives for Students
1. Apply the Christian metanarrative to teaching, the discipline, and Students. 2. Make distinctive curricular choices. 3. Integrate or add Christian practices. 4. Justify pedagogical approaches within the Christian narrative. 5. Be a spiritual, ethical, and pedagogical model for students.	1. Understand the implications of the Christian story for human persons and the discipline. 2. Develop a deeper relationship with God. 3. Learn to integrate a Christian worldview. 4. Cultivate Christian ethical thinking and behavior.

within most historical faith traditions, this approach can be applied in multiple settings. Of course, we should make it clear that our survey results come from a diverse set of largely theologically-conservative Protestant institutions. We think survey results from Catholic professors and from more mainline Protestant institutions could enrich this conversation even more. We discuss the more distinct emphases dependent upon a specific theological tradition in chapter 5.

5

Is There Really Baptist, Catholic, or Quaker Teaching?

The Unique Contributions of Particular Theological Traditions

> There is nothing wrong with the fact that our academic work is shaped by the traditions of faith and learning that have shaped us as persons. In fact, the particularities of our traditions can be construed as scholarly assets that allow us to discover or create things that others simply cannot see or do because their traditions are less attuned to those areas."
>
> —Doug Jacobsen and Rhonda Jacobsen,
> *Scholarship and Christian Faith*[1]

Religious identities, like most identities of any significance, remain complex. After all, most Christians do not simply identify as Christians. They also identify as Catholic, Baptist, Presbyterian, Eastern Orthodox, Pentecostal, Church of Christ, or Methodist, among many other labels. They may also identify as particular types of Catholics (e.g., Jesuit, Augustinian), Baptists (e.g., Southern, American), Eastern Orthodox (Russian, Greek, Romanian), and so forth. This multifaceted understanding of religious identity raises a question: In what ways is a Catholic, Presbyterian, Baptist, or Eastern Orthodox approach to teaching different from a more general Christian approach to teaching?

As recounted in chapter 1, beginning primarily in the 1800s, the idea that one's particular ecclesial Christian identity could and should influence one's teaching has been attacked and ridiculed. Many critics of this approach shared the view of the University of Michigan regents who in 1841 wanted to avoid "the morbid prejudices of sectarians"[2] because they found the focus on particular ecclesial identities politically divisive. After all, these particular religious identities create boundaries between individuals and prevent Americans from focusing on their common identity as citizens.

Mainline Protestant colleges and universities and later Catholic universities bought into this shame about their particular sectarian identity. As volumes by George Marsden, Philip Gleason, and James Burtchaell recount, during the twentieth century first mainline Protestant and then later Catholic institutional leaders sought to diminish the sectarian nature of their institutions.[3] They rewrote charters and abolished religious requirements for board members and faculty to receive private and federal funds and to make themselves more acceptable to the mainstream American academy. In a country and academy that supposedly sought increasingly to accept and embrace pluralism, these educational leaders saw reducing their particular Christian identity as the only path to acceptance and prestige.

Today, Americans claim to celebrate diversity to a greater extent than in the past, but ironically, they continue to appear averse to using more specific religious identity labels. For instance, a growing percentage of Americans refuse to identify with a particular religious group; scholars call this group the "nones."[4] Interestingly, despite their lack of *particular* identification with a specific religious affiliation, many of these "nones" still attend religious services.[5] In other words, it is not only nonreligious people who eschew religious labels, but also those who regularly attend religious services. We continually find this trend in our own qualitative research. In a recent study one of us conducted, we asked students how they would describe their religious or nonreligious identity. Here are just a couple of samples from these interviews: "Yeah, I go to a Baptist church, but I identify myself as a Christian, not a Baptist"; "I don't tell people I'm Lutheran, like I'm not Lutheran, I'm Christian. So generally I'll say I'm Christian." Many Christian participants in this study shared the general sentiment that these specific identifications created separation. In light of this fear, they expressed that they did not want to separate or set themselves apart from others.

Students also apply this view to professors with certain identities, even students at Christian colleges and universities. For instance, one of us undertook a study of students at a set of Protestant Christian colleges, providing this instruction: "Please rate how the following self-descriptors of a faculty member would influence your attitude toward that faculty member." Table 5.1 shows the responses.

Table 5.1 Effect of Religious Identity on Students' Opinions of a Faculty Member*

Religious Identity of Faculty Member	Significantly Lowers	Moderately Lowers	No Difference	Moderately Enhances	Significantly Enhances
Born-again	1.0%	2.3%	41.3%	21.9%	33.4%
Evangelical	1.5%	3.4%	52.2%	23.8%	19.1%
Mainline Protestant	1.7%	9.7%	76.8%	9.3%	2.5%
Denominational identity of institution	2.3%	5.3%	67.1%	17.2%	8.1%
Theologically conservative	2.3%	8.5%	57.5%	20.1%	11.6%
Charismatic	2.4%	11.4%	61.1%	16.5%	8.6%
Fundamentalist	6.2%	14.9%	70.1%	6.3%	2.5%
Theologically liberal	7.4%	18.3%	59.2%	11.0%	4.1%
Catholic	7.9%	24.4%	62.1%	3.8%	1.8%

* Values may not add up to 100% for all categories because of rounding.

Source: Phil Davignon, Perry L. Glanzer, and Jesse Rine, "Assessing the Denominational Identity of American Evangelical Colleges and Universities, Part III: The Student Experience," *Christian Higher Education* 12, 5 (2013): 315–30.

Although the majority of students in almost every case but one said it made no difference, particular religious identity descriptors still influenced a third of the students in virtually every case. Being Catholic at these Protestant institutions would lower almost a third of students' opinions of the faculty member. In contrast, being associated with the denomination of the sponsoring institution would raise the students' opinions for a quarter of students. Yet it also lowered the opinions of a significant minority of students (7.6 percent).

What, then, does a particular Christian identity offer a teacher other than the possibility of further separation and alienation or perhaps some enhancement in students' views? Interestingly, one rarely finds voices celebrating the contributions of specific religious identities; however, Douglas Jacobsen and Rhonda Hustedt Jacobsen provide a refreshing exception in *Scholarship and Christian Faith*. They contend that some previous scholars who discussed how their faith tradition influenced their scholarly practice did not acknowledge their debt to a specific tradition deeply *enough*.[6] They argue for our need to appreciate and draw upon a diversity of theological traditions when approaching the topic of how one's faith tradition influences scholarship. To this end, they provide helpful examples of the unique ways Catholic, Anglican, Lutheran, Reformed, Pentecostal, Wesleyan, Anabaptist, Baptist, and Church of Christ scholars' academic research endeavors have been shaped by their specific traditions.[7]

Although the Jacobsens primarily focus their analysis on scholarship and knowledge, we contend that the same point applies to how professors think about the relationship of their specific traditions to teaching. Certainly it would be helpful to understand how specific traditions can serve as a legitimate resource for teaching. As mentioned previously, however, much of this scholarly conversation has taken place without any broad-based empirical studies from the Christian faculty whose classroom practices writers critically appraise. To fill this gap, our study aimed to discover the influence of specific, theological traditions held by a large group of diverse Christian professors on their particular teaching practices.

The Diverse Results

As indicated in chapters 2 through 4, most faculty in our study reported that the broad theological traditions to which they subscribe regularly informed key elements of their classroom practice, including their ethical approach, personal motivations, and course foundations. As we mentioned previously, 40 percent of professors also wrote about how their specific Christian tradition influences their practice. Overall, we found four different types of claims professors made when describing the influence of a particular Christian tradition on some aspect of their teaching

A Common Theological Belief

First, in some cases professors identified a theological concept from their distinct Christian traditions that is equally shared by many other Christian traditions. The most obvious cases of this phenomenon were professors' mentioning how their tradition influenced their view of students as made in God's image or as children of God. The following four examples from four different Christian traditions provide helpful examples of this type of claim:

- "As an Anglican, I believe I (and others) are made in the image of God. We believe that God is calling us to our true selves."
- "Catholics believe that everyone is made in the image and likeness of God and I teach nursing with this approach to all patients. They are worthy of good care because they are children of God."
- "The thee/thou tradition of Quakers plays a big role in treating folks made in God's image (even folks of no religious faith and [different] sexual orientations) with respect and dignity."
- "The Church of the Nazarene believes in the worth of the individual as a child of God. Even the most annoying student is God's child and is valuable in His eyes. I try not to 'write off' students who may be slower or more difficult to work with—they deserve and need my time and attention."

As evidenced by comparing these quotes, almost all Christians share these views, not just those from one particular tradition. In other words, some professors merely identified a broadly held Christian belief and did not mention a theological belief particular to their specific denominational tradition. These professors likely believed that their tradition made a particular contribution by nurturing this belief.

A Common Ethical Teaching

Second, in other cases professors identified a common Christian ethical teaching they linked to their particular denominational identity. For example, a number of professors mentioned various ways that their traditions led them to emphasize certain virtues or practices. Following are helpful examples from five professors:

- "Because of Anabaptist convictions that the Christian life is a life of service to others, I see my role as a teacher in terms of being a servant of my students."
- "As an Evangelical, I believe I am called to serve God by serving others. As a professor, I am a servant leader, and my goal is to help and support my students as they work to learn and achieve."
- "Catholicism believes we each possess talents that God wants us to nurture and develop to serve others."

- "The Church of the Brethren teaches a simple lifestyle and a life of servanthood, modeled after Christ who humbled Himself to wash the feet of the disciples at the Last Supper."
- "My teaching should provide an example of servanthood and service to my students, which reflects the character and the qualities of Jesus Christ." (Wesleyan professor)

While the idea that Christianity teaches the importance of service may receive more emphasis in some traditions than others, this is not necessarily a distinctive belief of a particular Christian tradition. Nonetheless, these five professors specified a distinctive identity tradition that provided the impetus or motivation for maintaining this emphasis. In other words, they came to a deeper appreciation of commonly held Christian beliefs while participating in a particular tradition; they did not merely acquire this appreciation while participating in a generic form of Christianity.

In both of the types of the theological and ethical examples just illustrated, the particular tradition is important because it provides the nurturing context for the professors' convictions. To demonstrate this point, one professor noted, "The emphasis on ecumenism fostered by Catholics at Vatican II helps to emphasize the common essentials of faith common to most Churches willing to admit the overwhelmingly voluminous beliefs held by most Christians." In this case, the particular tradition nurtured an appreciation for seeking a common set of core Christian beliefs. The role of denominational particularity in supporting a common Christian belief (e.g., the importance of a teacher being a servant) followed a similar dynamic.

A Theological Belief or Element Shared by a Group of Traditions

Third, professors might identify an element that is particular to their tradition but also shared by a wider group of Christian traditions (although the teaching may not necessarily be emphasized in the same way by all Christian traditions). In other words, while all Christian traditions may support a *particular* emphasis, this element remains distinct to a certain group of traditions (e.g., conservative Protestants who emphasize the sole authority of the Bible). For instance, we found a number of professors who discussed the importance of the Bible within their particular tradition:

- "As a Baptist, I believe that the Bible is the Word of God and authoritative in all areas of life. Therefore, this influences my worldview, as I view everything (or try to) through the lens of Scripture."
- "The Anabaptist emphasis on the centrality of Scripture is a key part of my worldview."
- "I hold to the Reformed doctrine of *Sola Scriptura*. This is especially evident whenever I attempt to integrate worldview with my discipline because I share Biblical authority as often as possible."

In each of these cases, these professors were actually identifying a key aspect of certain forms of Protestantism, but they were not identifying something distinctive to their particular Protestant tradition.

Distinct Denominational Emphases

Finally, some professors pointed out a particular emphasis that is a unique, though not exclusive, emphasis within their particular tradition. For example, the Baptist and Anabaptist traditions have a long history of prioritizing the voluntary aspect of the faith.[8] One Baptist professor noted, "I try to teach students to be faithful and interested in the implications of Christianity for their worldview and choices. The Baptist side of it is that I also try to emphasize the importance of voluntarism as the spring of a vital faith." Although most other Christian traditions do not necessarily downplay or attack voluntarism, they usually do not elevate it to the same extent as the Baptist or Anabaptist denominations. In a case from the literature, we find a Catholic professor emphasizing the particular sacramental tradition that seeks to find God in all things:

> The design of the course is based on the pastoral circle of immersion, social analysis, theological reflection and the plan of action, something about which the students only become aware through the course of the semester. As Catholics we asked the question, "why should we care?" from a rich faith tradition which demands that we see God in all things.[9]

This focus on seeing God in all things is especially particular to the Jesuit tradition within Catholicism, although other traditions such as the Quakers may also make this kind of emphasis.

110 THE OUTRAGEOUS IDEA OF CHRISTIAN TEACHING

Table 5.2 Ways a Particular Christian Identity Animates Teaching

THE TEACHER	THE STUDENT	THE DISCIPLINE
Specific Ways of Talking about God and the Christian Metanarrative		
Sources of God's Wisdom/Knowledge		
	Ends of Teaching	
Curricular Sense-Making		
Pedagogy		

In the categorization we developed for this chapter, we focused on the last two types of examples because they pertained to elements emphasized by specific Christian traditions and not the Christian tradition as a whole. Using these two categories of examples, we found that the particular ways a tradition might influence teaching pertained to five different types of endeavors (see table 5.2). We provide explanations and examples of the specific types of activities in the remainder of this chapter.

Specific Ways of Thinking about God and the Christian Metanarrative

While different Christian traditions often share a significant amount of agreement about God's nature and story, each Christian tradition also has a unique way of summarizing and highlighting key aspects of God's character or other important elements of the Christian story. The professors in our study reflected this tendency in the way they discussed the contributions of their particular traditions to their teaching.

God's Role in the Metanarrative

One clear way teachers reflected denominational distinctions was the way they perceived and described the Triune God's role in shaping and influencing the cosmic drama in which teaching is enacted. As Richard Mouw once noted, "Christians play favorites with the members of the Trinity."[10] Christian teachers prove to be no different. Teachers associated with what are known as *high-church* traditions (e.g., ones in which the pastor wears a special collar, robe, etc., when preaching) focus on God. For instance, Catholic Jesuit teachers talk about "finding God in all things."[11] A Reformed professor proclaimed, "As a Reformed Christian, I see every square inch of the cosmos as belonging to God and in need of the redeeming power of his sovereignty and incarnation. That gives me excitement in every class." In contrast, Anabaptists and Baptists focus on another member of the Triune God: Jesus. One faculty member explained, "The Anabaptist tradition is one that highlights not only the teachings, but also the life, ministry, suffering, and death of Jesus as ethical example for the followers of Jesus. And I take that broad approach with all ethical issues." Finally, Pentecostals/Charismatics and Wesleyans often mentioned the role of another member of the Triune God in the Holy Spirit. Comments such as, "I believe that I rely on the Holy Spirit to guide my thoughts and life that helps me be open toward the needs of my students and share love" and "I often feature the role of the Holy Spirit which has played a major role in the Wesleyan heritage" represent professors who ascribe to these traditions.

These findings provide some insight into how a tradition may add to a fuller understanding of both Christian teaching and how specific, denominational beliefs and emphases may distort it. On the one hand, one might argue that *any* full understanding of the Triune God's influence on Christian teachers must involve contributions from *each* of these traditions' emphases. On the other hand, one might find that an inordinate focus on just *one* aspect of God may actually distort a Christian tradition of teaching. Although we believe such differences in emphasis result from the particular strengths of these traditions, we also believe those who identify with particular traditions may need to consider if and therefore *when* they are being theologically neglectful.

In addition, particular traditions may appeal to the whole Trinity, but how they talk about the ramifications of this appeal may be specific to the tradition or a set of traditions. We found this common outlook among professors who take the transformative view of teaching that the whole educational endeavor is something holy and spiritual and therefore do not separate what is done in the classroom into sacred and secular spheres. The theology behind this view often uses particular language linked to a specific Christian tradition. For instance, Catholic professors, particularly within the Jesuit tradition of education, emphasize the importance of the sacramental imagination. The sacramental imagination, as explained by Michael J. Himes, is linked to a common, Christian understanding of the Trinity: "The central point of the doctrine of the Trinity that God is least wrongly understood as a relationship, as an eternal explosion of love."[12] The sacramental principle then does not relate to the traditional seven sacraments in the Catholic tradition. Instead, in this case "sacramental" means "any person, place, thing or event, any sight, sound, taste, touch, or smell that causes us to notice the love which supports all that exists, that undergirds your being and mine and the being of everything about us."[13] Himes maintains that when understood in this way, "anything that awakens, enlivens, and expands the imagination, opens the vision, enriches the sensitivity of any human being is a religious act. Although we may not use this language, education is or can be training in sacramental beholding."[14]

Protestant or Eastern Orthodox professors who take the same transformative view of teaching may use similar or different theological language to come to the same conclusion. For instance, one Quaker professor in our survey used the same language:, "Quakers also believe in the sacramentology of all of life. God is present in all people and all things, so that DEEPLY affects how I teach and live." An Eastern Orthodox professor expressed it in a different way: "There is no separation between sacred and secular subjects, because there is nothing that is not created by God. . . . I believe that faithful adherence to my discipline is, in and of itself, an act of worship." For transformation professors from all these traditions, every part of education can and should be considered something sacred that can point us to God's love and grace, but their particular tradition formed the theological language and reasoning behind their outlook.

In addition, often each Christian intellectual tradition contains its own pedagogy for helping people take this view of the world. As Himes points out, "The whole Catholic sacramental life is a training to be beholders. Catholic liturgy is a lifelong pedagogy to bring us to see what is there, to behold what is always present, the conviction that if we truly see and fully appreciate what is there, whether we use the language or not, we will be encountering grace. We will see the love which undergirds all that exists."[15] This theological language and associated practice also provide a way to link all of learning in the disciplines together in a way that is different, or perhaps missing, from secular universities. While many thinkers tend to appeal to the democratic tradition or narrative to link together all of learning,[16] the Christian story about God provides this link for Christian professors. As Himes maintained, "Sacramentality conceives of God as active in, and through, the material world."[17] As a result, "approaching an enterprise through a sacramental imagination provides connective tissue that can lend a crucial kind of unity to any course of study. Undertaken in the context of sacramentality, students receive a cohesive, vigorous, and ultimately positive approach to their world, rather than a disconnected amalgam of classes."[18] In this way, something beyond a political or economic narrative makes sense of and connects the exploding array of knowledge and disciplines within the university.

An Emphasis within the Metanarrative

The second significant ecclesial uniqueness we found involved the particular way teachers from various traditions summarized the Christian story or emphasized a particular theme or themes within this metanarrative. For example, Reformed teachers often described how their tradition uses a three- or four-part way to think about the Christian story (e.g., "understand environmental issues within creation/fall/redemption approach"). They then commented about how they applied each or all parts of this framework to their subject or courses. One Reformed professor commented, "Reformed doctrine emphasizes that the world is good, though fallen, so that very much influences my approach to all my classes. There is a lot of good to be found in any area of study, but we must also seek to recognize the fallen-ness in our approach to any subject." This response illustrates the essential elements of this category. Here we see (1) a prior theological perspective or belief rooted in an identified tradition, (2) a particular theological emphasis drawn from that commitment, and (3) an implicit or explicit articulation of how it influences teaching.

While Reformed teachers tended to focus on a particular manner of summarizing the Christian metanarrative, professors from other traditions emphasized particular aspects of this narrative in ways that specifically directed their curricular approaches. For instance, the faculty members quoted in the following list provided specific examples of how their traditions underscored particular ways the Christian story shaped their interpretation of their teaching contexts:

- "The Anabaptist theological tradition places great emphasis on discipleship and 'following Jesus.' I view my course objectives (learning to read and exegete the Scriptures faithfully) as a tangible means to assist my students in that overarching calling."
- "If I believe that the evangelical understanding of the Bible is correct, and that a person's eternal standing with God pivots on how they respond to God, Christ, and the gospel, then I am very motivated to present a broad, well-argued case concerning what the Bible teaches about how we may be reconciled back to God, and about how we should live as a result."

In each of these cases, the professor focused on a specific theological theme emphasized by the particular Christian tradition and then reasoned from that theme.

Taken together, these teachers present a holistic Christian view of how to integrate faith into one's teaching. Integration could and should consider all aspects of the Triune God and all aspects of God's story. Yet, teachers also will want to consider how to draw out the implications of particular theological themes.

Sources of God's Wisdom/Knowledge

A second way that teachers' particular traditions influenced their teaching was the prioritization they placed on certain sources of knowledge, wisdom, or truth. Likely due to their denominations' emphasis on the limitations and fallenness of human reason, evangelical, Baptist, and Anabaptist professors tended to highlight the need to prioritize scripture and theology derived from scripture as the *primary* source of intellectual wisdom. For example, one professor claimed, "As a Baptist, I believe that the Bible is the Word of God and authoritative in all areas of life. Therefore, this influences my worldview, as I view everything (or try to) through the lens of Scripture." Another noted, "I teach with a general evangelical worldview, stating that the Bible should be our primary guiding document." An emphasis on biblically-informed teaching is one distinctive of many of the teachers we examined.

In some cases, professors from these traditions added that drawing upon both historical and present-day wisdom afforded to them by Christian community helped with making the Christian scriptures meaningful for their students. For example, one evangelical professor mentioned the importance of looking to the past Christian tradition for interpretive assistance: "As an Evangelical, I believe especially in the power of the written word—the Scriptures, foremost, but also writings of church leaders and the holy witnesses who make up our heritage. I encourage students with book lists and additional reading and writing and use primary sources so they can hear the voices of the church speak into their lives today." Another Anabaptist professor focused on the need to interpret scripture in light of the contemporary gathered Christian community: "The Anabaptist tradition is likewise one that highlights the discernment of the gathered group. And in all of my classes my students and I function intentionally as a community of learning where we work together to glean understanding from the Scriptures." Again, we do not mean to imply that other Christian traditions do not emphasize the importance of the Bible or the interpretive Christian community. What we are saying is that from the answers provided, these low-church professors clearly emphasized how certain communal ways of interpreting the Bible remain an important element of their teaching.

Though still prioritizing the Bible, other professors emphasized the importance of finding God's wisdom in *multiple* sources of revelation. As the following examples illustrate, faculty who identified with the Quaker tradition, in particular, emphasized the need for an expansive view of the source of wisdom in *all people*, not just the Christian community:

- "The Quaker tradition that God's truth and wisdom can come through anyone is the foundation for my student-centered teaching."
- "Quakers believe there is the light of Christ in every individual, and try to 'speak to that of Christ in everyone.' I take this approach, trying to find the unique ways each student reflects the light of Christ, and draw upon that, rather than trying to have everyone conform to one picture of 'goodness' or rightness. It's looking for the good, and building on that rather than looking for errors and trying to eliminate those. My motivation is to find what is true so I can resonate with and emphasize that."
- "The Quaker ethos discusses the light of Christ in each person; I try to speak to and honor that light in each of my students."

Since the Quaker tradition places much less emphasis on human fallenness and instead focuses on the light of Christ in all humans, the Quaker professors in our study tended not to mention scripture and instead talked about drawing insight from all individuals.[19]

While the Quakers focused on the importance of what one called "epistemological humility" when it comes to finding wisdom, both Quaker *and* Reformed professors expanded their sources of knowledge even further than human persons, to all of nature, defined as God's created order. For instance, one Reformed professor noted:

> The Reformed tradition values education, [and] recognizes that God reveals himself through both the Bible but also through the book of creation. By understanding and exploring the book of creation, we come to both comprehend and appreciate his attributes, which seem beyond comprehension. This leads to worship, which is the chief end of man (to glorify God and to enjoy him forever).

We add that these kinds of subtle nuances also end up influencing the types of academic programs and courses that receive attention in the curriculum.

The most expansive appeals to multiple sources of wisdom, however, came from professors who affirmed the Wesleyan tradition. These professors often shared something similar to these comments: "I believe all truth is God's truth so I want my students to have a wide range of knowledge. I believe in the Wesleyan Quadrilateral so I want my students to value scripture, reason, experience, and tradition in that order." As can be seen, while the prioritization of the Bible was similar, the mention of multiple knowledge sources first articulated by John Wesley proved the most expansive of all the traditions surveyed in our study. In fact, one professor pointed out how this approach differed from the method mentioned earlier: "I emphasize multiple sources of authority rather than *sola scriptura* (per the Wesleyan quadrilateral) in both biblical hermeneutics and in interpretive acts conceived of more broadly." In light of this emphasis, these Wesleyan professors continually highlighted the need to touch upon all these sources of knowledge in their classrooms.

Overall, professors' choices to underscore specific sources of knowledge stem from their traditions' tendency to emphasize different parts of the Christian story. The traditions that focus on the fall or human sinfulness tend to prioritize the need for God's special revelation. Those that do not place as much emphasis on human sinfulness or fallenness and have much more confidence in humanity's ability to obtain knowledge place increasing emphasis on the importance of receiving divine wisdom from sources beyond the Bible.[20]

Ends of Teaching

One of the challenges of allowing a particular Christian identity to influence one's teaching involves the ends, or larger purposes, of teaching. After all, even in a Christian university, where all or most students may be Christian, rarely are all students from the same Christian tradition. Thus, one may argue that in light of the diversity of students who are present in the classroom, the particular Christian identity of the teacher should not influence his or her particular understanding of the ends of teaching. The teachers whom we cite in the following examples, however, did not share this view. Yet the ways in which a particular faith tradition influences the ends of the teaching enterprise vary considerably.

In general, we found the examples our participants provided could be easily organized into a spectrum that comprises something similar to Bloom's taxonomy of learning.[21] On one end, we found the low-level learning ends (e.g., basic content knowledge and understanding), while we placed the more advanced skills on the other end of the spectrum.

First, at the basic level, some professors simply mentioned the need for students to know and understand the central beliefs of a particular tradition or traditions. For instance, one Anabaptist professor mentioned:

> It is very important to me that my students have a broad understanding of Christian history, in particular the Anabaptist insights—as these views have been frequently eclipsed by louder more strident voices. . . . Therefore, my objectives often read something like: Students will grasp the complex and textured historical purposes of baptism; or students will gain a broader understanding of salvation—not as simply a moment in time, but an ongoing stepping into discipleship that accompanies one's putting on Christ.

In some cases, the understanding that this professor hoped to cultivate might relate less to a *particular* tradition and might relate more to a *broad group* of traditions. Another professor explained this distinction in the following manner: "In courses in history and religion, I want to ensure the students understand the high-church traditions since almost all come from low-church backgrounds." In these instances, these professors saw themselves as providing a viewpoint students might not encounter elsewhere in their college experience.

Second, professors also not only mentioned helping students to understand a tradition but also highlighted the importance of helping students come to an empathetic understanding or appreciation of that particular tradition. For example, a Catholic teacher noted, "I teach French foreign language and culture; I hope that students will understand better after my courses that Christian community does not exclude all things Catholic." Another Anglican professor expressed, "One objective is to introduce evangelical Christians to the richness of their Protestant tradition as expressed in Anglican patterns of worship and theology." As this last response indicates, in some cases, minority Christian tradition professors (e.g., Anglican, Catholic) tried to increase majority Christian tradition students' understanding of the particular theological nuances of their tradition. These faculty members also attempted to help their students appreciate particular benefits stemming from their specific denominational traditions.

Third, professors also mentioned either directly applying these traditions to their course material or teaching students to learn how to apply a tradition to a particular subject by using its perspective to guide their interpretive lens within their discipline. In this regard, they wanted their students to experiment with the tradition and encounter it as a live intellectual option. Professors from a wide variety of traditions expressed this outlook, as the following examples illustrate:

- "When teaching criminological theory I relate the foundational assumptions of each theory to Baptist doctrinal beliefs."
- "From my syllabus for freshman composition: Strengthen your reading, viewing, and thinking skills by helping you interpret and assess a variety of essays, images, and lectures from a Reformed biblical perspective."
- "In my Psychology and Christian Thought class, for example, the class starts with an overview of [how] basic evangelical Christian assumptions form our worldview. The rest of the class explores how

this intersects with the epistemology, anthropology, theories, and current topic areas in the field of psychology."

As revealed in these examples, professors understand that for someone to engage in critical thinking about a discipline, he or she first needs to start from a particular identity, which in this case is a particular Christian identity. They then help students understand its presuppositions and evaluative framework. After reaching this appreciation, the student must then learn how to apply it. This additional step allows one to proceed to more sophisticated intellectual analysis.

We also found professors who mentioned what we would consider the next step in the learning taxonomy: helping students use their knowledge of the tradition to analyze and evaluate other traditions. For instance, one professor noted, "I seek to create an environment where students who are not Baptist are able to contrast their worldview with Baptists and by doing so are able to discover more about themselves and their worldview." While this type of comparative analysis requires a familiarity with multiple traditions, it also proves essential to a liberal education. Warren Nord observes, "A liberal education must be a conversation in which students come to understand the relationship of cultures, traditions, and disciplines to one another. Are they complementary, do they conflict, are they in tension with one another—and what are the implications for how we make sense of the world?"[22] Though it is often assumed that a liberal education requires one to appreciate the nuances of a broad range of traditions, certain professors in our study also recognized that liberal education also includes a robust understanding of the important differences among these broad traditions.

Curricular Sense-Making, Construction, and Content

Similar to the distinct approaches to understanding the content of the curriculum discussed in the last chapter, the influence of particular traditions on the curriculum again split between spiritual addition and Christian transformation professors. Spiritual addition professors insert content related to the particular tradition in a relevant course. The addition of specific content took two forms. In the first approach, the professor simply added the particular content to his or her course. The following examples demonstrate this approach:

- "I make a point of discussing Catholic Medieval thought—and of educating my students about the Saints."
- "Yes, the Lutheran church has a strong hymn-singing component and I stress hymn singing in all my music classes. We sing hymns and worship songs each week, and discuss the background, text, music, etc."
- "Anabaptist concerns about the teachings of Jesus and concern for the poor and marginalized influence my courses."
- "I try to introduce differing liturgical traditions, including Anglicanism to my students to show them their value, as many of them are predisposed to distrust any denomination other than their own."

As can be seen from these examples, these cases usually involved courses in which such inclusion was quite natural (e.g., theology, liturgy, music, and history).

In other courses, the addition involved devoting particular attention to certain themes or theories understood to be consistent with the professor's particular theological tradition. In these cases, the professor did not understand the emphasis as opposed to the field or exclusive to the particular tradition. Still, it emerged as an outgrowth of identifying with the tradition. The following examples provide insight into how professors perceived their particular theological tradition as shaping this more indirect influence. One professor shared, "Church of the Brethren and Anabaptist traditions value service to others, living out your beliefs and pacifism. These are not directly course objectives but may motivate me to include certain books, examples, articles rather than others." A philosophy professor gave the following example: "I spend time talking about virtue ethics (which I believe exemplifies an Anabaptist understanding) in contrast to deontological or utilitarian ethics." An evangelical professor who taught ministry courses wrote, "Since I teach Ministry courses, my own tradition cannot help but come through in the way I teach. Specifically, I tend to favor textbooks that represent an evangelical point of view."

Again, this kind of influence is perhaps what first comes to mind when discussing the role a particular identity may play in shaping one's teaching. Moreover, this type of inclusion or favoritism raises some of the core questions about ethics and favoritism that we discuss in latter chapters.

The Christian transformation approach focused on how the larger theological story emphasized by the particular tradition shaped one's overall approach to the curriculum. As scholars have noted, this outlook is often associated with the Reformed tradition.[23] One Reformed professor demonstrated this approach in the way he described rethinking the entire course content in light of the Christian narrative:

> The Reformed (or broadly Augustinian) theological tradition informs our institutional mission with speaks of inspiring and equipping learners to bring renewal and reconciliation to every walk of life as followers of Jesus Christ, the Servant King. An emphasis on the goodness of God's creation, the pervasiveness of sin and evil, the cosmic sweep of redemption and the reign of God, and on our human calling to participate in God's redemptive work are characteristic of this tradition, and provide orientation for the entire curriculum.

While other Christian professors also took this approach, we found it most often emphasized by those from a Reformed or more Calvinist tradition. Here, we see the scholarly emphasis on the themes of creation, fall, redemption, and restoration among Reformed scholars making its way into the classroom.[24]

Pedagogy

Is there an Anabaptist, Reformed, or Wesleyan way to teach that touches upon what is traditionally understood as pedagogy or method? Similar to the typology discussed in the preceding section and in chapter 4, here we can divide the respondents once again into spiritual addition and Christian transformation teachers. Spiritual addition professors simply added a method or approach that linked to their tradition to their other teaching methods. For instance, one professor who drew upon the Anglican liturgical tradition noted, "Being an Anglican has made me approach the devotional portion differently. I now lead devotions with a *lectio divina* (or the students do) of one Psalm per semester." Another professor mentioned the incorporation of the following particular interpretive method: "This might have less to do with theological tradition and more to do with academic discipline, but the Reformed emphases on lay reading of scripture and on 'interpreting scripture with scripture' undergirds my emphasis in courses on reading/interpretive skills, particularly those which 'take the text seriously' and interpret it first in its own terms." While examples from spiritual addition teachers were more limited in scope, responses from Christian transformation professors more broadly discussed how they believe their specific tradition justified particular methods commonly used by teachers, especially when considering the general tone or point of emphasis found within these approaches. The following four examples from different denominational perspectives capture four different perspectives on this practice:

- "I'm increasingly moving away from lectures toward informed class discussion and small group activities, even though these are not my personally favored models, partly because I think the habits learned in such activities support an Anabaptist understanding of decision-making and moral discernment."
- "Dialogical-Reflective-Community approach to learning involving interplay/reflection of scripture, tradition, reason, experience" (a blend of Paulo Freire's pedagogy and Wesley's Quadrilateral).
- "The decentralized authority structures of the Evangelical church have given me a model for class structure. While I provide the class with regular guidance, I also allow considerable latitude for student participation, and I am always open when the students wish to take the class in a new or innovative direction."
- "I believe that the emotions and will need to be educated along with the mind, much as the Wesleyan tradition has valued all of these in the process of conversion and sanctification."

While there is nothing inherently *Christian* about these methods, a professor's particular tradition provided a thick narrative framework from which the whole range of pedagogical methods or types of emphasis unfolded. One finds this similar approach among Catholic teachers in the Jesuit tradition, who use the methods of journaling and service learning to help students "find God in all things."[25] In the same way that an emphasis on democratic education leads to methods that respect a student's autonomy, these professors described how a particular aspect of their tradition led them to embrace particular pedagogical methods. In many of the cases cited, the professors viewed their tradition as supporting student participation and engagement.

Ethics

As mentioned in chapter 4, teachers often cited general forms of moralism one might hear from any professor, unless one focused on what we call redemptive virtues. Specific Christian traditions also provide a theological rationale for focusing on, or even favoring, certain kinds of ethical principles or virtues (e.g., "I think I am more egalitarian in my relationship with students as a result of both Anabaptist and Quaker influences."). A number of professors offered helpful examples of this kind of connection with regard to inclusivity. One Anglican professor explained, "The Anglican tradition is a 'big tent,' making it clear that 'all are welcome.' I try to bring a similar attitude of hospitality to my students, even when I might disagree with them." Another Wesleyan professor shared, "As I understand it, the Wesleyan tradition is also more accepting of people with various theological frameworks—more open-minded in its own theology. It is important to me that differences (of all kinds) are not only accepted, but highly valued in my classroom." These quotes reveal that while particular Christian traditions may emphasize various virtues, the reason for such points of emphasis likely is the historic tendency to focus on particular biblical texts that emphasize certain moral teachings.

Combining the Strands

As we did in chapter 4, we want to end by pointing out that these areas of influence rarely exist in isolation from one another. After all, our illustrations come from singular examples offered by professors who usually spend at least 45 hours a semester in a specific classroom for each class. How they integrate their particular tradition into their teaching likely proves much more complex than the strategies we have outlined in this chapter. Indeed, we found a number of examples of teachers who demonstrated complex forms of integration involving a focus on multiple strands. A professor who identified with the Quaker tradition noted how this theological understanding transformed the classroom setting (to one of worship) and changed his identity (to that of being a Christ-like servant):

> As an evangelical Friend, my goal is to serve my students well; that is why I work them hard and seek to engage them in the subjects I teach. I am a

servant-teacher. As a believer in the present Christ, accessible wherever two or three are gathered in his name, I have sought to design several of my courses as "the meeting for worship in which learning is welcomed"—facilitating the student being enrolled in the school of Christ.

Here we see a Christian transformation approach in which the whole classroom and endeavor of learning become envisioned as an extension of worship. In this approach, the teacher takes the role of Christ, a servant-teacher.

Another teacher illustrated the merging of different strands as she discussed how her particular tradition emphasizes certain theological elements of the Christian metanarrative reflecting clear, ethical content:

> The Church of the Brethren teaches a simple life style and a life of servanthood, modeled after Christ who humbled Himself to wash the feet of the disciples at the Last Supper. In the same vein, I advocate to my students through the course objectives that as public school teachers they are answering God's calling to teach His children in our public schools. I emphasize through the course objectives the importance of differentiating instruction to meet the learning needs of every child they teach.

As this example illustrates, this professor identified the virtues of humility and servanthood as exemplified in the Last Supper narrative, but then applied them to a particular way that a teacher could or perhaps should behave in a future professional position.

Conclusion

Our overview of how ecclesial traditions influence teaching provides evidence of two important phenomena. First, while professors identified a whole range of tradition-related specifics, some comments proved less distinctive to particular denominational traditions and more applicable to the general Christian tradition. For example, some professors identified a theological or ethical concept that is really shared by all Christian traditions, although it may have been nurtured in the distinct Christian tradition. Still, other professors identified a specific belief that is particular to their tradition but also may be shared by a wider group of Christian traditions. In other words, this type of belief could be a unique, although not exclusive, emphasis of the particular tradition.

Second, we found that Christian teachers perceived their particular traditions as influencing five areas of their teaching: (1) specific ways of talking about God and the Christian metanarrative, (2) particular sources of God's wisdom and knowledge, (3) the ends of teaching, (4) curricular sense-making construction and content, and (5) pedagogy. In the first area, teachers understood that their tradition highlighted key aspects of God's nature, character, and/or important elements of the Christian story. The second way that the teachers' particular tradition influenced their teaching concerned the prioritization they placed on certain sources of knowledge, wisdom, or truth. Baptist and evangelical professors emphasized the importance of the Bible, while Reformed, Quaker, and Wesleyan professors emphasized gaining insight from God's general revelation in human reason, experience, reflection, nature, and the church tradition.

Teachers provided examples of ways their tradition influenced the ends of teaching from what could be categorized as low-level learning goals (e.g., basic knowledge and understanding) to more advanced skills (e.g., critically evaluating one intellectual tradition using the narrative framework of another tradition). With regard to the curriculum and teaching methods (the fourth and fifth areas in the list), professors could once again be divided into spiritual addition and Christian transformation types. The spiritual addition teachers simply supplemented what they perceived as the regular curriculum and methods with some denominationally related spiritual material. Christian transformation professors attempted to reframe the whole curriculum and their entire pedagogy to align with the larger Christian narrative.

Overall, the findings we described in chapters 2–5 come from Christians teaching at Christian colleges and universities. Many people think that allowing one's Christian identity to shape one's teaching is fine and perhaps should be encouraged at an institution that espouses a Christian identity. For example, Stanley Fish made clear that his argument against bringing moral opinions associated with one's additional identities, especially religious identities, into the classroom was not directed against teachers at faith-based institutions.[26] The tougher question is: *How should teachers handle the relationship between their professional and Christian identity at the pluralistic university (whether public or private)?* Should such contributions be welcomed and nurtured in higher education as a whole, first by encouraging specific, ecclesial forms of higher education and second by allowing both *generally* Christian and *particular* Christian teaching influences to be manifested in a pluralistic university setting? These important normative questions are addressed in the next three chapters.

6

Christian Teaching in the Pluralistic University

> Reticence about one's religious or spiritual convictions is the default mode today for most scholars in most secular colleges and universities... We faculty rarely mention our personal religious or spiritual convictions in our scholarship or teaching.
> —Mark U. Edwards Jr., "Why Faculty Find It Difficult to Talk about Religion"[1]

In early August 2017, a group of white supremacists held a rally at the University of Virginia on a Friday evening. While some fighting between the supremacists and counter-protestors reportedly took place that night, a Saturday rally led to additional outbreaks of street fighting. The violence culminated when James Alex Fields, a rally attender who had earlier been seen marching with a fascist group, drove a car into a crowd of antiracism protesters, killing 32-year-old Heather Heyer and injuring more than a dozen other participants.[2] Astoundingly, in the aftermath, rally organizer Richard Spencer, a University of Virginia alumnus, still called the original event "beautiful."[3]

A German professor named Chad Wellman, who was just beginning a term as principal of one of the university's residential colleges, had just moved onto the University of Virginia campus earlier that week. In an article for the *Chronicle of Higher Education*, Wellman described the teaching challenge the events produced for him: "White supremacists had marched not just across my yard, but also alongside the dorms where this Saturday I will welcome more than 200 students—and will have to explain to them what happened here."[4] He also mentioned that he had three children, whom he told to stay inside while the march occurred. He would also have to explain the march to them.

Wellman then went on to describe how he would choose to use two different types of moral language in his conversations with these two groups:

> When I welcome my students this Saturday, I will discuss white supremacy and the march, but I will use language different than the one my wife and I used with our three children. To them we spoke in the language of our faith tradition—in terms of the image of God, the church, and Christian love. When I speak to my students, I will do so in the language of the university and its traditions—in terms of open debate, critique, and a love of knowledge.[5]

Like a good teacher, Wellman acknowledges the need to speak a different moral language to his different audiences. With his students at a pluralistic university Wellman consciously chose to limit the influence of his primary nonteaching identity due to the diversity of his students' various worldviews. Here, Wellman seems to be following Stanley Fish's admonition that good teaching at a pluralistic university requires faculty members to constrain the influence of their extraprofessional identities.

Yet Wellman also noted that the need to speak in the limited moral language linked to the modern university's identity, story, and ends created problems:

> The university has moral limitations. Universities cannot impart comprehensive visions of the good. They cannot provide ultimate moral ends. Their goods are proximate. Faculty members, myself included, need to acknowledge that most university leaders lack the language and moral imagination to confront evils such as white supremacy. They lack those things not because of who they are, but, as Weber argued, because of what the modern research university has become. Such an acknowledgment is also part of the moral clarity that we can offer to ourselves and to our students. We have goods to offer, but they are not ultimate goods.[6]

For Wellman, these specific limitations of the modern research university also caused problematic but understandable moral limitations in the face of events such as the white supremacist march. As a result, university leaders only condemned the march in emotional or vague moral terms. For instance, he analyzed the moral language and reasoning of the University of Virginia's president, Theresa Sullivan in the following manner:

She wrote that she was "saddened" and "disturbed" by the "hateful behavior" of Friday's protesters. In a second statement, sent later that day, after the Unite the Right rally had spread into sporadic violence across downtown, she said that the "ideologies and beliefs" of Friday's protesters "contradicted our values of diversity, inclusion, and mutual respect." In neither statement did she name the particular ideology—white supremacy—or express the moral outrage so palpable across Charlottesville. She spoke instead of vague values and of disappointment.[7]

Overall, while vital and understandable for promoting learning among a pluralistic community, the limited moral tradition on which the contemporary pluralistic university is built could not give President Sullivan the specific moral language Wellman believed the occasion required.

Wellman's testimony provides a helpful example of some of the tensions regarding Christian teaching in the pluralistic university that we address in this chapter. We define a pluralistic university, whether public or private, as an institution of higher learning that uses only academic requirements and identities to exclude students or faculty. In other words, *in theory*,[8] a pluralistic university does not discriminate based on nonacademic identities unless that discrimination fosters particular academic ends (e.g., admissions decisions using metrics such as grades and test scores).[9]

Moreover, *in theory*, the pluralistic university does not espouse a particular religious or ideological identity, among other identities, and only educates with common human identities ends in mind (e.g., enhancing our flourishing as human beings by discovering truth) or academic/vocational identities (e.g., fashioning good biologists, sociologists, or economists). Of course, *in practice*, most pluralistic universities still make appeals to particularistic national or political identities (e.g., encouraging good democratic citizenship, helping to improve America's economy), since many pluralistic universities are not only funded by the government but have also implicitly inherited Georg Wilhelm Friedrich Hegel's idea behind the original German research universities that the state is primary.[10]

Pluralistic universities, such as the University of Virginia, provide the most extensive place for teachers and students with varied identities to interact and challenge one another, as well as to make decisions about how their non-teaching identities might shape their work. In a pluralistic university in a diverse country such as the United States, teachers often do not share various identities with a significant portion of their students (e.g., race, worldview, class). Consequently, professors in these institutions must learn how to steward the power entrusted to them so that the integration of extraprofessional identity traditions into the classroom does not undermine the ends of the pluralistic university (we discuss what those ends are or should be in subsequent sections of this chapter).

Although we set forth some general views about how teachers should address this matter, in the next two chapters we focus specifically on how Christian teachers should determine when and how to draw upon their nonprofessional identities in their professional practice. Our sources of moral guidance come from both the Christian tradition and the liberal moral tradition of the contemporary pluralistic university. Although the justificatory narrative that supports these narratives differs in important respects, we believe the commonality provides enough of a thin consensus by which to make our case in ways that show integrity to both of our identities as Christians and professors. This particular chapter focuses on this role of teachers' background beliefs in light of the pluralistic university's goals and purposes.

Basic Intellectual Awareness about Identity Influences

The pluralistic university is not pluralistic if professors do not recognize and examine the implications of ideological and identity pluralism for their teaching. Every identity and its accompanying narrative has different implications for professors' motivations, views of students, each part of the curriculum, and the overall purpose of education and life. Only by first understanding the complex relationships their prioritized identities have with their teaching will professors be able to understand when and when not to draw boundaries regarding the influence of those identities on their teaching. Consequently, if leaders of pluralistic universities expect professors to navigate wisely how our different identities influence our teaching, they must support and encourage this exploration.

The Importance of a Liberal Education

This encouragement starts with our graduate education practices. If professors have primarily received a narrowly specialized education, they may not be intellectually prepared to undertake the reflection and exploration we suggest is needed. We agree with Warren Nord's view:

> First, and most important, teachers need to be liberally educated. They need to be more than specialists, they should be intellectuals, at home in the world of ideas. This is clearly important quite apart from religion. Teachers should have some sense of how they teach relates to other subjects and disciplines, and to broad moral, political, religious, and existential issues, concerns, and controversies. Alas, few teachers—indeed, few undergraduates—receive a good liberal education.[11]

A liberal graduate education would help teachers become conscious of the influence of their primary identities and narratives on their teaching. If they have not received this kind of education, the pluralistic university may have to help nurture it.

Here pluralistic universities may have to learn from identity-focused institutions. Professors at specifically female or male colleges, historically black colleges, tribal colleges, faith-based colleges and universities, or other institutions with a particular identity focus or mission (e.g., military academies) cultivate this type of identity-informed awareness. At a pluralistic university, however, professors will likely not experience communities that cultivate this kind of consciousness, except within certain "studies" departments or groups, such as gender studies and African American studies. Therefore, the university will have to encourage a more broad-scale awareness about the influence of particular identities on teaching within their faculty development programs.

Still, the advantage of pluralistic universities is the possibility that professors will receive exposure to a wider variety of colleagues with different worldviews. In this sense, pluralistic universities have the potential to provide a form of liberal education about how worldview diversity influences teachers and teaching. For instance, to encourage faculty development in this area, pluralistic universities could hold forums to discuss how their wide array of professors' primary and secondary identities influences their pedagogy.

Unfortunately, two realities will likely hinder this project. First, pluralistic universities are actually becoming less pluralistic when it comes to ideological diversity.[12] The failure to address this problem in the contemporary academy means that "pluralistic" universities are really not pluralistic. In fact, it would be fair to call many universities politically liberal universities, which is much different than being true liberal universities.[13] Second, professors rarely watch each other teach. We think graduate students or young faculty could learn from seeing online or digital recordings of professors who demonstrate a sophisticated approach to identity-informed teaching.

Addressing Religious Identity

In addition, the intellectual awareness we hope the pluralistic university may provide, particularly regarding religious identities, is more difficult to achieve at a pluralistic university than at a university that prioritizes a particular religious identity (e.g., a Protestant or Catholic university). The contemporary academy devotes inordinate attention to the importance of identities such as race, ethnicity, gender, and sexual identity, but it usually does not give the same amount of attention to religious identities.[14]

There are cultural reasons for this phenomenon. Most Americans are educated in public schools and universities, where they are usually taught to privatize their religious identities, beliefs, and practices. A student we recently interviewed who started attending a Christian university provides a helpful example of this intellectual conditioning. She observed, "Before college, I had always attended public schools and I remember being taken aback on one of my first days of college when a professor opened up class with a word of prayer. My initial reaction was 'Wait, you can't pray in school.'" This sort of habituation occurs with more than just the practice of religious rituals. As Warren Nord found in his extensive study of the curriculum, "Schools and universities systematically privilege secular over religious ways of making sense of the world." He went so far as to maintain that, "Most public schools and universities border on secular indoctrination (and many cross the line). In doing so, they encourage (secular) faith and undermine critical reason."[15] The pluralistic university, if it is actually pluralistic, should do the opposite.

Ironically, most professors have spiritual identities, and many want to integrate this aspect of themselves into their lives. For example, in her national study of college faculty, Jennifer Lindholm found the following:

> Nearly nine in ten (87%) say that they believe in the sacredness of life. Roughly three in four indicate having an interest in spirituality (77%) and

say that they believe we are all spiritual beings (73%). Fully three fourths say that they are searching for meaning and purpose in life, and 70 percent report having discussions about the meaning of life with friends. Nearly two-thirds (65%) say that to at least "some" extent, they seek out opportunities to grow spiritually, and 54 percent believe that "we cannot really understand the world that lies outside of us without understanding the deeper spiritual aspects of ourselves." Overall, 47 percent give high priority to integrating spirituality in their lives.[16]

Teachers need to, and many want to, understand their religious and/or spiritual identities, their colleagues' religious and/or spiritual identities, as well as the influence of these identities on their teaching. Moreover, these identities should not merely be acknowledged; more importantly, they must be understood as possible resources for advancing the goals and outcomes of the pluralistic university.

Learning from Christian Colleges and Universities

In this area, pluralistic universities could learn from identity-shaped universities. As the examples presented in the last four chapters illustrate, Christian college and university faculty often engage in conversations about what difference Christianity makes for teaching and scholarship—even in the sciences. These examples reveal that when professors become aware of extraprofessional identity influences on their teaching, they cannot and should not draw a simple boundary between their professional teaching identity and the background beliefs supplied by their other identities. For example, the results presented in chapter 2 reveal how Christian teachers draw upon the Christian metanarrative to inform their motivations for teaching and their views of students. We do not believe teachers can or should somehow disengage themselves or unlearn this approach when teaching in a pluralistic university. In fact, it would be impossible to expect teachers to discard the views that they are called by God or see their students as made in God's image. Of course, the same statement could be made about the professor who teaches with little to no sense of divine calling who views students through a materialistic lens and does not ascribe metaphysical value or worth to them.

We also contend that encouraging professors to draw upon their extraprofessional identity narratives helps nurture their teaching motivations. Here, Parker Palmer's admonition that excellent teaching stems from the identity and integrity of the teacher holds the most weight. He writes, "[W]hen I devote myself to something that does not flow from my identity, that is not integral to my nature, I am most likely deepening the world's hunger rather than helping to alleviate it."[17] For instance, if Christian faculty members are discouraged from drawing upon the belief that they need to glorify or worship God in their teaching practices, respond to God's presence or call, view students as made in God's image, or enact God's character in their pedagogy, educational leaders are contributing to creating in professors what Palmer calls the divided self—a self that is disconnected from one's true identity, one's subject, and one's students.

In sum, we maintain that if educational leaders in the pluralistic university set forth Weber's objective, scientific teachers as the ideal teacher, they compromise the identity and ends of the pluralistic university. A contemporary vision for teachers, however, needs a much different ideal: one that recognizes the whole host of identities and stories that form professors, including religious identities. Educational leaders in pluralistic universities must then encourage teachers to become aware of how these identities influence their teaching. This awareness starts with how those identities may inform the ends and rules of the academy.

The Ends and Rules of Teaching in the Pluralistic Academy

Professors often take the goals of good teaching in the pluralistic academy for granted. For instance, the 1975 American Association of University Professor's (AAUP) "Statement on Teacher Evaluation" spent little time setting forth the ends of teaching. It mentioned the end of good teaching by which teachers should be evaluated in only one brief sentence: "The most valid measure is probably the most difficult to obtain, that is, the assessment of a teacher's effectiveness on the basis of the learning of his [or her] students."[18] The AAUP acknowledged what almost everyone recognizes, that the good professor advances learning.

Agreeing upon simple phrases, such as "advancing learning," however, may mask important disagreements, such as what exactly we think "learning" entails. An example from another field helps illuminate this point. Consider the statement, "The end of the game is to place the ball in the goal." Simply stating this end does not clarify whether we are playing soccer, basketball, or lacrosse; each involves different identities, narratives, and rules regarding how one can place the ball in the goal. Academic ends and associated rules can also suffer from similar terminological vagueness. For instance, phrases such as "advancing learning" and "teaching critical thinking" do not necessarily bring clarity to the ends of teaching. If anything, they may simply disguise deeper disagreements. In fact, even though we may agree upon the phrases describing certain broad ends, we argue that many in the academy are playing different games with different rules.

Stanley Fish's Proposal: Do Your Job

Considering the limits of simply-phrased goals, it helps to provide ends that are more descriptive for teachers in the pluralistic university. As mentioned in the introduction, Stanley Fish suggests a few purposes for teachers to follow. Instead of setting forth broad goals (e.g., learning or critical thinking), he describes two increasingly specific ends: "(1) introduce students to bodies of knowledge and traditions of inquiry they didn't know much about before; and (2) equip those same students with the analytical skills that will enable them to move confidently within those traditions and to engage in independent research should they choose to do so."[19]

While these purposes do not encompass the goals of every type of teacher in the university (e.g., art, drama, music), they cover the ends expected by administrators of many university teachers. These purposes would also be consistent with some of the purposes of teachers described in chapter 3, even when the subject related to Christianity (e.g., "In African American literature, we analyze how the Biblical text and Christian faith were used both to justify slavery and work for its abolition.").

Fish claims these two purposes provide guidance regarding the rules of the university, especially the limits of academic freedom. He argues that the principle of academic freedom is not meant to enable a teacher to hijack the classroom for other purposes:

> Of course, one is free to prefer other purposes to the purposes appropriate to the academy, but one is not free to employ the academy's

machinery and resources in the service of those other purposes. If what you really want to do is preach, or organize political rallies, or work for world peace, or minister to the poor and homeless, or counsel troubled youths, you engage in those activities after hours and on weekends, or, if part-time is not enough time, you should resign from the academy . . . and take up work that speaks directly to the problems you feel compelled to address.[20]

Fish wants teachers to stick to doing their job—as he defines it.

Unfortunately, Fish's point is not very precise. After all, teaching students how to preach, help the poor and homeless, or counsel troubled youth may be the domain of teachers in a divinity school, a school of social work, or an educational psychology program. Yet Fish's desire to prevent the purposes of the academy from being corrupted by problematic ends is a good one; it merely needs to be phrased differently.

We believe Fish's concerns center on teachers who seek identity conversion in a context in which identity conversion is not anticipated, stated, or desired. In other words, students who study in a pluralistic university primarily expect to be initiated into what it means to be excellent in particular academic identities. They want to be taught what it means to be a good historian, psychologist, social worker, biologist, and more. In this context, students likely do not expect or even want teachers to try to convert them to a particular ideology or political or religious identity, or to follow a particular vision of the good life. Consider this reaction from a student named Katie when she went to hear one of her Catholic professors preach:

> *I was so shocked and upset when I heard you in church saying exactly the same things you been saying to us in class. What gives you the right to be preaching to us in a class this way, without warning us that this is what you're doing? You're not supposed to do that! You're supposed to keep your own beliefs out of teaching not force us to believe as you do.*[21]

This quote reflects Steven Glazer's point that people are concerned about spirituality in education because "they are afraid of the *imposition of [a specific] identity.*"[22]

Of course, students have many problematic expectations when they enter the university. For example, one of us recently interviewed over 100 students about their expectations of college life.[23] Several students explained that they believe "the purpose of higher education is to get a job." Is the nonconversion to another identity idea a problematic student expectation in the pluralistic university?

Regarding the nonconversion expectation, we think important ethical reasons exist for it that go beyond students' expectations. Like liberal democracy, the pluralistic academy functions under an implicit social contract that recognizes that despite the significant amount of agreed-upon knowledge and wisdom, a pluralistic society also contains a wealth of divergent identities and narratives. Calling them "comprehensive doctrines," John Rawls argues, "Political liberalism assumes that, for political purposes, a plurality of reasonable yet incompatible comprehensive doctrines is the normal result of the exercise of human reason within the framework of the free institutions of a constitutional democratic regime."[24] Liberal democracies accommodated this pluralism by creating organizations, including pluralistic educational institutions that respect this diversity in the name of promoting justice among comprehensive doctrines or what we call diverse identities and narratives. Private pluralistic universities also follow this model. If Fish's argument is that professors should not seek unexpected identity conversions out of respect for students' human dignity and the implicit social contract between teachers and students functioning in a liberal democratic society, then we agree with him.

Obviously living out this ethical view in a pluralistic university limits the application of many of the specific goals mentioned in chapter 3 by Christian professors (e.g., "My primary objective is that they encounter Jesus Christ and grow as his disciples in love of God and neighbor."; "I want students to see that God wants all the areas of culture to be redeemed."). In a Christian college or university, students expect teachers to explore what it means to be a good Christian historian, accountant, or psychologist. In a pluralistic university, they do not.

We also think professors need to be careful even if they express identity transformation goals in broader language. Recently, a prominent group of scholars has used the term "spirituality" in higher education conversations.[25] Some of the professors we quoted earlier in this chapter also use this language (e.g., "I aspire to see my students growing spiritually as well as intellectually."; "Some courses have spiritual development as a goal."). We think these kinds of goals would be inappropriate in the pluralistic academy. Atheists, agnostics, and nonbelievers can rightly contend that they have not consented to these kinds of spiritual goals.

Of course, this limitation should also apply to other identities and other attempts at identity conversion in the classroom. Both of us once had a student who told one of us about a philosophy class he took at a state university. In the opening class, the professor stated, "My goal is to make you an atheist. If I can't do that, my goal is to at least make you an agnostic." Our guess is that this professor would claim that academic freedom allows him to make this end one of his goals. Yet the same professor would likely object to a faculty member claiming that one of her class goals is to make students Christians, Muslims, or Jews. The purpose of a philosophy of religion class should not be to change someone's identity.

A subtle distinction exists between *converting* students to an identity and *teaching them to understand* a position the way a person who holds that identity might experience it. In other words, helping students to try to get inside someone's skin is the professor's job. As Katie's Christian teacher in a pluralistic university clarified to her, "Students shouldn't be made Christian, but they should be able to hear the Christian challenge."[26] This kind of teaching should enhance the student's identity as a critical thinker. In this respect, we agree with Fish's insistence that teachers prioritize their professional identity in these cases.[27] We call this the "no unwanted identity conversion rule."

This rule has important implications for Parker Palmer's view: "*Good teaching cannot be reduced to technique; good teaching comes from the identity and integrity of the teacher.*"[28] This rule requires the teacher to limit the influence of his or her primary identity or identities in one particular way. *It requires that professors in a pluralistic university have the courage not to teach students to be exactly like them.* In this sense, the rule may limit what Palmer understands as good teaching out of respect for human dignity and the prevention of the abuse of power.

Should the "No Unwanted Identity Conversion Rule" Apply Only to the Religious Professor?

When thinking about matters of religious identity and teaching, many teachers immediately jump to the First Amendment. We have delayed addressing this topic, because the First Amendment does not apply to all pluralistic institutions. The pluralistic universities that are private yet profess no religious identity, such as the Ivy League institutions, do not have to abide by the religion clauses in the First Amendment ("Congress shall make no law respecting the establishment of religion, or prohibiting the free exercise thereof"). We have also delayed addressing this topic because we think it is helpful to think first about some particular ethical issues. After all, the First Amendment is built on ethical principles. For instance, one of the guiding values underlying those two clauses in the First Amendment pertains to the matter of justice toward those with different religious or nonreligious identities and convictions.

With that being said, we want to address how the First Amendment, and particularly its religion clauses, might apply to a religious or nonreligious teacher at a state-funded pluralistic university. First, the Supreme Court has not ruled directly on the matter of religiously informed teaching in state *universities*.[29] Consequently, it is not clear how a professor's rights to free speech and free exercise of religion should be balanced with concerns about a government employee promulgating or supporting religion.[30] In cases covering K–12 education, the Supreme Court has generally ruled that teachers employed by the state cannot use their position of power to promulgate or help "establish" government favoritism toward a particular religion, religion in general, or nonreligion. A well-known distinction the Court has suggested is that *teaching about religion* is permissible, but the *teaching of religion* is not (sometimes described as indoctrination).[31]

It is particularly important to recognize that the Supreme Court indicated state sponsorship could also apply to nonreligious teachers. In *Abington Township v. Schemp* (1963), a case addressing devotional Bible reading in public schools, Justice Tom C. Clark wrote that government-funded educational institutions could not establish a "religion of secularism," preferring "those who believe in no religion over those who do believe."[32] Similarly, Justice Arthur J. Goldberg warned in a concurring opinion that an "untutored devotion to the concept of neutrality" could lead to a "brooding and pervasive devotion to the secular and a passive, or even active, hostility to the religious."[33] Behind this perspective is the ethical advocacy of the classical liberal concept of justice as fairness toward competing identities and worldviews.[34]

At the university level, most scholars do not believe the religion clauses severely restrict religious or nonreligious professors, apart from the obvious abuses of indoctrination and proselytization. Mark Edwards Jr. noted this point:

> So long as the scholar and teacher avoids blatant proselytization and remains sensitive to the unequal power relations between faculty and students (or between senior faculty and junior or probationary faculty), the explicit mention of religious or spiritual conviction in scholarship or teaching may remain problematic for other reasons, but not because the First Amendment requires such beliefs to remain private.[35]

While we agree with Edwards's general interpretation of Supreme Court jurisprudence in this area, the Court's interpretation of what constitutes an Establishment Clause violation still leaves many questions unanswered. For example, if a philosophy professor stood up and said his goal was to show students that belief in God is rational, would that be understood as "teaching religion" or "blatant proselytization"? We do not think so, granted that this type of reasoning exercise is germane to the course. Would it be blatant "proselytism" or "teaching religion" if an education or nursing professor mentioned, as some did in our survey, that they seek to show their students the love of Christ? Again, announcing one's particular religious motivation for being ethical in the classroom does not even come close to approaching an establishment clause violation, because it does not ask students to affirm that identity, espouse its beliefs, or participate in Christian practices.

We think our "no unwanted identity conversion rule" is a better way to think about religiously related teaching than trying to discern between "teaching about religion" and "teaching a religion." The former is usually understood, mistakenly, as being more objective than the latter.[36] Yet as Douglas Jacobsen and Rhonda Jacobsen maintain:

> Every act of teaching—whether the course is about religion or anything else—requires making choices about what topics to include, what metaphors to use in introducing new concepts, how to explain the subject being studied. All this involves interpretation, and interpretation is never purely neutral or objective. . . . Viewed in this light, claims that teaching *about* religion is inherently more "objective" than teaching about religion itself become difficult to sustain[37]

They also point out that good teaching may require going beyond merely teaching information or knowledge *about* religion. Referring to the meditation techniques found in many religions as an example, they point out that describing the activity of meditation is not the same thing as actually meditating. They provide one other example that goes beyond merely teaching about religion:

> One professor of Hindu studies who is herself Hindu (and also teaches at a public university) told us that she requires students who enroll in her introductory level course to participate in a workshop on Hindu dance "because this is the essence of the tradition." Students cannot understand Hinduism, she said, without experiencing dance. But recently some of her students refused to take part, protesting that she was essentially requiring them to worship a Hindu deity.[38]

Here we see why it helps to think in terms of identity conversion. In the pluralistic university, the faculty's job is *not* to try to make students agnostics, Christians, atheists, Muslims, Hindus, or even Marxists or feminists. Instead, their job is to expose students to the arguments and practices relevant to their subjects within their discipline and to help students gain the moral imagination to place themselves in another religious or nonreligious person's shoes. Certainly it is important to recognize that these arguments and practices may include drawing upon Christian, Marxist, or feminist perspectives or perhaps something like a religious practice.

Nonetheless, asking someone to engage in an activity, such as meditating, singing, or dancing, violates the "no unwanted identity conversion rule" if professors specifically ask students to direct this activity to a particular deity or deities. In other words, just as one begins to become a baseball player or a trumpet player by engaging in baseball or trumpet practice, if professors ask students to practice being a Christian, Hindu, or Buddhist in some way, it means they are asking students to take on that identity. For example, if they ask someone to learn about worship by singing in a Christian worship service or dancing to a Hindu deity, they ask the student to become a Christian or Hindu in that action. Similarly, asking a student to think or act purely as an agnostic or atheist would also violate the no-conversion rule. If the First Amendment prohibits favoritism toward "a religion of secularism" or "devotion to the secular," then in our view, the "no unwanted identity conversion rule" applies to both religious and secular identities.

Christian Contributions to the Pluralistic Academy

While we support the "no nonacademic identity conversion rule" that appears to underlie one of Fish's principal concerns, we have some problems with his desire for professors to function exclusively from their professional identity. Since Fish focuses so exclusively on the way other identities can corrupt academic purposes, he ends up stressing the importance of maintaining a general boundary between one's professional identity and other identities. He does not explore the way other identities could and even perhaps *should* enhance a professor's role. This becomes especially important when professors are aiming not for the identity conversion of their students but to be good teachers. Since Fish fails to acknowledge the positive contributions such visions could make to teaching, he ends up supporting several boundaries that cannot and do not need to be maintained.

In contrast to Fish's argument, our findings indicate that other identities can help enhance or reinforce academic purposes. This contribution occurs when teachers draw upon the narrative associated with the identity that motivates them to fulfill their academic purposes. One Christian teacher we interviewed articulated this kind of perspective: "Because I believe that I am teaching immortals who are created in the image of God and beloved in Christ, I want more for them than knowledge of facts and skills to earn a living. I teach for knowledge, skills, and wisdom for the whole of life, including making a living." As our findings suggest, Christian professors indicated that their motivation for becoming teachers grows from their Christian identity. It nourishes their calling and sense of vocation as a professor.

One also can find examples of this type of reinforcement in the scholarly literature. For instance, in *A Theology of Higher Education*, Mike Higton discusses ways that the pluralistic university can be a school for intellectual and moral virtue: "A Christian may know, for instance, that she is called to honesty—but that does not mean that she knows what the exercise of the virtue of honesty looks like in all contexts."[39] Thus, the university initiates students into disciplines, which are themselves "communities of training in virtuous perception, and in the judgment that springs from it."[40] Such initiation requires a willingness to judge and to be judged. In this respect, Higton sees his work in a pluralistic university as producing in students "a life of openness to judgement that in its own way echoes the dynamic of crucifixion and resurrection that shapes discipleship."[41] That Higton views his work this way empowers and motivates him, but it does not mean he engages in identity conversion. In other words, understanding the importance of Christian teachers' placement of their vocation in a larger theological narrative helps elucidate the benefits of encouraging Christian teachers to bring this identity to the profession.

Moreover, sometimes corrupt university environments can be reformed by teachers who draw upon their nonprofessional identities. Chris Anderson, a professor at a state university, gives testament to this outlook: "My faith gives me strength to remain a teacher within an institution that tends not to value teaching, but only when I remember where this strength comes from. From Christ. From the One."[42] In other words, professors' religious identities and their accompanying narratives about reality may even help nurture a deeper motivation for teaching in academic settings where the production of research is valued over teaching.

Fish's description of the purpose of the academy also appears to leave little room for teachers to add purposes that stem from their identity. In contrast, we believe that identity-informed objectives could be added in ways that augment Fish's purposes. For instance, one professor in our survey shared, "Even when I taught at a state university, I saw my role in the classroom, as well as in advising, as one of needing to reflect God's love towards my students." A psychology teacher noted, "Teaching counseling and psychology courses with an emphasis on the Christian value of love in relationships is fundamental to my approach to meeting the teaching objectives of my courses." Hopefully the pluralistic academy thinks it is appropriate for professors to show agape, sacrificial love, to their students! We certainly think these purposes are compatible with the purposes Fish identified and therefore that Christian teachers can add them to the purposes of the pluralistic university.[43]

Other purposes teachers in our survey expressed could also be compatible with or perhaps reinforce the purposes Fish identified (e.g., "I seek wholeness in restoring the image of God in students over information acquisition."; "I believe that God wants us to be all we can be, so improving ourselves through study is Biblical."). These additions do not aim for wholesale identity conversion; instead, they aim to advance human flourishing, which could be the goal of any institution of higher learning.

Finally, there are ways that drawing upon one's identity can further the particular academic ends Fish has in mind. After all, this is *why* we value diversity in the academy. Professors confessing a particular identity can help students understand the identity and its intellectual tradition from the inside and therefore help them adopt an empathetic understanding of the tradition. As the examples in previous chapters reveal, Christian professors can model how to apply an identity with an intellectual tradition by using it to guide their interpretive lens within their discipline. In this way, students encounter the intellectual tradition as a live option.

A "No Contested Ethical Conversion Rule"?

One of the boundaries erected over the past century by Max Weber and others who embrace the ideal of the objective professor is the belief that professors should not inculcate particular nonacademic moral beliefs in students. To be clear, those who hold to this view believe a teacher can and should expound professionally and even morally about what it means to be a good accountant, chemist, or sociologist. But they hold that professors should not instill in their students ethical views outside a specific professional identity. In general, they should not try to persuade students of particular controversial moral viewpoints unless they are making arguments for both sides of an issue. Moreover, professors themselves should not be judged morally by any particular view of the good life. They should *only* be judged according to professional virtues.

Stanley Fish's postmodern perspective provides a helpful example of this view. He does not think professors should venture into persuading students about contested ethical matters. Instead, he contends that if a university's employees pressure students to accept contested ethical views as their own, the institution "is using the power it has to impose a moral vision on those who do not share it, and that is indoctrination if anything is."[44] Here, it is important to note that Fish makes a distinction between persuading students of contested ethical views versus helping to promote more universally agreed upon moral positions. Fish holds to the same view when it comes to the assessment of professors: "Job performance should be assessed on the basis of academic virtue, not virtue in general. Teachers should show up for their classes, prepare lesson plans, teach what has been advertised, be current in the literature in the field, promptly correct assignments and papers, hold regular office hours, and give academic (not political or moral) advice."[45] Overall, Fish's outlook extends even further than the "no unwanted identity conversion rule." It applies to particular moral positions that may be linked to a variety of identities. One might call it the "no contested ethical conversion" rule.

Again, we find ourselves agreeing with this general rule if it simply means professors in pluralistic universities should not pressure or indoctrinate students into a contested moral position. In this regard, Palmer's admonition to teach from one's full identity, we believe, could lead to unhealthy forms of indoctrination and the abuse of the professor's power. Professors *could* end up using the classroom as an opportunity to pressure students to adhere to their own contested moral views, all in the name of being authentic and teaching from an "undivided self."

We should not let a focus on this rule, however, lead us to dismiss the important ways that our other identities and their associated narratives function regarding our pedagogy and our ethics. Parker Palmer argued that teachers need to connect both their vision of good teaching and the ends of education with their broader identities. This remains true *even if* the ethical views they hope to transmit are commonly agreed upon views. To understand this point, it helps to examine our findings about how Christian teachers think about ethics and teaching in general.

As we mentioned in chapter 2, hundreds of professors in our study discussed the particular virtues they hoped to cultivate in students. Many were what we consider common virtues and moral principles, (e.g., respect, honesty, empathy, love, and the golden rule).[46] Indeed, our findings demonstrate that even teachers at Christian universities usually focus on principles or virtues about which a wide variety of traditions might share some at least thin agreement.

Where differences emerge pertains to the source of the virtue or principle and the reasoning behind it. The virtues and moral principles Christian professors in our study supported did not come simply from their professional, disciplinary traditions. Instead, our participants mentioned they had the theologically- informed goal of transforming the whole person in light of an ideal set forth or personified by God. Consider again this comment from a professor mentioned in a previous chapter:

> I have one course where we discuss ethics of human subjects in research. My theological tradition is "care for one's neighbor," especially those who may not be able to care for themselves. We discuss the biblical tradition

of how one cares for one's neighbor and relate that to designing human subjects research that respects a patient's right to make an educated decision about the benefits and risks of the study and to protect the patients from being misused.

This teacher understood the justification for a commonly-accepted ethical norm in the academic world as being connected to a particular aspect of her theological tradition. It also helped expand the definition of "care for one's neighbor" to include those with less power.

What would the "do not inculcate controversial moral views" rule mean in this situation? It certainly does not mean a Christian teacher cannot encourage students to be loving, empathetic, or caring toward their neighbors. It merely sets forth the view that the Christian teacher should try to find reasons or justifications for virtues that will appeal to the broad student audience. Appealing to the Bible or other forms of special revelation when teaching non-Christians will likely prove ineffective. As George Marsden writes, "It simply does not advance the discussion to introduce an authority that other people do not accept."[47] That being said, it would be appropriate for Christian teachers to mention the justifications they find persuasive for adhering to a common moral virtue or principles. Indeed, we should expect a variety of justifications for commonly-agreed upon moral virtues and principles to exist in a pluralistic university.

Moreover, it would not be problematic for a Christian teacher to focus on what we call the "redemptive virtues" or "redemptive principles," such as forgiveness, humility, servant leadership, love for one's enemies, and nonviolence, in a pluralistic context. While some of these virtues and principles may be emphasized more within the Christian tradition, it does not mean they are not emphasized in other traditions, or even in academic fields such as positive psychology and secular forms of ethics.[48] The teacher would merely be more likely to persuade students of these virtues using commonly agreed upon moral justifications.[49]

A Revised List of Teaching Ends in the Pluralistic Academy

Considering our concerns with Fish's approach, as well as some limitations we see with the ends he proposed, we want to set forth a somewhat different set of purposes that we think should define the pluralistic academy. The first three describe goals we think teachers in the pluralistic academy should use to guide their work:

1. Transmit culturally agreed-upon views about truth, goodness, and beauty in various fields of knowledge.

2. Initiate students into a set of common academic and professional practices associated with academic identities (e.g., what it means to be a good historian) that help students create, discover, and/or care for truth, goodness, and beauty.

3. Educate students about the similarities and differences between various identities and traditions and the implications for views of truth, goodness, and beauty, as well as academic and professional practices.

Regarding the first objective, Stanley Fish admits that he ultimately has at least part of this end in mind when he teaches. He confesses, "If anything is a value, truth is, and the implicit (and sometimes explicit) assumption in the classroom as I envision it is that truth, and the seeking of truth, must always be defended. . . . You will never hear in any of my classes the some-people-say-X-and-others-say-Y-and-who's-to-judge-dance."[50] Fish merely limits his end to truth, while we want to expand that important end to include goodness and beauty as well.

Regarding the second purpose, we believe it is important to recognize that an introduction into a field of study and training in a field requires a certain amount of submission to the authority of those well versed in that specific tradition. Like learning a practice from an athletic coach or music teacher, one must be inculcated in the basics of that activity. This is why Stanley Hauerwas makes the following claim about theological education:

> I start my classes by telling my students that I do not teach in a manner that is meant to help them make up their own minds. Instead, I tell them that I do not believe they have minds worth making up until they have been trained by me. I realize such a statement is deeply offensive to students since it exhibits a complete lack of pedagogic sensitivities. Yet I cannot imagine any teacher who is serious who would allow students to make up their own minds.[51]

Hauerwas claims this approach is like the one taken in science courses, in which students are initiated into a tradition of study:

> Would you trust a physics instructor who thought she or he could teach physics in a manner that students could make up their own minds about whether atoms do or do not exist? Do you think you could study molecular biology and doubt the existence of cells? Can you study geology and wonder whether a strong distinction can be made between different kinds of rocks? Why is it students are ready to submit to authority in the sciences but yet think they ought to be able to make up their minds when they take courses in the humanities and, in particular, theology?[52]

Fish also believes that students need this kind of initiation into a tradition of inquiry: "Opinion-sharing sessions are like junk food: they fill you up the starch and leave you feeling both sated and hungry. The sustained inquiry into the truth of the matter is an almost athletic experience; it may exhaust you, but it also improves you."[53] Like Fish, we think athletic or musical examples are helpful to elucidate this point. In both cases, students submit to a certain kind of training under a person of authority. After all, if they could make up their own minds about how to achieve excellence, they would not need the mentor.

Our third goal for teachers in a pluralistic academy addresses the heart of liberal education. A liberal education takes place within a tournament of identities and narratives. If universities hope to teach their students to think critically, they must not simply educate them about commonly agreed upon forms of knowledge and professional practices. In addition, they should not merely help students learn about different identities and their associated traditions. They must also help students understand the implications of these different identities and traditions for views of truth, goodness, and beauty, as well as academic and professional practices.

Moreover, both professors and students must acquire the necessary critical thinking skills to evaluate the strengths and weaknesses of various intellectual traditions (including one's own). If there is one end that most educators will agree upon, it is that they wish to help their students become critical thinkers. Of course this term, and therefore the goal, is often quite vague. At a minimum, what helping teachers and students to become critical thinkers should mean is facilitating their understanding of the ontological, epistemological, and ethical assumptions related to various identities and their associated traditions of thought. It also means helping them to appreciate the possible strengths, weaknesses, and limitations of various traditions. Warren Nord helpfully points out that for teachers to help students experience a liberal education, students "must be initiated into conversations in which they learn to assess the assumptions and claims of contending disciplines and the traditions and worldviews within which they are embedded."[54]

Achieving this end would require teachers to discuss their identity differences, which is a practice that is not always encouraged even among scholars. In *The End of Education*, Neil Postman suggests that teachers and students should exclude "narratives that lead to alienation and divisiveness."[55] He continues by asserting that the task of public schooling is to make students less hyphenated Americans or to "erase the hyphens or make them less distinct."[56] We contend that neither educators nor students should be expected to drop their other identifies and the narratives associated with these identities at the door of the pluralistic university. This treats the pluralistic university as if it has the same function the established church had for many countries: to provide the necessary form of ideological unity. Certainly we need to find commonality and overlapping consensus, *but* we should not do so by downplaying everyone's particularity. The ability to live with our deepest differences will not be developed if teachers merely stifle our worldview differences as Christians, materialists, utilitarians, capitalists, Marxists, or feminists.

Scholars from the group Heterodox Academy summarize the problem that will result if teachers in a pluralistic university fail in this endeavor: "We fail as teachers to teach students the most important skill—*how to think*. When we shield them from strong counter-arguments on the issues they care most about, we set them up for confusion and anger when they later encounter people who think differently."[57] What students need to hear are the best arguments, not only from scholars who share a common professional identity (e.g., psychologists, sociologists, physicists), but also from those with a wide range of identity commitments, including religious identity commitments.

Considering the arguments set forth in this chapter, we suggest two additional principles for teachers in a pluralistic academy:

4. Teachers seeking identity conversion or conversion to controversial moral beliefs may threaten or corrupt the previously mentioned

ends of the university. Yet, the teachers' own identities, beyond that of being a teacher, can be used to strengthen, amplify, or add to the three previously listed purposes. To strike the proper balance, teachers need to learn how to show fairness to the various traditions represented in the classroom.

5. Teachers must model this commitment to pluralistic education in their teaching. To do so, they will need to exercise certain virtues, such as intellectual awareness and humility, and engage in certain practices, such as confession about the identity or identities that may influence their approach to teaching a particular class.

We expand on the importance of principles 4 and 5 in chapter 7.

Conclusion

In light of our views, it should come as little surprise that we think University of Virginia professor Chad Wellman clearly understands the moral limitations of pluralistic universities. Accommodating moral pluralism leaves such universities few ethical resources. Certainly new students at the university need to learn their university's thin moral tradition. Moreover, the variety of students will likely only find agreement regarding the reasoning for opposing the evils of white nationalism or supremacism if the language and forms of reasoning are agreeable to most of them. In addition, Wellman is right not to try to *persuade* students to affirm his particular Christian reasons for opposing white nationalism. In these respects, we can understand why Wellman seemed to follow Fish's approach and avoided Palmer's advice to teach from one's full identity.

Yet because Wellman understandably does not want to speak to students with a moral voice that many will disregard, he may have missed an important teaching opportunity for his students. We do think that students need to be taught that they should not leave their thick moral traditions at the academy's door. Wellman could have let students know his deeper reasons for opposing racism, as did the following group of Christian scholars who wrote in an open letter: "As Christian scholars, we affirm the reality that all humans are created in the image of God and should be treated with respect and dignity. There is no good moral, biblical, or theological reason to denigrate others on the basis of race or ethnicity, to exalt one race over others, or to countenance those who do."⁵⁸ Here, we think it is best to eschew Fish's strong boundary lines and to follow Palmer's call to teach from one's identity with integrity. Christian teachers in the pluralistic academy *can* and *should* let their students know about this identity-specific line of reasoning in the classroom. If they do not, they may leave their students less educated and potentially less-equipped critical thinkers.

7

Identity-Informed Teaching in the Pluralistic University

Important Virtues and Practices

[T]he key to reasonableness (and critical thinking) is not some particular method—[the] scientific method, for example—but the willingness to think critically about one's most basic assumptions, engaging in conversation.

—Warren Nord[1]

"I am a teacher." Claiming this identity immediately places moral demands on the person making such an assertion. When someone identifies as a teacher, that person inherits a professional identity with a moral tradition that guides and orients his or her actions. Indeed, because humans have practiced teaching virtually as long as recorded history, we have a fairly well-developed moral tradition associated with the professional practice of what it means to be a good or bad teacher in the classroom.[2]

In addition, since universities have been around for over 800 years, a long historical conversation also exists about what it means to be a good or bad professor—a vocation that includes a combination of teaching and scholarly work. This commentary does not look kindly upon professors who only focus on being a good scholar. Consider the following comment by Ludwig Heinrich Jacob in 1798:

> An orderly, upright man with a well-ordered erudition and a gift for communicating is more suitable to become a professor than a scholarly monster who labors only for himself and world or who does little for his students, or a genius who has offensive morals and who does not think it worth the labor to employ diligence on lectures for his students, or a rhapsodic-polymath who strews everything together without any connection and has no proper method of instruction.[3]

These conclusions about the ideals a good professor should embody have not changed much in the last few hundred years. For example, Steven Cahn's *Saints and Scamps: Ethics in Academia*, first published in 1986 and reprinted again in 2011, presents similar conclusions. The book starts with a description of a professor Cahn knew who was a respected scholar. However, this faculty member failed to reach even the lowest levels of decency in his teaching:

> He regularly canceled classes. At those he attended, he arrived late, and when he did arrive he was generally unprepared. He gave no examinations, so he would have none to correct. In each course, he assigned one term paper, to which he gave a cursory reading. If he liked the few pages he read, he gave the paper an A. If he didn't like them, he gave the paper a B. Students who submitted no paper received a C. This grading system avoided most complaints.[4]

Both Jacob and Cahn grant that the professors they describe might be good, or even great, scholars. Yet, they share a general agreement about the type of professors who violate some of the basic agreed-upon standards of what it means to be a good teacher.[5]

Cahn continues by specifying the particular practices that one should perform to be a good and even a great teacher. Overall, the advice that Cahn provides is hardly controversial. In fact, although his book is subtitled "Ethics in Academia," it contains minimal moral argumentation in which he explains reasons for his ethical positions. Instead, Cahn fills his pages with general moral admonitions to which nearly everyone would likely assent (e.g., "Professors are obliged to be at every class session. . . . Professors are also obligated to be available to students for consultations outside of class. . . . Assignments should always be returned with detailed comments."[6]). One gives these pieces of advice to beginners; they are the basic moral rules and virtues of teaching upon which almost anyone in a pluralistic university would agree. Cahn's book likely still resonates with readers since its ethical advice to teachers remains largely uncontroversial.

Teaching in pluralistic settings, where the tournament of identities and narratives is more complex, requires more than following the basic moral rules of the profession or being conscious of the particular influences of one's identities on one's instruction. It also demands more than a simple recognition of how one's identity and guiding narrative may influence one's own ends or the pluralistic university's understanding of the purpose of teaching. For instance, teachers cannot always heed Parker Palmer's call to teach from their identity in the pluralistic academy. Sometimes they need the courage *not* to teach from who they are. They need the discernment and discretion to know how to wield their incredible power to influence young minds. In other words, teaching in a pluralistic university also requires the use of certain kinds of advanced virtues and practices in the classroom. These advanced virtues and practices help professors learn how to draw boundaries and connect their extraprofessional identities to their teaching in appropriate ways.

In this chapter, we present our thesis that the most effective approach to managing the tournament of identities and narratives in the classroom requires the civic virtues that Plato and Aristotle taught more than 2,000 years ago. These include virtues such as courage, honesty, self-control, and justice. Alasdair MacIntyre observed that while virtues sustain traditions, vices destroy them.[7] This is also true for the professional practice of teaching in the pluralistic university. If we want teachers to have honest and productive conversations with students about the tournament of identities and narratives, they need to demonstrate these virtues in combination with the practices of confession and modeling.

Courage, Intellectual Honesty, and Confession

As discussed in chapter 6, professors in pluralistic universities do not only need to be conscious about the influence of their primary identities on their teaching practices; they also must also be honest with themselves about which identity or identities they prioritize in their lives and teaching (e.g., religious, sexual, racial, gender, national, or economic identity). This ordering will affect how they educate their students and their overarching pedagogical goals, curriculum, and methods. They also then need to demonstrate the courage to confess how this prioritization might influence the class and their view of knowledge. While personally revealing, this form of confession is simply the practice of intellectual honesty.

Teaching, in particular, requires this kind of vulnerability. After all, most students are likely not preoccupied with whether their dentist is a born-again Christian, a feminist, or an environmental activist. They probably merely want their dentist to be well trained, gentle, compassionate, and honest about his or her billing practices. Students in a university, however, are having their heads filled, not their teeth. While we must understand that students are not simply passive receptacles of academic knowledge, we also must recognize that professors explicitly or implicitly seek to form students' views of the natural world, humanity, and themselves. Thus, the identities and associated stories that faculty members bring with them into the classroom possess serious significance. Teachers need to be both conscious and honest about *how* their identities and accompanying stories influence their approach to classroom objectives, curricular construction, and pedagogy. The courage to be honest about how one's primary identity influences these elements of one's teaching is needed whether this identity pertains to race, gender, religion, or any other identity the professor may prioritize.

The professor bell hooks provides an intriguing example of this phenomenon. Out of respect for the "no unwanted identity conversion rule" discussed in chapter 6, she admitted that she once stayed silent about her spiritual identity, and maintained: "Throughout my educational experience, both as a student and during the early years of my teaching as an assistant professor I felt it was crucial that I say nothing about spirituality in the classroom so that I would not in any way be imposing my concern with spiritual development on my students."[8] This silence changed while she taught at Yale University. She confessed:

> When students would ask me how I survived, how I made it without falling apart, I was compelled to give them an honest account of the sustaining power of spirituality in my life. Honestly naming spirituality as a force strengthening my capacity to resist enabled me to stand within centers of dominator culture and courageously offer alternatives. I shared with my students the basis of my hope.[9]

What is important to note about this process, however, is that bell hooks did not impose her spirituality on students. Instead, the students themselves initiated this conversation with her, thus providing the impetus for her confession about spirituality's power in her life.

Although we think it is appropriate for individual teachers to start their courses with a confession of how their primary identity influences their teaching, we also maintain that this practice should be common to all scholars. After all, scholars consider the practice of including some sort of positionality statement an essential component in qualitative research.[10]

What we are proposing here is merely an extension of this practice to the classroom. George Marsden, a Christian historian, provides a helpful example of the way he incorporated practice when he taught at the University of California at Berkeley:

> [W]hat I decided was that early in the semester [I] would acknowledge my religiously informed viewpoint, presenting the disclosure as analogous to truth in advertising. Since everyone who teaches about religion has an interpretive bias, I said, students do not really benefit from teachers posing as neutral objective observers, when in fact their interpretations reflect a particular point of view. So, I told the students that they should be aware of my point of view. At times, I would be making interpretive statements, sometimes explicitly identified as reflecting my perspective. I would not expect anyone to agree with my more biased interpretations, and I would respect different points of view. That approach seemed to work eminently well. No one, so far as I know, objected and many students told me they appreciated my frankness.[11]

In a pluralistic university, we think that every professor, or at the very least those in the humanities and social sciences, should begin each semester with this sort of confession. Moreover, we want to make clear that this confession should not be used as cover for oppressive opinion pushing.

This confessional practice, even when made from a religious identity, is not only the expression of academic honesty; it is also an expression of humility and courage. Sharing one's story is something we do with those we trust, especially since after sharing the story there is a chance that it might be used against us. R. Eugene Rice writes, "Self-disclosure comes with a price: the forfeiture of some of the protections afforded by the status and prestige that faculty have labored so hard to achieve that are frequently invoked in the university environment."[12] Just as self-disclosure to students requires courage and humility, so does revealing oneself to colleagues, peers, and educational leaders.

This courage and humility is also important because not every Christian professor has the same experience as Marsden when being open about his or her positionality. Chris Anderson, a Christian professor who teaches in a pluralistic university, describes the current perspective of his students and colleagues regarding this matter:

Students willingly and rightly accept the committed feminism of their other professors. They willingly and rightly accept the committed environmentalism of their other professors. They willingly and rightly respect the gender of their professors in women's studies and the race of their professors in ethnic studies, realizing as they should that who we are in our bodies and our lives is everywhere connected to what we think and what we know. But when it comes to Christianity, when it comes to the Christian professor teaching a Christian text, when it comes to any contact with Christian ideas, suddenly my students and even my colleagues devolve into old-fashioned Enlightenment rationalists, suspicious of bias, on the lookout for any trace of commitment.[13]

The reason for this apparent double standard could involve multiple factors. According to Anderson's report, it may stem from a failure to consider the importance of showing justice to different identities. Alternatively, it may stem from a misunderstanding of the First Amendment, as discussed in chapter 6. Whatever the reason, this change in treatment simply fails to demonstrate fairness toward religious identities.

We must also recognize that the kind of disclosure we recommend is an expression of academic freedom. Warren Nord writes, "But if academic freedom protects the right of scholars to be critical of a particular religion or religion generally, shouldn't it also protect the right of scholars to be supportive of religion?"[14] In other words, academic freedom allows a professor to confess whether he or she is a Muslim or an atheist, a political liberal or a political conservative.

Of course, this confession should serve the ends of the class and the pluralistic university and should not merely fulfill the professor's emotional needs or desires. For instance, Mark C. Edwards Jr. describes a chemistry professor who introduces "green chemistry" using this approach:

> Her pedagogical goal is for students to value innovative chemical technologies that reduce or eliminate the use or generation of hazardous substances in the design, manufacture, and use of chemical products. She typically disclosed some of her own personal, religious commitments regarding the environment as a means of getting the students to engage questions about the morally responsible use of chemical knowledge.[15]

It would appear in this case that this confession helpfully served larger pedagogical goals and was not made solely to support her own agenda. Such a confession helps students experience something essential to a liberal education: learning to understand a particular tradition from the inside. A liberal education that does not expose students to individuals who embody a variety of perspectives and fails to help them learn how to understand empathetically the particular reasoning of different identity traditions also fails to fulfill its overarching purpose.

We also want to acknowledge a danger. Once students know a teacher's prioritized identity and its accompanying narrative, they may interpret everything a professor has to say through a hermeneutic of suspicion. We argue that the way to allay that suspicion is through the practice of justice in the classroom.

Justice in the Postmodern Classroom

We consider the moral argument made by Stephen Cahn regarding how a professor should handle his or her own views in the classroom a helpful description of the standard teachers in the pluralistic university should follow. He sets forth the following position based on what he terms an academic golden rule, grounded in a general concept of fairness or justice:

> For an instructor to defend personal opinions is appropriate, but serious alternatives should not be neglected. A faculty member should consider the question: if another qualified instructor were in my place, might that individual offer opinions that conflict with those I have presented? If the answer is yes, the faculty member should alert students, thereby increasing their understanding of the relevant issue.... An instructor is well-advised to imagine that intellectual opponents are in the classroom while the instructor presents their viewpoints.[16]

In Cahn's approach, the bad professor is not the teacher who expresses his or her own opinions to the exclusion of others; it is the *unjust* professor. In addition to being unfair to other approaches, such professors engage in intimidation and expect acquiescence. Cahn explains, "Their aim is not education but indoctrination. Such attempts to foster ideological zeal may be in order at a political rally but are entirely inappropriate in a college classroom."[17] While Weber also wanted to make sure professors did not politicize classes, unlike Weber, Cahn is more interested in fairness than in objectivity.

Clearly Cahn sets forth a high moral ideal. We think it is likely that few professors give their intellectual opponents this kind of respect in the classroom. In this regard, we find much to admire in Cahn's outlook. Nonetheless, we think his view warrants an important caveat. For many academics today, different views about knowledge and ethics are not simply what Cahn calls "personal opinions"; they are personal convictions about knowledge, truth, and the good. Professors often connect these convictions to their identity in significant ways. To call them "opinions" treats them too lightly.[18]

Scholars often set forth the ideal of the objective professor and exalt Fish's exclusive emphasis on teaching solely from one's professional identity because they perceive these approaches as the way to preserve justice or fairness in the classroom. These scholars think professors who allow other identities to influence their teaching will be guilty of favoritism and therefore will corrupt the purposes of the pluralistic university. For instance, Christian teachers who allow their religious identity to shape their teaching could show favoritism toward Christian texts, ideas, or students who share the same identity. Palmer himself recognizes this point as well as its root in Christian theological thinking: "Indeed, the commitment to objectivity has good spiritual grounding. It can be a hedge against the sin of self-centeredness which affects everything we do, including knowing, and has since Adam and Eve."[19]

It is helpful to illustrate this common concern by quoting a student who complained about the practices of a Christian professor who teaches about the Bible in a course in a pluralistic university. This teacher confessed his identity and talked about his personal experience during certain class sessions. The student wrote:

> What I really want from you is an objective look at the reading. I understand that the Bible has played a large role in your life, which I consider personally admirable. But I do not think that you should express how much effect the book has had on you as much as you do in class. I think we all would be able to think clearly about it if we could further detach from the religious implications of what we are reading. I think you should supply as many multiple interpretations of the Bible as you can, even if they are negative.[20]

We think this student's comment is useful for several reasons.

First, the example demonstrates the student's valid concern about whether the professor demonstrated justice to different viewpoints in the classroom. This concern was likely magnified because the professor confessed his religious identity and shared experiences related to the identity in class. The core issue really is how teachers handle their own overt expressions of their identity in the classroom in a way that fosters and does not undermine both justice and a liberal education.

Yet, the student needs to recognize that supposedly objective professors who do not confess their identity may not always demonstrate justice to all perspectives. For instance, bell hooks describes her own experience with "objective professors" as a student:

> Throughout my student years I noticed that the professors who valued objectivism highly were often individuals who lacked basic communication skills. Often pathologically narcissistic, they simply could not connect. At times they experienced as a threat any efforts students made to emotionally connect with them. It was their inability to connect that helped me interrogate their overvaluation of objectivity. They stood at a distance from us (students) and the world, and yet I could see no evidence that this distance made them see everything more clearly, or enabled them to be just or fair. Certainly, the argument in favor of objectivity was that it freed us from attachments to particular individuals or perspectives.[21]

Although we do not want to cast all those who seek objectivity as emotionally stunted, we think hooks's observation that the quest for objectivity can be used as an excuse either to avoid interrogating one's own emotional connection to a subject or to avoid connecting to or caring for students is an important one. Overall, injustice in the classroom may not be rectified by being "objective," which leads to our second point.

This student's story also demonstrates how students in general may misunderstand what a liberal education is and have multiple, conflicting ideals in mind. The student's last statement ("supply as many interpretations of the Bible as you can") holds up the liberal arts ideal of exposing learners to diverse views. Yet, his previous sentence ("I think we all would be able to think clearly about [the Bible] if we could further detach from the religious implications of what we are reading.") demonstrates a different kind of ideal that excludes particular types of readings of the Bible. In this example, the student has succumbed to the modern, secular ideal of what education should be, described at the end of chapter 1. In this later view, the student wants the professor to help students study and read a text secularly, in a way that divorces one from any religious readings that seem too personal or subjective. We argue that there are multiple problems with this view. If a professor is atheist or agnostic, why would a secular reading not be understood as subjective or personal and a religious reading as something a bit more distant from the professor?

The real difficulty, however, is the modern view of knowledge articulated by the student that we described at the end of chapter 1. One contemporary literature teacher summarized this view: "that knowledge is true knowledge only when it's 'detached', that effective reading is reading that never shows the 'personal effect' of the text on the reader."[22] The overarching problem with this viewpoint is that it is simply not true. Often, as Parker Palmer argues, we get to know something or someone better by becoming more attached to the thing or the person.[23] Indeed, the *best* form of liberal education seeks to help students understand the broad variety of disciplines, intellectual traditions, and cultures by teaching learners how to examine them empathetically from the inside. As Warren Nord states:

> If students are to understand different cultures, intellectual traditions, and academic disciplines they must be able to get inside them. They must acquire some sense of how their members or advocates understand them, not how we understand them given our preconceptions and values. If we screen alternative traditions through our own conceptual filters, assuming that we know how to interpret the world, we will gain no critical perspective on our own assumptions.[24]

We believe the student's comments illustrate Nord's point. The student's claim is problematic, not just because the Bible is historically significant, but because it is a religious book. If you do not learn how people read it with religious implications, you will fail to understand its role in the lives of individual Christians in the Christian community today as well as throughout history. While one might still consider this approach a kind of attempt at empathetic objectivity, like that of an anthropologist, it requires more than detachment.

Furthermore, if this student wants to understand the Bible from multiple perspectives, it would help if he encounters people who take the religious implications of the Bible seriously. As Warren Nord pointed out, students need to encounter religious perspectives as live options and not relics of a past era.[25] Ultimately, this "secular only" approach undermines the liberal vision of exposing students to different interpretations of the Bible that the student articulated. Both students and teachers need to be aware of how their worldview and identity shape their approaches to course material.

Moreover, while teachers can have strong identity-based convictions, they can also still hold to the "no conversion rules" discussed in chapter 6 as well as to the principle of maintaining justice to different identities and their associated narratives in classroom discussions. While teachers always have the *potential* to use their favored identities and narratives for justice or injustice in setting up their classroom learning environments, the particular worldview professors develop from these identities and associated convictions hopefully supports justice. We find examples of this support in the following reflections provided by Christian professors in our study:

- "I try to be considerate, fair, patient, and kind to all students, thinking this is what Jesus would do."
- "I like to feel I have a compassionate ear to the class influenced by my personal faith, along with a desire for them to experience both justice and grace/mercy."
- "I approach ethics as the fair, just, and merciful treatment of other people in keeping with 'Do unto others as you would have them do unto you.'"
- "I am constantly praying and asking the Lord if I am being fair to everyone in my class."

These professors' Christian identity magnified and supported their concern for justice in the classroom.

In fact, we contend that it is vitally necessary for professors to connect their conception of justice in the classroom to their primary identity. Otherwise, they may experience what Palmer calls "violence to the self," in which a person follows an ethical norm without being able to connect that norm to his or her identity. In the end, both the person's identity and integrity are violated.[26]

We also think that particular religious narratives, such as the Christian narrative, can help Christian teachers promote principles of justice in the classroom even when they see others with different identities acting unfairly.

Ultimately, the question is: When others do not play fair, what motivates someone to stay true to the ethical ends, virtues, and rules of the academic game? Perhaps, as Fish argues, their simple conscience and thin convictions regarding professional standards will be enough to help professors maintain justice toward different worldviews. Yet, we think that acting justly when others do not requires a kind of faith that in the end, truth and justice will prevail—perhaps not in this life but in the next one. Without such a conviction, if they see little empirical evidence for such hope in this life, we think it is doubtful that professors will continue to play by the rules of the academic game when others do not. All too often, they will want to grab power and use it for their own ideological ends.

In fact, some Christians go so far as to claim that in light of this tendency, using justice language is not very helpful. Stanley Hauerwas writes, "As Christians we will speak more truthfully to our society and be of greater service refusing to continue the illusion the larger social order knows what it is talking about when it calls for justice."[27] While we concur with Hauerwas that Christians and those identifying with other moral traditions will not always agree upon the specifics of what justice entails, especially in the political realm, we do think that we can still hope to establish some thin accord in the academy about what justice toward different identities and their associated traditions of thought might entail.[28]

Overall, what we are proposing is somewhat similar to Alasdair MacIntyre's solution to what he perceives as the failure of the liberal university. He proposes what he calls a "postliberal university." This university is "a place of constrained disagreement, of imposed participation in conflict, in which a central responsibility of higher education would be to initiate students into conflict."[29] Professors in this university would have two responsibilities. First, they would advance teaching and inquiry from a particular perspective while also fairly presenting and engaging rival viewpoints. Thus, in classes a professor would not pretend to present objective and neutral knowledge to every reasonable person but would instead acknowledge a personal commitment to some particular partisan standpoint. Second, professors would also need to play a role in ordering the conflicts among intellectual traditions and sustaining institutionalized forums for such conflicts to occur. They would act as

> someone concerned to uphold and to order the ongoing conflicts, to provide and sustain institutionalized means for their expression, to negotiate

the modes of encounter between opponents, to ensure that rival voices were not illegitimately suppressed, to sustain the university—not as an arena of neutral objectivity, as in the liberal university, since each of the contending standpoints would be advancing its own partisan account of the nature and function of objectivity—but as an arena of conflict in which the most fundamental type of moral and theological disagreement was accorded recognition.[30]

In the remainder of this chapter we address in more detail what thin virtues and practices would be required if the teacher takes this approach.

Curricular Sense-Making, Construction, and Content

To what degree should professors' identities beyond their professional identity influence the curriculum they use in the pluralistic university? This issue pertains to more than the interpretational issues mentioned previously. This matter also includes the choice of material covered, the books students read, and the interpretive lens or lenses teachers use to evaluate the subject matter.

Overall, we do not believe a professor can ever put together some sort of objective curriculum. In fact, we find it surprising that a progressive educator such as bell hooks talks about the effort "to transform the curriculum so that it does not reflect biases or reinforce systems of domination."[31] A curriculum *always* reflects biases and *always* privileges some voices over others. Yet, we think hooks's second point gets to the heart of our concern. Justice at three different levels should guide curricular choices when it comes to identity.

First, professors may teach whole courses that they limit solely to their particular identity (e.g., feminist literary interpretation, Muslim ethics). We contend that the professors in pluralistic universities should be encouraged to create and teach these types of courses within the bounds of justice. To promote justice, we think that such courses should not be required, since a pluralistic university should not favor particular identities beyond academic identities. With that being said, we recognize that some courses attract more students than others and that some departments may have professors with certain kinds of expertise. Consequently, a pluralistic university may only offer certain identity-related courses based on student demand and the expertise of professors in the department.

Second, professors can alter the content of a general course based on their identity commitments. In some cases, these changes are quite general. As demonstrated in chapter 6, some faculty members only alter the curriculum in broad ways, particularly regarding ethics (e.g., "I choose texts that emphasize ethical issues."; "It can influence my focus on spending more time addressing ethics."). Here, their curricular alterations do not necessarily favor a specific identity, but instead appeal to a realm that is important for any and every student. The same can be said for a curricular emphasis on common virtues such as honesty, kindness, and patience, which are important within the context of this profession. Even an emphasis on what we call redemptive virtues (described in chapter 3 as sacrificial love, forgiveness, humility, and service), while often emphasized by Christians, is not exclusive to the Christian tradition.

Third, these alterations could relate to specific Christian content. We demonstrated how some spiritual addition professors tended to do this in chapter 3 (e.g., "I make a point of discussing Catholic Medieval thought—and of educating my students about the Saints."). These types of professors in a pluralistic university must usually let the ideal of fairness, the context, and the academic standards of the field guide them. We say "usually" because scholars at times may not accept revolutionary, but legitimate, views but understand that students still need exposure to them. This may be particularly true in areas where consensus does not exist. Warren Nord explains this point: "If there is as yet no consensus about how to make sense of the world in many of its enduring problems, and if religious ways of making sense of the world continue to be influential, then humility suggests that it may be reasonable that religious voices be included in the curricular conversation."[32] In these instances, it would certainly make sense to add religious perspectives and views to the content of the course.

The way Christian transformation professors would alter a course could be less invasive and possibly more transformative than what spiritual addition professors do. Since Christian transformation professors understand all of life to relate to sacred and spiritual matters, their curricular approach may not be different than that of other non-Christian professors because they do not separate certain parts of a curriculum as being more spiritual or religious than others. Yet, to promote justice, Christian transformation professors would likely set forth a *Christian* interpretive perspective alongside a myriad of other interpretive perspectives. As Warren Nord maintains, "[I]f we are to take religion seriously, we must take seriously religious claims to truth as *truth is understood within various religious traditions*."[33]

For instance, Christian transformation professors are often keen to point out how certain totalizing secular theories function as a religion, such as how Marxism functioned in the former Soviet Union and presently functions in current communist countries. Scholars in the field of sociology have long noted this phenomenon, and as noted previously, a wide variety of scholars have observed the religious nature of certain totalizing secular theories.[34]

In addition, Christian transformation professors may aim to show how the ethical rationales behind the common ethical content mentioned previously may differ widely depending on one's identity and supporting moral tradition. They may also wish to communicate the theological rationale behind their own ethical views. These endeavors do not minimize the aims of the pluralistic university, and in truth, they enhance them.

Of course, no matter the content or interpretive additions, we do not believe teachers should show justice to every theoretical view, whether secular or religious (e.g., the flat Earth perspective or the denial of the Holocaust). Teachers must establish some criteria. In general, when it comes to considering the basis for including content or interpretive views from particular religious traditions in the curriculum of a course, Warren Nord provides five helpful criteria for inclusion:

> First, only live traditions need be taken seriously as live options, though there may be very good reasons for studying dead traditions in the context of history. . . . Second among living traditions, we may justifiably give priority to those that are most influential. . . . Third, it is justifiable to give some priority to traditions depending on proximity. . . . Fourth . . . liberal education addresses questions of existential depth, this provides a criterion for choosing among contending alternatives. Some traditions are more important [to] people's lives [than] others. . . . Fifth, it is justifiable to discriminate on the grounds of what is intellectually serious.[35]

If a Christian professor wishes to include Christian material or interpretive perspectives in his or her course, and if this content meets these criteria, we see no reason why it should not be included in a course. In fact, where significant and legitimate controversies emerge, one can usually find influences of secular and religious worldviews behind these disagreements. In most cases, there is a side that must be heard that is being drowned out by other, louder perspectives.

Pedagogical Practices

Parker Palmer maintains that when teachers extract their identity from the classroom, their pedagogy often becomes lifeless.[36] When this occurs, classrooms become places of stagnation and unquestioning dullness. We believe Palmer should nuance this argument. After all, we have multiple identities, so the more important question is whether we can recognize which identities are important for giving a pedagogical practice life.

Moreover, we must acknowledge that teachers may not believe that even one of their primary extraprofessional identities influences their pedagogical practice. Indeed, most Christian teachers we surveyed in our study did not consider their particular faith identity relevant for their teaching methods or were unsure if it mattered. Yet, individuals who did see a connection between their Christian identity and their teaching practices shared important insights. For spiritual addition professors to adjust their pedagogy to the pluralistic university, they would merely need to discard praying or doing a devotional before class. In a similar manner, Christian transformation educators would also want to avoid the insertion of prayer and Bible connections when teaching a pluralistic student body.

Still, one can imagine other inclusive pedagogical practices professors could follow. In fact, K–12 teachers already practice one of these rituals, observing a moment of silence before class. One could also incorporate similar practices described as Christian that would be suitable for a pluralistic university setting. For instance, one Christian professor described opening a class by having students share their joys and concerns, while another discussed integrating hospitality into this context.[37]

This leads to the issue we noted in chapter 3 regarding pedagogical practices. Often, practitioners justify a pedagogical practice for particular reasons related to their identity, but this does not mean the pedagogical practice would and could not be shared by others with different identity commitments. An example from another identity can be found in Danica

Savonick's article "Timekeeping as Feminist Pedagogy." Here, she tells a story about what motivated her to focus diligently on timekeeping:

> But the day I was scheduled to present my work, I was assigned to go last. (By now, I'm sure you know where this is going.) I remember sitting in my seat and watching the hands of the clock tick by as the students before me shared their work and engaged our seminar in a lively dialogue. But apparently I was the only one watching the clock, because before I knew it there were only 10 minutes left in the class, and it still was not my turn. And then there were only five minutes. I will never forget the feeling of sitting in that chair, fidgeting with sweaty palms and unable to contribute to the conversation because I was so anxious that my turn would never come. And that's basically what happened.[38]

Yet, Savonick provides more than a simple personal experience to justify her concern with justice and timekeeping. She provides an identity-related rationale for her concern with equitable timekeeping among students: "Feminist pedagogy teaches that silence is not an absence but the effect of power. It encourages us to listen to those voices that have historically been silenced and to change the structural conditions so that their voices are heard."[39] Both of us also have concerns about timekeeping in class that flow from a concern with equity and justice. However, we would not say that our beliefs arise primarily from a belief in feminism. Instead, they arise from a theological concern with human dignity and justice.

In a similar manner, many of the Christian transformation professors we quoted also shared pedagogical practices that they chose or emphasized that linked to their Christian or denominational identity. Consider the following professor's reasoning:

> I see my students as made in the image of God. I assume they can recognize truth for themselves, at least when the ground is cleared of gross misconceptions through argumentation and their own investigation. I stress their reading and interpretation of key documents for themselves, with a little help if needed, I am a history guy, primarily history of thought. The individual is responsible before God for what he or she does with truth and whether they embrace it. All real truth is God's truth, there are not separate truths, hence my job is to expose the students to truth and to help them fall in love with truth finding and its processes.

The fact that Christian professors might choose particular pedagogical practices partly or wholly for theological reasons should not be a problem in the pluralistic university. Professors do not always explicitly state their rationales for their pedagogical practices. If theological beliefs play a role in professors choosing group projects, service learning, or the use of primary sources, the pluralistic university cannot and should not police them. Moreover, most of the examples of specific teaching methods we found in our study fell within the normal range of pedagogical practices.

Professors can take a similar stance regarding ethical ends and pedagogy. In chapter 4, we noted that Christian professors usually saw their faith expressed through demonstrating particular virtues in pedagogical practices. Chris Anderson writes of his own teaching, "I am trying through example analysis to encourage my students to think in a certain way themselves, I am urging on the values that are also Christian values, I am trying to convert them into reading in ways that Christians also read—not to become Christian but to take from Christianity its humility and precision."[40] While his rationale for demonstrating these virtues in the classroom came from a theological narrative, this expression does not contain content that would violate the "no conversion" rules discussed in the previous chapter. For instance, seeking to show hospitality, justice tempered with grace, servanthood, respectfulness, forgiveness, and other virtues in a pluralistic context would likely enhance students' learning. In other words, there is a subtle distinction between converting students to an identity and encouraging them to practice virtues in a professional context that professors understand as growing out of their Christian tradition.

It should be obvious by now that one of the major pedagogical strategies that teachers discussed in chapter 4, that of modeling "Christ-like behavior" or justifying particular virtues using their Christian worldview, would be unproblematic in the classroom. The pluralistic university should be quite pleased if a teacher demonstrates virtues such as honesty, respect, justice, grace, mercy, love, care, humility, forgiveness, patience, hospitality, wisdom, courage, and service, among all the other virtues teachers mentioned.[41] In addition, modeling specific professional identities related to one's discipline (e.g., being a good nurse, scholar, teacher) would all be unproblematic when taking this approach.

Combining pedagogical practices and specific identities may become problematic when a teacher suggests that a particular method should be used as a comprehensive method for finding knowledge about all of life. For instance, the methodological secularism applied in science often becomes elevated to the status of a comprehensive worldview about all knowledge. The use of the scientific method then becomes methodological atheism about all of life. In contrast, Christians will take a much more limited approach. George Marsden writes:

> Methodological secularization means only that for limited ad-hoc purposes we will focus on natural phenomena accessible to all, while not denying their spiritual dimensions as created and ordered by God or forgetting that there is much more to the picture. The pilot who follows the radar in the instrument panel may even sense those tasks differently if she believes she is ultimately dependent on God and that she has spiritual responsibility to her passengers.[42]

As he recounts, the good pilot will employ a type of methodological secularization when landing a plane when it comes to the technical parts of this endeavor, but this limited type of reliance does not mean other spiritual realities do not relate to this particular task, or for that matter, to life as a whole. An example of how this might work relates to a teaching practice that often does not receive as much attention since it does not involve pedagogical methods used in class: grading.

Grading

Often issues of identity politics and matters of injustice become especially pronounced in the practice of grading. Consider this example from Timothy Larsen's article "No Christianity Please, We're Academics." He recounts the story of a prospective graduate student named John who had been a straight A student until he took a particular English class. In the class, the teacher asked students to write about traditional marriage. As a Baptist, he decided to give his honest views, which relied on the Bible. Larsen recounts, "The paper was rejected as a 'sermon', and given an F, with the words, 'I reject your dogmatism', written at the bottom by way of explanation."[43] Larsen notes that he did not think the student's paper was an A paper, but it certainly did not deserve an F. This was not the end of this particular student's problems with the professor's grading:

Thereafter, John could never get better than a C for papers without any marked errors or corrections. When he asked for a reason why yet another grade was so poor he was told that it was inappropriate to quote C. S. Lewis in work for an English class because he was "a pastor." (Lewis, of course, was actually an English professor at Cambridge University. Perhaps it was wrong to quote Lewis simply because he had said something recognizably Christian.) Eventually John complained to the department chair, who said curtly that he could do nothing until the course was over. John took this to mean that the chair would do nothing and just accepted the bad grade.[44]

Just as Parker Palmer might hope, this was a case in which a professor brought his or her identity into grading. Yet the overarching result *may have been* an injustice to the student. We say "*may have been*" because whether John was treated unfairly depends, of course, on the overall context. Larsen acknowledged, "Maybe John is just one of those uppity believers who don't know their place. Maybe. Maybe John got an F purely as an academic judgment. . . . I'm not in a position to hear the professor or the chair's explanation of the broader context." Still, he noted, "I've seen the marked paper (and my own view is that it is academically weak, but certainly not deserving of an F)."[45] If the latter is the case, it is an injustice based on a professor teaching from his or her whole self.

Would Christianity make any difference in a professor's grading practices in a pluralistic university? For one French professor in our study, it meant doing the opposite from the English professor discussed in the previous example. The French teacher shared how Christianity influenced "the ethics of grading." By this, she meant the following: "While I try to facilitate student growth in understanding of diversity in cultural and religious settings, I do not let their theological tradition or their reluctance to accept other traditions influence my grading of their progress in the French language." For some professors, Christianity simply reinforces their commitment to certain professional standards. For instance, the following professors we surveyed indicated that their Christian tradition influenced certain practices, but the specific practices they mentioned had no explicit Christian content or justification:

- "I treat all students with respect, value their time and money at university, treat all students fairly, and grade fairly."

- "I don't penalize late work severely; I penalize slightly and consistently, but still encourage the student to get it in—I still want them to learn."
- "I believe in the importance of justice in grading and providing students with feedback that provides them guidance on how to improve their scholarship."

In a few other cases, our participants talked about how the particular Christian themes of justice and mercy influenced their approach to grading. They sought to balance these two themes. One professor noted, "Because God is redemptive, I seek to enforce justice tempered with mercy. Thus, if I catch students cheating, I flunk them, but if they confess cheating, I only give them a zero on the assignment." Another respondent simply shared, "God's justice concerning plagiarism. Grace given in individual situations." Again, we find that bringing one's identity into classroom practices is a two-edged sword. It may promote justice or injustice. It depends on the teacher and the identity involved.

Conclusion

Overall, teachers who want to incorporate an ethic of justice into their classrooms need to do three things. First, as outlined in the previous chapter, professors need to recognize, reflect upon, and admit the influences of their personal guiding identities and narratives on their teaching. Second, they need to connect their personal identity and narratives to a vision of moral and intellectual virtue that applies to the classroom in pluralistic educational institutions. We contend that, although it is arrived at through one's particular identities and narratives, this moral vision is one that most educators will likely share. Finally, educators must learn how to practice the intellectual and moral virtues necessary to hold discussions about these connections.

Ethical issues do not emerge only at the classroom level, however. Attention to social justice requires that we think about the American university system as a whole and how it treats religiously-based, identity-informed teachers and their communities. After all, despite Robert Bellah and company's famous description in *Habits of the Heart* of the individual Sheila, who had created her own religion called Shelism, most religious and nonreligious individuals share more social similarity to the female one of us interviewed for another book, whom we called Katie Marsh.[46] She shared that her nontheistic family, along with a couple of other neighborhood families, would hold general character education lessons on Sunday along with nature hikes. She observed, "My parents don't identify with agnostic or even atheist, but they joke that we have our own religion of Marshish—cause that's my last name."[47] Individuals, like this student, are rarely just functionally religious by themselves. Therefore, the next chapter considers the important question of how we show social justice to various educational communities when it comes to religion.

8

In Praise of Diverse Teaching Contexts

> American university culture is still shaped by a powerful impulse toward homogeneity and uniformity.
>
> —George Marsden[1]

Both of us, at different times in our careers, have taught or been educated in the three types of contexts we discuss in this book: (1) denominational colleges or universities, (2) interdenominational Christian universities, and (3) pluralistic universities. We find all three contexts provide different strengths when it comes to identity-informed teaching, and all also have certain challenges. We think chapters 2 through 7 demonstrate these strengths and challenges, and this concluding chapter attempts to summarize and expand upon them. Our overall argument is that higher education as a whole, and identity-informed teaching in particular, benefits from the diversity of postsecondary institutions in the United States. Furthermore, we think that considerations of social justice require sustaining and incentivizing a just pluralistic system of higher education.

We want to be clear that our argument focuses primarily on the strengths and benefits for teachers engaged in expansive forms of identity-informed teaching. Much of the discussion about the strengths and weaknesses of Christian teaching has rightly focused on the implications of this kind of teaching for students (e.g., concerns about indoctrination).[2] While we understand that those matters are vitally important, we also think we need to consider the degree to which these different contexts allow freedom for identity-informed teaching.

The Value of Constrained Disagreement

Some contemporary professors still believe in that noble modern dream: the idea of creating a university characterized by skeptical and unrestricted exploration of the truth that could then arrive at commonly agreed upon objective truths. For instance, not too long ago Peter Conn, emeritus professor of English at Penn University, published an article in the *Chronicle of Higher Education* arguing against the accreditation of religious colleges. He declared:

> By awarding accreditation to religious colleges, the process confers legitimacy on institutions that systematically undermine the most fundamental purposes of higher education. Skeptical and unfettered inquiry is the hallmark of American teaching and research. However, such inquiry cannot flourish—in many cases, cannot even survive—inside institutions that erect religious tests for truth. The contradiction is obvious.[3]

Certainly this broadside comes from another age. Today, fewer and fewer believe that teaching is "unfettered." Even Conn appealed to some abstract ideal of "American" teaching, although he probably means to refer to particular Enlightenment ideals of the university. As we mentioned in the introduction, we take it as relatively uncontroversial, except for certain modernists such as Conn, that all of us have multiple identities, and many of them have intellectual traditions of thought associated with them that influence our teaching.

Considering this fact, Alasdair MacIntyre claimed that if pluralistic societies should foster the development of "postliberal universities"—universities that support identity-informed teaching and scholarship from a particular tradition—what would occur is that different interpretive traditions would create rival universities. As a result, "the wider society would be confronted with the claims of rival universities, each advancing its own enquiries by its own set of exclusions and prohibitions, formal and informal."[4] Oddly, MacIntyre called his vision "utopian." We believe it is quite realistic to expect that the current American system has the potential to function in this manner. The American university system, which is the most pluralistic in the world, already contains tribal colleges; historically black colleges; men's and women's colleges (in which many of the women's institutions further feminist thought); Christian universities; Jewish universities; *supposedly* pluralistic private universities, many of which often function as identity-oriented universities; and pluralistic public universities and colleges. We believe MacIntyre's vision could continue to become reality, especially if we understand the strengths and weaknesses of different types of universities for identity-informed teaching.

Academic Freedom and Identity-Informed Teaching

Before we begin discussing those limits and strengths, we need to address a common complaint that has emerged over the past century about colleges and universities with religious identities. Critics claim that faith-based institutions of higher education limit the academic freedom of professors.[5] When discussing this critique, it helps to distinguish between efforts to preserve the *corporate* freedom of teachers to establish diverse academic communities and the *individual* academic freedom of professors.[6] Corporate academic freedom is the first known form of academic freedom that developed in the West. This freedom, according to Anthony Diekema, is "the privilege of college and university, as corporate bodies, to be reasonably secure from meddling by political or religious authorities, special interests, pressure groups, or any group that wields power in our society."[7]

The emphasis on protecting individual academic freedom of professors, however, emerged in the last two centuries through the influence of the German universities. Diekema described this freedom as entailing the protection of professors "from all of those forces, both internal and external, which tend to prevent them from meeting all the obligations of the professional office in the pursuit of truth."[8] The protection of this freedom was the impetus behind the formation of the American Association of University Professors (AAUP) in 1915, the AAUP's original "Declaration of Principles" defining academic freedom, and the AAUP's later "1940 Statement of Principles on Academic Freedom."

The AAUP recognized that a tension could also exist between corporate and individual academic freedom regarding religious institutions. This tension concerns the individual academic freedom of professors and the ability of religious institutions to define themselves and preserve the religious identity of the institution by imposing hiring standards. The AAUP resolved this tension by asserting in its 1940 statement that "religious commitments or other aims of the institution should be clearly stated in writing at the time of the appointment."[9]

We think the AAUP encouragement to state, in writing, the limits on academic freedom should actually apply to all institutions. As Elmer Thiessen points out, "All institutions have *limited* academic freedom."[10] For example, political entities have helped create and support many pluralistic universities, and most are usually committed to endorsing certain ideological perspectives, which often leads to the exclusion of others. As mentioned in chapter 6, state universities have restrictions on what a professor may or may not teach with respect to religion. One of the positive aspects of most liberal democracies, though, is that they usually respect and encourage pluralism beyond state-run institutions, since there is acknowledgment that uniformly state-run institutions place their own limits on academic freedom.

Furthermore, we contend that faith-based universities' ability to hire based on religious identity is a necessary expression of both corporate and a particular kind of individual academic freedom. Numerous scholars recognize that whether Christian colleges and universities can hire based on their mission is a matter of both their survival and their religious and academic freedom.[11] Moreover, most professors hired by ecclesial and interdenominational Christian universities want the academic freedom to build a university in which professors agree on certain first principles and share a particular understanding of what it means to be fully human. George Marsden notes, "Persons who work from religious perspectives . . . do so voluntarily. The same is true of people who choose to teach at institutions that set some religious boundaries. Since their guiding viewpoints are held voluntarily, their freedom is hardly infringed by choosing to work within those restrictions."[12]

The common agreement upon first principles allows professors to advance scholarly work and conversations that are enhanced when engaged by common epistemic communities. In other words, these unique academic communities can support the very purpose of academic freedom: the advancement of knowledge and learning through shared agreement on deep questions. For example, many of the professors we surveyed believed that "all truth is God's truth" gave them an expansive view of knowledge and an impetus to work for the integration of knowledge:

- "I come at my courses from the perspective of science and relationship with God, not seeing these two as separate entities, but both working toward the same thing—truth."
- "I believe all truth is God's truth, so I want my students to have a wide range of knowledge."
- "Belief that all truth is God's so encourage students to ask hard questions about their learning as it relates to their faith."

Of course, simply because Christians hold some common views about God and the importance of truth does not mean they are very different from other academics. As Jacobsen and Jacobsen write, "Like anyone else who has a point of view, religious believers think, they evaluate options, they make choices about what they consider to be better and worse interpretations of reality, they debate with themselves and others, and sometimes they change their views based on new evidence and improved arguments."[13] What faith-based universities and colleges allow is teaching that takes certain first principles, such as that God is the creator of all and humans are made in the image of God, for granted. Teachers can then proceed from those principles to more sophisticated arguments and practices arising out of their common identity tradition. This is a strength of both the ecclesial and the interdenominational Christian university that we discuss in the following sections.

The Ecclesial Christian University

As chapter 1 explained, for the first three centuries of American higher education, the dominant form of higher education in America was what has variously been called the sectarian, denominational, or church-related college. Today, church-related colleges and universities comprise a much smaller subsection of American higher education. In addition, many colleges and universities with tenuous church relationships (e.g., Duke University, Georgetown University) function in a manner very similar to that of pluralistic universities. Thus, we focus more explicitly on institutions we label *ecclesial* colleges and universities. We define these institutions as those that still show favoritism to their ecclesial affiliation through their mission, membership policies (faculty, administration, or board members), curriculum decisions, and/or co-curricular programming. These institutions also differ from *interdenominational* Christian colleges and universities that only show favoritism to the *Christian* identity in their mission, membership policies (faculty, administration, or board members), curriculum decisions, and/or co-curricular programming.

The Strengths

Regarding teaching, the key strength of the ecclesial college or university is that it allows professors from that particular religious tradition (e.g.,

Catholic, Reformed) to teach from an undivided self. In other words, it allows educational leaders and faculty to agree upon a particular identity and theological interpretation of the Christian narrative. It also provides them the social support to work out the implications of this intellectual agreement for an academic discipline and a community. Although a pluralistic university allows an individual professor to work out the implications of different views about knowledge, the environment it facilitates does not make this kind of corporate or communal cooperation possible. Furthermore, faculty members face some constraints upon their freedom to work out their views in the classroom. Elmer Thiessen helpfully summarizes the difference:

> Although there may be some plurality at secular universities, it is primarily a plurality of individuals. If truth is found within epistemic communities . . . then perhaps a healthier kind of pluralism could be found in a plurality of educational institutions, each is committed to finding truth based on its particular standpoint. Individuals by themselves are in a position of weakness in terms of challenging established opinion.[14]

Overall, professors at institutions with a matching ecclesial identity can explore the implications of that ecclesial identity for teaching in the classroom with the support of an *entire* academic community.[15]

Many teachers whom we quoted in chapter 6 expressed an appreciation for this environment. While the implications of these benefits may be subtle, they are important for helping professors teach from an undivided self. For example, one professor shared:

> Pentecostalism includes a strong emphasis on personal experience and personal relationship with Christ as well as responsibility to bear witness. Some of my course objectives (depending on the course) will identify for students how they can apply the material to their personal growth (spiritually, intellectually, socially) or its relevance to their bearing witness to their faith. It's a tangential connection with the tradition, but I was not as free to make this connection at other types of institutions where I have taught.

This freedom to teach from an undivided self applies to more than just one particular teacher's experience. For example, Anabaptist professors at Anabaptist institutions are afforded the freedom to assume that their colleagues and some percentage of students share a degree of agreement with a certain set of beliefs and therefore can focus on the implications of their commonly agreed upon views about issues (e.g., pacifism). In addition, a community of Anabaptist faculty can then work out the implications for their views in their college or university. For instance, Anabaptist institutions usually do not have political science departments because of their particular theological views about politics and the relationship between the Kingdom of God, the church and politics.

It should come as no surprise, then, that respondents in our survey of denominational institutions were more likely than those at interdenominational (or what some call nondenominational) institutions to claim that their particular tradition influenced various aspects of their teaching (see table 8.1). Moreover, professors at interdenominational institutions may not consider themselves to have the freedom to teach from their *particular* Christian identity (e.g., Anglican, Wesleyan, Reformed) as opposed to their *general* Christian identity, since their institutions focus on what a number of Christian traditions have in common. Interestingly, the greatest difference had to do with matters of pedagogy.

Some argue that ecclesial institutions are too narrow, since these colleges or universities affirm the tradition through some form of constrained disagreement regarding hiring, curriculum, or programming. We contend that in many ways these institutions are still religiously diverse. In fact, many have a unique kind of diversity that allows for a certain type of academic conversation to take place that would not occur at pluralistic universities.

Table 8.1 Respondents Whose Teaching Is Influenced by Theological Tradition

Aspect of Teaching Affected by Theological Tradition	Professors at Denominational Institutions	Professors at Interdenominational Institutions
Ethical approach	90%	79%
Motivations for or attitude toward the course	85%	76%
Course foundations, worldview, or narrative	85%	80%
Teaching methods	61%	39%
Course objectives	58%	50%

Except at certain Reformed, Assembly of God, and Church of Christ institutions, where the leaders require all faculty members to belong to the particular tradition,[16] most ecclesial institutions continue to hire faculty from a variety of Christian traditions,[17] which creates a diverse Christian faculty. In our survey of faculty at ecclesial universities, while close to three-fifths expressed some degree of affinity with the sponsoring denomination, we still found faculty with a wide range in affinity with the denomination of the institution (table 8.2). They also indicated a wide variance in agreement with the particular beliefs of their institution's sponsoring tradition (table 8.3).

While anywhere from half to almost three-quarters of teachers share commonality about what C. S. Lewis called "mere Christianity" (e.g., the existence of God, the Trinity, Christ's salvific role), not all professors have the *exact same* theological stance as the college or university on other, more contested issues (e.g., women's ordination, evolution, and same-sex marriage). This is particularly true at the clear majority of Catholic institutions, whose hiring requirements often allow for the hiring of large numbers of non-Catholics or even non-Christians.[18]

The students at the ecclesial colleges and universities we surveyed have also become increasingly diverse over the past 20 years.[19] In fact, the growing diversity of ecclesial universities' student bodies is one of the greatest challenges to maintaining their distinctiveness. Yet this diversity within an ecclesial university allows for a certain kind of discussion that teachers would be less likely to foster in a pluralistic university or even a university with an interdenominational Christian identity. For example, in a study one of us undertook some time ago, a teacher from George Fox University, where less than 5 percent of students come from the sponsoring

Table 8.2 Respondents with Strong Sense of Affinity with Denomination of Institution*

Strongly agree	28%
Agree	31%
Neither agree nor disagree	21%
Disagree	15%
Strongly disagree	4%

* Values do not add up to 100% because of rounding.

Table 8.3 Respondents' Beliefs Compared to Positions of Home Institution's Sponsoring Denomination*

Belief/Position	More Liberal	The Same	More Conservative	Don't Know
Biblical Authority	20%	66%	12%	2%
Hell	17%	71%	7%	5%
Salvation of those who do not believe in Christ	18%	71%	7%	4%
Same-sex marriage	25%	64%	9%	2%
Satan	13%	73%	6%	8%
Women's ordination	29%	53%	13%	4%
Role of government	23%	55%	13%	9%
Evolution	31%	52%	10%	7%

*Values do not add up to 100% in some categories because of rounding.

Source: Jesse Rine, Perry L. Glanzer & Phil Davignon, "Assessing the Denominational Identity of American Evangelical Colleges and Universities, Part II: Faculty Perspectives and Practices," *Christian Higher Education* 12, 4 (2013): 243–65.

Quaker tradition, discussed how the pacifist and social activist dimensions of its Quaker tradition sometimes created healthy intellectual tension with evangelical faculty and students who were not pacifists:

> Our Quaker ethos gives us a strong sense of social justice. . . . The war in Iraq is a classic example. We had quite a discussion on our campus because several of our faculty and students were opposed to the war in Iraq because of the Quaker ethos and peacemaking. We also had a number of faculty/staff and students who were in favor of wanting to support the troops and we had a special chapel where it was really a time of prayer for the whole situation. We had a person from the Christian peacemaking team share, [but] we also had a former armed forces vet share, and we had an international student share from an international perspective. Then we gave students the opportunity to write cards either to Iraqi families and children that would be delivered through Christian peacemaking teams or to write letters to the troops and/or to do both if they so desired. . . . It wasn't as though there was this great division, I think it was great conversation both ways.[52]

This example illustrates the unique type of academic conversation an ecclesial community can have. It seems quite unlikely that teachers would foster this kind of Christian disagreement in a secular pluralistic university or college or even at an interdenominational Christian university or college.

Considering this freedom, it should come as no surprise that over half of the Christian faculty members we surveyed did not want their institutions to adjust the statement of faith so that it would become a more "generic" Christian institution (see table 8.4). Only 14 percent of professors would prefer that their institution change its statement of faith so that the institution would be a "merely Christian" institution.

In addition, the clear majority of faculty in our survey were satisfied with the emphasis placed on denominational affiliation by the president, administration, and trustees (see table 8.5).

Most students, it should be noted, were also satisfied with how denominational institutions treat diverse views in the classroom, and their satisfaction was not appreciably different from that of students at interdenominational institutions (see tables 8.6 and 8.7).

Table 8.4 Respondents Who Wished Institution's Statement of Faith Was More Generic/Took "Mere Christianity" Approach

Strongly agree	4%
Agree	10%
Neither agree nor disagree	35%
Disagree	38%
Strongly disagree	13%

Source: Jesse Rine, Perry L. Glanzer & Phil Davignon, "Assessing the Denominational Identity of American Evangelical Colleges and Universities, Part II: Faculty Perspectives and Practices," *Christian Higher Education* 12, 4 (2013): 243–65.

Table 8.5 Importance Placed on Denominational Affiliation by Specific Administrative Roles

Degree of Importance	President and Administration	Trustees
Too much	11%	21%
About right	80%	73%
Too little	9%	6%

Source: Jesse Rine, Perry L. Glanzer & Phil Davignon, "Assessing the Denominational Identity of American Evangelical Colleges and Universities, Part II: Faculty Perspectives and Practices," *Christian Higher Education* 12, 4 (2013): 243–65.

Table 8.6 Denominational Identity's Effect on Institution*

	Greatly Enhances	Enhances	Neither	Hinders	Greatly Hinders	Don't know
Recruitment and admissions	8%	43%	35%	9%	1%	4%
Financial health	8%	34%	35%	13%	3%	7%
Perception of academic quality	5%	19%	51%	19%	2%	4%
Attracting high-quality faculty	4%	19%	48%	22%	3%	4%
Campus ethos and moral climate	22%	54%	18%	3%	1%	2%
On campus worship	22%	45%	27%	3%	0%	3%
Governance and leadership	16%	34%	29%	11%	2%	7%

* Values do not add up to 100% in some categories because of rounding.

Source: Jesse Rine, Perry L. Glanzer & Phil Davignon, "Assessing the Denominational Identity of American Evangelical Colleges and Universities, Part II: Faculty Perspectives and Practices," Christian Higher Education 12, 4 (2013): 243–65.

Table 8.7 Satisfaction with Faculty's Respect for Expression of Diverse Beliefs*

	Students at Denominational Institution	Students at Interdenominational Institution
Dissatisfied or very dissatisfied	9%	10%
Neutral	19%	16%
Satisfied or very satisfied	72%	73%

* Values do not all add up to 100% because of rounding.

Source: Jesse Rine, Perry L. Glanzer & Phil Davignon, "Assessing the Denominational Identity of American Evangelical Colleges and Universities, Part II: Faculty Perspectives and Practices," Christian Higher Education 12, 4 (2013): 243–65.

The Limitations

While we have presented some of the strengths of identity-informed teaching at ecclesial universities, there are, of course, other limitations for ecclesial institutions. As table 8.6 indicates, about one-quarter of faculty who teach at these institutions think their college or university's ecclesial identity might hinder attracting high-quality faculty and the larger perception of academic quality. It would appear that a significant minority of faculty wonder if their ecclesial identity lowers the quality of their peers.

In addition, while a certain kind of pluralism exists at these types of universities, faculty and students may not receive extensive personal exposure to others with non-Christian or in some cases different denominational identities. Encountering someone with opposing views in a face-to-face setting, such as a classroom discussion or one-on-one faculty conversation, is much different from simply reading about these types of ideas or encountering them at professional conferences.

Yet, this limitation actually does not apply to the vast majority of ecclesial colleges. Our survey results demonstrated that 92 percent of the institutions we surveyed did not require all faculty to be part of the sponsoring denomination. Most only required this of the theology faculty or not at all (see table 8.8). Furthermore, only a small minority of Catholic institutions require their entire faculty to be Catholic.[20] Teachers at most types of Catholic institutions will also be exposed to faculty with a plurality of worldviews.[21]

In addition, most faculty at Christian institutions are *not* convinced that it is important or extremely important to hire faculty belonging to

Table 8.8 Employment Expectations Based on Denominational Affiliation of Faculty (n = 63)

Question	Yes (All Are)	Some Are	No (None Are)
Are faculty members required to hold membership in the sponsoring denomination?	8%	51%	41%
Has this requirement changed in the past 20 years?	11%	0%	89%

Source: Perry L. Glanzer, Jesse Rine, & Phil Davignon, "Assessing the Denominational Identity of American Evangelical Colleges and Universities, Part I: Denominational Patronage and Institutional Policy," Christian Higher Education 12, 3 (2013): 182–202.

Table 8.9 Importance of Having a Majority Belong to Institution's Sponsoring Denomination*

Degree of Importance	Students	Faculty
Extremely important	2%	7%
Important	20%	34%
Neither important nor unimportant	42%	32%
Unimportant	23%	15%
Not at all important	13%	11%

* Values do not all add up to 100% because of rounding.

Source: Phil Davignon, Perry L. Glanzer, and Jesse Rine, "Assessing the Denominational Identity of American Evangelical Colleges and Universities, Part III: The Student Experience," Christian Higher Education 12, 5 (2013): 315–30.

Jesse Rine, Perry L. Glanzer & Phil Davignon, "Assessing the Denominational Identity of American Evangelical Colleges and Universities, Part II: Faculty Perspectives and Practices," Christian Higher Education 12, 4 (2013): 243–65.

the institution's sponsoring denomination (table 8.9). Most of these institutions also do not require faculty in their respective Bible, theology, or religion departments to be members of the sponsoring denomination (see table 8.10). Even though all the institutions we surveyed were Protestant, the vast majority of faculty support hiring Catholic or Eastern Orthodox faculty (see table 8.11). Interestingly, ecclesial college faculty were even more open to Catholic and Eastern Orthodox faculty than faculty in nondenominational colleges and universities.

Another possible limitation of the ecclesial college that we already touched upon is that Christian professors who are not of the same tradition as their university may experience some restrictions on teaching according to their *particular* Christian identity (but not their broad Christian identity). In fact, as was explained in the previous chapters, teachers from different traditions may also believe that they must adhere to the "no conversion rule." For instance, in our survey a Catholic teacher at a Protestant institution shared, "If what you are asking is whether I promote Roman Catholicism, then the answer is 'no.' Do I present Christian ideals or teach

Table 8.10 Employment Expectations: Denominational Affiliation of Religion/Theology Faculty (n = 63)

Question	Yes (All Are)	Some Are	No (None Are)
Are faculty members in religion/theology required to hold membership in the sponsoring denomination?	43%	18%	39%
Has this requirement changed in the past 20 years?	13%	0%	87%

Source: Perry L. Glanzer, Jesse Rine, & Phil Davignon, "Assessing the Denominational Identity of American Evangelical Colleges and Universities, Part I: Denominational Patronage and Institutional Policy," Christian Higher Education 12, 3 (2013): 182–202.

Table 8.11 Roman Catholics and Eastern Orthodox Should Be Acceptable as Full-Time Faculty

	Ecclesial Faculty	Nondenominational Faculty
Strongly agree	34%	33%
Agree	33%	23%
Neither agree nor disagree	15%	15%
Disagree	13%	18%
Strongly disagree	5%	11%

Source: Jesse Rine, Perry L. Glanzer & Phil Davignon, "Assessing the Denominational Identity of American Evangelical Colleges and Universities, Part II: Faculty Perspectives and Practices," *Christian Higher Education* 12, 4 (2013): 243–65.

from a Christian perspective? Of course, I do. This Christian perspective is influenced by the tradition from which I came but it is not the only religious ideals that have influenced me." We do not view this limitation as a weakness, but Christian professors of another denominational confession, while having much in common with their particular ecclesial college or university, may still face limits on teaching from their full religious identity. Of course this may also prove true for a professor of the same ecclesial identity who also prioritizes another identity or school of thought (e.g., feminism, Marxism) that he or she perceives to be in some tension with the ethos of his or her ecclesial institution.

The Interdenominational Christian University

Interdenominational or nondenominational institutions are a uniquely American creation. Although a few of these types of colleges and universities were founded in the early 1800s, most emerged after the Civil War. After that time, a significant number of historical Christian colleges and universities became more interdenominationally Christian, and less sectarian in nature.[22] Some started as Bible colleges and grew to be nondenominational colleges or universities through expansion and/or mergers (e.g., Asbury University, Azusa Pacific University, Biola University, Colorado Christian University, Gordon College, Taylor University, and Wheaton College). Others simply began without denominational affiliation (e.g., Westmont College). This trend has increased in recent years, and individuals with prominent media ministries have started many of the newer nondenominational universities (e.g., Oral Roberts University, Regent University). These institutions provide evidence of a common evangelical tendency throughout American history: the propensity to focus on certain shared Christian beliefs about the Bible, Christ, salvation, and activism that cross denominational boundaries and provide a source for common partnerships.[23]

Some ecclesial colleges and universities connected to a specific tradition are also slowly loosening their ties with their tradition by altering hiring requirements.[24] For example, although historically Baptist, our university (Baylor University) functions in many respects as a broadly Christian university. There are no hiring requirements regarding the Baptist identity for faculty, except in the religion department. Members of the Board of Trustees also do not need to be Baptist. We should also note that the weakening denominational bonds, such as the decline in denominational funding and the number of students from the sponsoring denomination, might not be under the institution's control.[25] Overall, these trends mean that what we write about the interdenominational Christian university can apply to these types of denominationally-related institutions as well.

As chapters 2 through 5 indicated, even when we asked professors at denominational institutions about the influence of their particular ecclesial tradition on their teaching, most provided examples that draw upon and focus on a common Christian tradition. These responses support part of Samuel Schuman's claim that "most of the faith-based colleges and universities today are, in name or in fact, nondenominational."[26] Although these institutions are not nondenominational in either name or official status, they often focus on common Christian beliefs.

Furthermore, the other quantitative elements of our study revealed that although most faculty who serve in ecclesial colleges also attend a local congregation connected to the university's denomination, when given a list of religious identifiers (e.g., evangelical, mainline Protestant, and the name of their particular denomination), only one-third of our respondents identified their particular denominational affiliation as their primary religious identity.[27] Instead, faculty in our study often selected a more general, transdenominational term associated with basic Christianity to describe their primary religious identity. In many ways, most faculty at denominational colleges and universities still identify and teach with their general Christian identity as primary.

Students also appear to care more about a general Christian identity. In a survey one of us helped conduct recently of Christian college students at 31 institutions, the institution's denomination played the second least important role in students' decision to attend their college compared to the other options offered, with only 15.3 percent claiming that their institution's denomination was "very important" for them in choosing to attend that college.[28] In fact, 13 percent of students could not even tell us whether their institution was denominationally affiliated. Even though denomination was rated as being relatively unimportant, the Christian identity of the college was rated as highly important, with 73.0 percent of respondents claiming that Christian identity was "very important" in their college choice.

The Strengths

The strengths of an interdenominational Christian university have several similarities to the advantages provided by ecclesial colleges and universities, although in some cases interdenominational institutions broaden these advantages. First, Christian teachers of all denominations do not have to teach from a place of a divided self. There is no privileged denominational voice, but there can be a unique Christian voice. For example, we both have taught graduate courses about faith-based higher education, and one of us has taught a course about the relationship of Christian faith to education. Neither one of these courses can be found at a pluralistic university in the United States. In other words, the mere existence of faith-based universities allows for prioritizing and teaching certain subjects that Christian professors think are important. We also teach these courses with a common understanding and expectation that students will understand that theological perspectives are important and will take them seriously. Although we unpack the prominent theories being discussed within the current academic conversation on our subjects, teaching from this point of view at these types of universities allows us to more easily ask and explore questions such as: "What might be a Christian evaluation of this theory?" In this regard, the advantage of a Christian university also extends to Christian students. Within this context, our master's degree students in student affairs learn how to think about what it means to be Christians in student life divisions. Even if they work in a secular context, they will have learned how to integrate their Christian identity into their work in appropriate ways. This practice helps them to learn how to teach from more fully human, less divided selves.

Of course, while some students come from different faith backgrounds, they recognize that when attending faith-based institutions, teachers will take theological perspectives and thinking seriously. For instance, as mentioned previously, one of us (Perry) teaches a course called Christian Faith and Education. As this title makes clear, the entire class focuses on exploring Christian perspectives in education. While teaching this class over the years, I have had Buddhist, agnostic, and atheist students. At the beginning of the course, I often discuss with these students some background passages within the Bible that they should read to become familiar with Christianity. By the end of the course, most of them demonstrate a significantly better understanding of how various Christian traditions have understood education in both the past and the current eras. In other words, by the end of the semester, they know how to think about the Christian tradition empathetically and with more sophistication than at the start of the semester.

A second advantage of the interdenominational Christian university, as of the ecclesial institution, is that the constrained disagreement among faculty allows each scholar to share a common worldview from which to teach and work. This foundation nurtures Christian epistemic communities and helps a specific type of knowledge advancement to occur in these contexts. These settings encourage the formation of unique academic communities that support the very purpose of academic freedom. As the 1915 AAUP "Declaration of Principles on Academic Freedom and Academic Tenure" states, universities "should be an intellectual experiment station, where new ideas may germinate and where their fruit, though still distasteful to the community as a whole, may be allowed to ripen until finally, perchance, it may become a part of the accepted intellectual food of the nation or the world."[29] Consequently, an open university system will need to allow *some* experimentation with both individual and corporate academic freedom, since communities that have agreed upon certain first principles will want to undertake some unique forms of experimentation, discovery, and teaching based on those principles. A Christian university, for example, can engage in communal research or teaching projects based on agreed upon first principles that cannot be undertaken at secular pluralistic universities.

Furthermore, as in ecclesial universities, building communities of scholars with common agreement about certain basic questions and epistemic views also allows for different kinds of teaching and conversation in interdenominational universities. Jon Stackhouse, who has taught at both interdenominational Christian and pluralistic universities, observes, "The synergy that comes from such shared intellectual commitments is simply not to be found in the secular university. It is an obvious and yet important trade off: the exciting stimulation of radical plurality versus the reinforcing energy of coherent perspectives. Both are truly education, and both therefore deserve the support of the academy."[30] These types of communities may also produce knowledge and conversations that are not supported in other settings (e.g., the pluralistic university). If professors are truly to have the freedom to experiment, they need to be able to form unique kinds of academic communities that may produce a variety of results.

Of course various religious perspectives can still exist in the interdenominational Christian university. For instance, in our university, we not only have Baptist professors, we also have professors who are different kinds of Baptists (including those who range on a theological spectrum from very conservative to very liberal). We also have faculty members who are Catholic, Jewish, Eastern Orthodox, Presbyterian, Mennonite, and Anglican, among other denominational and religious identities. In fact, neither one of us teaches our department's faith-based higher education course in the same way due to our different theological traditions. Therefore, what the interdenominational Christian university allows is a broad mixture of faculty within Christianity to work together. For instance, one of the teachers in our survey shared, "The Catholic Church's epistemology is largely charismatic; hence it gives 2,000 years of support to the superordinate goals and values of Oral Roberts University. There are an estimated 150 million Catholic Charismatics on earth; why then, should there be hostility and division?" Our guess is that this charismatic Catholic professor may feel more at home at a university like Oral Roberts than, say, a school like Georgetown University. Moreover, at interdenominational Christian universities, students themselves tend to come from a wider variety of traditions, including Muslim, Hindu, atheist, and agnostic perspectives. At these types of institutions, students will still be exposed to a wide plurality of viewpoints within the Christian tradition.

A third important advantage of Christian universities comes from the greater ability to form a common moral community. In a study of character education, James Davison Hunter found that character thrives when young people "inhabit a social world that coherently incarnates a moral culture defined by a clear and intelligible understanding of public and private good."[31] Hunter describes this *comprehensive moral culture* as a milieu "where the school, youth organizations, and larger community share a moral culture that is integrated and mutually reinforcing . . . where intellectual and moral virtues are not only naturally interwoven in a distinctive moral ethos but embedded within the structure of communities."[32] Hunter continues by observing that these cultures do not separate education from "the concept of what constitutes a good life and good community."[33] Due to their ability to agree upon a common metanarrative, interdenominational Christian colleges and universities provide this kind of comprehensive moral culture.[34]

Thus, it should be no surprise that scholars find that Christian colleges and universities give more attention than pluralistic universities to character and moral education.[35] In addition, studies comparing moral or character education at different kinds of religious and secular institutions reveal that Christian colleges and universities show greater attention to and greater effectiveness with this matter in five different ways: (1) faculty attitudes,[36] (2) ethics in the curriculum,[37] (3) measured or reported impact on character or moral attitudes,[38] (4) students' moral reasoning,[39] and (5) alumni views about moral education.[40] Interestingly, ecclesial colleges and universities have demonstrated the greatest ability to engage in a wide variety of approaches to moral education that include attention to virtue development, community service, and social justice.[41]

The Limitations

The limitations of the interdenominational Christian university may be similar to or different than those of the denominational university. Depending on the hiring requirements, faculty may not receive extensive personal exposure to those with Christian identities outside of their institution's tradition or to those with non-Christian identities. Furthermore, like the ecclesial university, Christian universities expect some agreement upon first principles regarding beliefs about God, Christ, and the Bible that will involve voluntarily chosen limits on certain kinds of academic freedom.

Depending on the admission requirements, the same principle applies to the student body as well. In some cases, interdenominational institutions may have more restrictive hiring or admissions policies than denominational institutions. For instance, institutions such as Wheaton College and Taylor University require students to be Christians, whereas the University of Notre Dame, Calvin College, and Baylor University do not have any religious requirements for students' admission to the institution.

An Aside on a New Kind of Christian-Pluralistic Online Hybrid

At the tail end of the recent economic recession, Christian colleges and universities have worked hard to demonstrate that they are cost effective, contribute to the economy, and respond to student demand for workforce-ready education. *U.S. News & World Report* touted this success (and its own rankings) in an article entitled, "Why Enrollment Is Rising at Large Christian Colleges."[42] The authors attributed this growth to, in addition to the attractiveness of Christian mission and recent major philanthropic gifts, the expansion of online education. Such changes have contributed to an explosion of growth in some quarters. Liberty University, with about 15,000 residential students, was the country's second largest higher education provider by 2015, boasting some 95,000 students who were seeking a credential remotely.[43]

Although Liberty is clearly an outlier in terms of scale, online programs, degree completion programs, graduate programs, and even two-year degrees have all come to represent opportunities for local service and revenue generation for Christian colleges over the past several decades.[44] For example, of 536 Christian colleges and universities in a Department of Education data comparison group, 447 (or 83 percent) had some sort of graduate degree offering in 2016. This was an increase from 396 institutions (or 74 percent) in 2001.[45]

Given the likelihood that these and other curricular strategies will continue to be attractive as Christian colleges seek financial stability, this expansion raises important questions about the potential effect on Christian teaching. Although the Christian teachers in these programs may not experience the same lack of restrictions or pressures as pluralistic institutions, a similar dynamic might be in play. Students enrolled in such programs may not be admitted with the same expectations for faith commitment as those who come as traditional undergraduates. Furthermore, students not engaged in the traditional residential experience, due to either delivery method (e.g., online) or degree type (e.g., graduate, professional), may bring with them an instrumentalist expectation of education in addition to a lack of interest in faith topics. Those with such a perspective might be impatient with or even intolerant of professors' active integration of faith perspectives, approaches, materials, examples, or other strategies that they might view as ancillary and distracting from their focus on learning material for professional advancement. This might be particularly true for areas, such as teacher education, in which the professional expectation that teachers bracket their personal beliefs in public school settings is pervasive.

On the professor side, some auxiliary educational programs rely on teachers hired under different terms or expectations than are applied to the traditional core faculty. For example, we are familiar with a Christian university where the vetting process for tenure-system faculty is extensive, including exploration of the prospective teacher's personal faith. However, a newly-installed online degree has resulted in a spate of hiring in which both academic and religious qualifications are far less rigorously examined, due in part to the expedited institutional timeline.

In these scenarios generally, the confluence of student, teacher, and curricular focus and expectations may contribute to an educational environment much like that of a pluralistic institution, where neither the teacher nor the student sees Christian commitments as directly relevant. Given these special circumstances, we encourage Christian colleges and universities to pay close attention not only to hiring well, but also to preparing teachers well, particularly for these educational environments. Professional development that aligns expectations for nontraditional teaching with the expectations of the traditional classroom requires additional effort and resources on the part of administrators and faculty leaders but is a necessary step. For individual faculty members, especially those who may be teaching ancillary to their work as professionals, part of allowing their Christian faith to invigorate learning may require having direct conversations with students about the norms of personal/professional bifurcation that they collectively feel. For those teachers who experience discomfort about their own religious identity in the classroom, admitting their feelings could open fruitful dialogue with students.

The Pluralistic University

As chapter 1 recounts, the current model of the pluralistic university, which tries to rely *only* on professional qualifications for employment or academic qualifications for student admissions, is a rather recent development and has only emerged within the past century. In addition, this phenomenon exists for the most part only in liberal democratic countries. After all, most state universities in China are primarily communist universities. Ironically, in liberal democracies with a plurality of worldviews, some current professors and accrediting authorities believe we should follow the statist model and make the pluralistic university the only model of the university that is allowed accreditation or government recognition.[46] In truth, many liberal democratic governments outside of North America often make it difficult for any other kind of university to exist.[47] In contrast, the United States and Canada still nourish the most pluralistic systems of higher education in the world, especially with regard to religion.[48]

The Strengths

The most obvious strength of the pluralistic university for the Christian teacher is "the exciting stimulation of radical plurality" that Stackhouse mentioned. This kind of plurality can help Christian teachers sharpen their thinking with other teachers and students. Since the best faculty members acquire knowledge from both other teachers and their own students, Christian teachers can learn from the full range of different types of faculty and students at the pluralistic university.[49]

Another obvious strength of the pluralistic university is that it allows for a certain degree of academic freedom regarding one's teaching. A teacher who does not have the same religious identity as the institution in which he or she teaches may be freer to engage in identity-informed types of teaching about certain kinds of subjects. In addition, as chapter 6 outlined, the freedom to address religion in a pluralistic university is much broader than many understand.[50] Interestingly, many scholars believe that more freedom to explore religion exists for students in these institutions. For example, the following comment is quite typical: "[T]he secular institution is the ideal place for students to explore their spiritual sides, because, unlike many sectarian institutions, there is no official perspective or dogma when it comes to spiritual values or beliefs."[51] Christian teachers in these contexts can also participate in helping students explore religious ideas due to the lack of a guiding, institutional metanarrative.

Finally, as our findings indicate, Christian professors uphold and support many of the ends promoted by the pluralistic university. In fact, the pluralistic university does the best job of supporting particular academic ends, as attested by the fact that these types of universities dominate the top of every type of academic rating such as the *U.S. News and World Report* rankings.[52] Christian professors can also participate with a wider group of professors and students in advancing virtuous, sociable, and inclusive conversations about the common good in these kinds of settings.

The Limitations

Yet obvious limits exist for the Christian teacher in a pluralistic university, especially if the institution is a state university. Christian teachers cannot fully offer their whole selves to students. If good teaching, as Parker Palmer claims, comes from the identity and integrity of the teacher, then good religious teachers are also handicapped at private and state pluralistic universities. Professors at state universities are primarily government employees,[53] and as a result, they must have the courage *not* to seek identity conversation and controversial moral conversions. They must teach from a divided self. In fact, pluralistic universities may have trouble reaching agreement about important concepts, such as what it means to be a well-developed human being.[54] As a result, it becomes more difficult to create thick moral communities at these institutions, so teachers are left to rely on only thin agreement about moral goods.[55]

Second, we need to acknowledge that teachers and students at pluralistic universities may have an inordinate fear of conservative forms of Christianity. In reality, even at universities that claim to be pluralistic, identity-based prejudices may still play a role in faculty hiring practices and student admissions.[56] A recent interview one of our colleagues conducted with a homosexual male working on staff at a pluralistic university provides insight into this problem:

> The attitude that professional staff in our department have towards hiring religiously conservative or religious Christian people is shocking and appalling. If it was applied to even another religious group or another social identity would be appalling, and they would be called out for that as inappropriate but it's okay to casually talk about how we don't want to hire Christians.[57]

Even faith-informed teaching that respects the "no conversion rules" discussed in chapter 6 will likely face hostility. As a result, secular universities often fail to provide the kind of space needed for robust conversation about religion to take place.[58]

We think that too often scholars exalt pluralistic universities as a better environment for those exploring spirituality. Quite often though, teachers are encouraged to privatize their religious beliefs. For instance, bell hooks shared, "I was trained to keep all discussions of religion and spirituality out of the classroom."[59] Her experience is not unusual. In one study of four graduate degree programs preparing student affairs staff for higher education, most of the interviewees felt equipped to deal with matters of race, gender, and sexual identity, but felt ill equipped and even resistant to discuss religion and religious identity.[60] The encouragement to privatize religion may be particularly pervasive if teachers' beliefs run counter to the prevailing culture in a university. In other words, this kind of diversity may not be welcome. As George Marsden summarized when relating Will Herberg's argument about American universities, the problem is that "pluralism that welcomed religion only when it was another bland version of the 'American Way of Life' was not a true pluralism."[61]

Indeed, a disconcerting tendency exists for pluralistic universities to become less ideologically pluralistic. Empirically and politically speaking, professors are predominantly more politically liberal than ever before.[62] Scholars affiliated with the Heterodox Academy argue that this lack of ideological pluralism is hurting teaching in the academy. They claim that uncritical leftist orthodoxies are being upheld in the university without being questioned. Consequently, "promoters of orthodoxies often create an environment of intolerance for diversity of ideas and dissent in the very institution in which free exchange of ideas is its raison d'etre."[63]

Finally, what a Christian teacher thinks the ends of education should be will sometimes conflict with what the pluralistic academy thinks the ends of education should be. Christian teachers ultimately want to love God by knowing more about God and God's creation and communicate that wisdom to students. They want students to reflect the image of the God who created them. They not only want students to be excellent biologists, psychologists, and accountants; they also want them to demonstrate the Triune God's character of sacrificial love, justice, mercy, forgiveness, humility, servant leadership, and more. Faculty at pluralistic universities will not see those ends as part of a professor's job description. One student described the message she received from her teachers at a pluralistic university as we "don't believe that you need to care about this [religious] identity as much as you care about others or the way you engage with students."[64] Helping students understand their religious identities simply does not rate as highly as understanding other identities at pluralistic universities.

A Forum for Identity Gladiators

As already mentioned, Alasdair MacIntyre claimed that since epistemological pluralism (and we would add identity pluralism) among postliberal universities is a reality, we need institutionalized forums in which rival universities can engage in debate, especially about the moral and theological underpinnings of their perspectives.[65] Yet as Marsden's quote at the beginning of this chapter reminds us, the elites in American higher education have usually feared this kind of conversation, especially when it concerns religion. As chapter 1 recounts, this fear started in the early colonial period with the Rhode Island College (today Brown University) forbidding conversations about diverse theological beliefs in the classroom. Later, both Madison and Jefferson expressed concern at the University of Virginia about creating an "Arena of Theological Gladiators." In contrast to the founders of Brown University and the University of Virginia, we think that if the world of American academe is to be truly pluralistic, it should welcome the creation of an "Arena of Theological Gladiators," or what we would prefer to call the "tournament of identities and identity narratives."[66] After all, we *must* figure out how to prioritize our own identities, or as Augustine described it, we must learn how to order our loves.[67] Academia must allow this same identity tournament to take place, especially through its professional conferences, publishing, and other endeavors. We must encourage academic conversations about what we love and how to love, since, as Parker Palmer explains to us, "Knowing is loving."[68]

When Christian Teaching Is Really Outrageous

Is Christian teaching really *that* outrageous? We think it is only outrageous in America when a critic *or* practitioner takes a simplistic understanding of it and tries to critique or apply that simplistic understanding. If Christian teaching just involved adding a prayer, inserting some Bible verses, and sharing one's personal religious experience, then it would be easy to caricature, criticize, and privatize it. In this book, we have tried to make clear that most Christian professors move beyond these mere "add ons." The Christian narrative shapes the setting and story in which their entire practice of teaching takes place. It influences how professors view their calling (God calls them) and their students (as made in God's image). It forms their whole array of motivations and their understanding of how their identity as a teacher fits with their other identities (sometimes other identities that support but also trump the teacher-student relationship). It involves additions to or transformation of the ends of classroom teaching (loving their students), and it shapes curricular sense-making and construction. Ethical considerations, particularly the modeling and teaching of specific virtues, remain vitally important in areas such as the curriculum and pedagogical practices. Professors also think about and justify their teaching methods within the overall Christian narrative. As the range of examples cited in this book illustrate, Christian teaching is multifaceted and complex.

This complexity, combined with the "no identity conversion" rules set forth earlier, means that Christian teachers in pluralistic universities, particularly state-funded institutions, can neither simply teach from their professional identity and story, as Stanley Fish suggests, or teach from their whole selves, as Parker Palmer admonishes. After all, Christian teaching is not simply a vital form of self-expression or something that can and should be easily privatized. The calling to love and teach students requires that Christians respect the dignity of the student and the agreed-upon purposes of the academic context in which one teaches. It therefore necessitates that we sometimes refrain from the temptation to make those students exactly like us. However, it is also helpful for their education if they understand religiously-based identities, including our own. Still, in a pluralistic university, we must respect what we call the "no unwanted identity conversion rule" and the "no contested moral conversion rule." Even if others violate those rules, our faith in God gives us reasons to live with integrity, knowing that justice will prevail, in this life or the next. Furthermore, within the stimulating environment created by those rules, there is a tremendous amount of freedom and creativity for combining these elements of one's identity.

Our contemporary academy must also be careful. The request that teachers rein in additional parts of themselves beyond these two rules while engaging in their calling can lead to deeper problems than just what Palmer termed "the divided self." When unjust requests are made to privatize or even rid oneself of an essential identity when teaching, unfairly oppressed teachers will and must then learn a new kind of practice: active rebellion against the repressive powers. Reminiscent of those made by Stanley Fish, calls for teachers to simply teach from their professional identity, while potentially problematic, have little force unless they are institutionalized.

Throughout history, the most dangerous oppression in the university has come from the government.[1] When the government represses Christian teachers and Christian universities, Christian must then turn to other models for inspiration to learn a new type of pedagogy. At this point, Christian teaching must become outrageous not only to individuals and groups opposed to Christianity, but also to the powers in authority.

When Christian Institutions Are Oppressed

Sometimes outrageous Christian teaching will take place within a repressed Christian institution or in the name of that institution. For example, in 1918 the Polish Episcopate established a new Catholic university in order to resist the secularization of higher education occurring throughout Europe.[2] With "For God and Fatherland" as its motto, the University of Lublin, renamed the Catholic University of Lublin in 1928 (Katolicki Uniwersytet Lubelski, or KUL), established as its mission "to conduct scientific research in harmony with reason and faith to educate a new Catholic intelligentsia."[3] One unique characteristic of this university proved vitally important. KUL sought to challenge European secularization as a privately-financed university, which is not a phenomenon that is considered unique in North America but was unique in Europe at that time.[4]

Twenty years after its establishment, the university faced significant persecution. After the German invasion of Poland in 1939, the Nazis forced the university to shut down. A summary of KUL's history gives some idea of the hardships endured by the whole university: "The rector was imprisoned, many of the professors and students were executed, while others were forced to go work in Germany or sent to concentration camps."[5] When Christian teaching became outrageous in this setting, the Christian professors acted with what often becomes the pedagogy of the oppressed.[6] They took their teaching underground in Lublin and other Polish cities.

After the takeover of Poland by the Soviets in 1945, KUL was the first university to reopen in postwar Poland, but it merely traded one persecutor for another. When the university grew from 1,600 to 3,000 students between 1946 and 1951, the Polish Communist Party considered KUL "the most threatening place in higher education."[7] Party leaders sought to weaken KUL through a variety of measures:

> The Potulicka Foundation was taken over and made state property, student entries and enrolment were severely limited, aiming at closing the most popular faculties of KUL. . . . The rector, Rev. Antoni Słomkowski, was then imprisoned. The right to grant doctorates and professorships was taken away from the Humanities Faculty, and academic exchange with foreign countries was blocked. KUL alumni were denied employment in state positions. . . . The government's treating KUL as a profit-making institution obliged it to pay high taxes, and due to delayed payments buildings and university property were confiscated.[8]

Once again, Christian teachers responded by taking both their teaching and scholarship underground. According to their own history, "In the whole so-called 'block of socialist countries' only at our Catholic University it was possible to practice philosophy free of Marxist-Leninist ideology."[9] Karol Wojtyla, one of KUL's professors who engaged in and helped sustain this subversive Christian teaching, was named Pope John Paul II in 1978. His influence, including a visit to his old university in

1987, helped sustain and guide the institution during the last days of communism and allowed this Christian university, the only independent university in the entire Soviet bloc, to survive the attack of communism upon Christian higher education.[10] These Christian teachers fought bravely to sustain Christian education in the face of a regime that made Christianity outrageous.

A Pedagogy for Oppressed Christian Teachers

Sometimes, oppressed Christian teachers must engage in outrageous teaching without the help of an institution. Many Christian professors at pluralistic universities in *illiberal* democracies may fall into this category. They live in countries that allow voting, but the country is largely ruled by one political party and does not respect basic human rights. At this point, these teachers will likely need to turn to the church for help. With the support of the church, these teachers may feel compelled to model a completely different kind of pedagogy to their students.

Yu Jie provides an example of this kind of outrageous Christian teacher. The Chinese secret police warned him, "You are number one on the personal list of 'two hundred intellectuals to bury alive' kept by Zhou Yongkang" (at the time, Yongkang was secretary of China's Central Political and Legal Affairs Commission).[11] What had made Yu Jie such a dangerous intellectual? He was a Christian political dissident.

More importantly, he had made his Christian identity his foremost identity. Similar to the Christian transformation professors we profiled, he shared, "Christianity has transformed how I see myself as a dissident."[12] He apprehended that before he became a Christian, he had made an idol of democracy. Instead of treating it as simply the best political arrangement among alternatives, he had let it become his primary metanarrative. Yet after becoming a Christian, Yu Jie realized democracy "is not the horizon of all human hope and longing. If one does not believe in something other than democracy, one is no better off than the Communists, making a god of a political system."[13]

Yu Jie also learned, similar to the teachers in our study, that fundamental Christian practices, such as confession, transform both one's perspective and one's pedagogy. He recalled, "When I became a Christian, I learned to recognize myself as a sinner. In doing so, I developed a sensitivity to sin that helps me recognize evil and injustice when I see them. As I point out the tyranny of the Communist regime, I reflect on and judge myself." Once again, this unique pedagogical practice altered his teaching as a Christian political dissident: "This interior work of repentance for my own sins has transformed my fight against totalitarianism. No longer am I merely pointing out faults in the world. I also recognize them in myself."[14]

Finally, similar to our teachers, the models that Yu Jie uses now change the way he teaches. While he still fights for democratic reforms to occur in China, he now looks to Christ and other Christian models to help him. For instance, he wrote, "No one's influence, though, has been greater on me than Dietrich Bonhoeffer's. His warning that, 'A state that threatens the proclamation of the Christian message negates itself, has become a motto for China's Christians, on whom he exerts a great influence."[15] He also claims that Bonhoeffer's writings about "life together" have changed his view of the church as a community that can sustain a new and different type of communal life. He notes, "Of course, God has a personal relationship with each of us, but it is the fact that we love one another, help one another, and pray for one another that makes it possible for us to complete our pilgrimage."[16]

Through the church, Yu Jie has discovered a new kind of democratic pedagogy that is based in Christ, Christ's church, and a theological understanding of the human person. He insists, "The Chinese must undertake a profound spiritual transformation in order to restore the freedom and dignity God has bestowed on them when creating them in his image. The way forward requires a turn away from ourselves and toward the divine."[17] Our teachers also proclaimed this same theological basis. This kind of divinely-based pedagogy calls for a unique kind of pilgrimage for transforming society. It calls for a Christian witness to the state based in the theology of the Christian church. Yu Jie asserts:

> Though Communist China is a totalitarian society, Christians can learn and practice a democratic way of life at church, and then act as a leaven in society. For instance, to this day the Chinese have no real voting rights, but congregants can elect their own board members and administrative leaders. For those inexperienced with running and voting for office, churches are a seedbed of civic activity.

He also points to the church as teaching people how to be active members of civil society instead of relying solely on government institutions:

> Churches are already involved in charity, education, culture, and other public sectors, further expanding China's public space. For example, in the aftermath of the 2008 Sichuan earthquake, hundreds of churches quickly formed the China Christian Action Love volunteer association to provide relief, which many disaster victims praised as besting government efforts in both speed and constancy. In addition, some churches have established schools for members' children as an alternative to the statist curriculum of public schools. Through the churches, Chinese Christians are becoming active agents in society rather than passive subjects controlled by the government.

This kind of "student-focused pedagogy" that does not rely on authority to direct one's efforts reflects something many of the Christian teachers in our study also endorsed.

Yet when Christians engage in this kind of pedagogy of the oppressed through the support of the church, they will face resistance. Yu Jie himself has personal experience of the cost of the outrageous idea of Christian teaching in an oppressive country that tries to douse his flame. Through his work, he became friends with Liu Xiaobo, the winner of the 2010 Nobel Peace Prize for defending human rights in China, including the rights of Christians and their churches. Due to this relationship, Yu Jie became a model for the truly outrageous kind of Christian teaching that Christ exemplified:

> On the night of December 10, 2010, as the Nobel Peace Prize ceremony honoring Liu was taking place in Oslo, I was kidnapped by the secret police and taken to the outskirts of Beijing. They beat and tortured me for hours, breaking my fingers one by one. I blacked out and was taken to a hospital. A hospital in Changping, a suburb of Beijing, refused to take me, saying I was "hopeless." Then I was taken to a hospital in Beijing. My life was saved.[18]

Today, albeit in a different venue, Yu Jie continues to strive to engage in outrageous Christian teaching. He leads a Sunday school and Bible study at a

Chinese Christian church in Washington, DC, where his wife is a preacher, and he continues his work as a Christian political dissident through his writing. He also finds that God continues to amaze him through a divine form of ironic teaching. While he used to be number one on the personal list of "two hundred intellectuals to bury alive" kept by Zhou Yongkang, Yu Jie now writes:

> Who would have imagined that today I would be writing freely, praying freely, breathing freely, standing on free soil, while Zhou, once nicknamed China's "security tsar," would be sentenced to life in prison for corruption by his political enemies? In God's plan, tyrants count for little. As Mary said in her great hymn of praise, the Magnificat: "He has shown the strength of his arm. He has scattered the proud in their conceit. He has cast down the mighty from their thrones, and has lifted up the lowly."

That is certainly outrageous teaching.

APPENDIX

Methodology

The findings used in this book are part of a larger data set generated from an online survey of instructional faculty members employed at Council of Christian Colleges and Universities (CCCU) member institutions. Of the 110 institutions that were CCCU members at the time of the survey, 79 participated in phase I of the study. The first phase surveyed institutions about their denominational affiliations.[1] Forty-eight institutions (61 percent) participated in the second phase of the study, directed at the faculty of these institutions.[2] The survey contained both qualitative and quantitative responses.

We took an interpretive approach to our qualitative findings, since participants' interpretations of their classroom practices were the only source of data from which we drew.[3] Therefore, we had to rely on the meaning they had constructed from their classroom experiences.

Qualitative Response Coding

We used an inductive approach to analyze the short-form responses because our desire was to generate frameworks from the particulars of faculty responses, rather than to impose theory upon them. To do this we used a two-cycle coding process through which descriptive categories could emerge (first cycle) and then be combined into thematic categories (second cycle).[4]

In the first cycle, we used a holistic coding process to identify broad categories of response, initially resulting in 31 codes. In holistic coding, data are examined in sentences or even paragraphs, and a summative word or phrase (one or more than one) that represents the meaning of that passage is identified to represent it. This approach was congruent with our short-form data type, in which responses typically varied between a short phrase and a short paragraph. Following the holistic coding process, we performed a second round of coding that then pulled these disparate parts together to identify patterns and elements of greatest salience. To do this, we used an axial coding approach often associated with grounded theory development.[5] The purpose of the axial approach is "to determine which [codes] in the research are the dominant ones and which are the less important ones . . . [and to] reorganize the data set: synonyms are crossed out, redundant codes are removed and the best representative codes are selected."[6]

In our second cycle process we re-examined the first cycle subsets within the largest meta code categories ("Discipline or Course-Specific Implications and References," "Specific Denominational Reference," and "Impart Biblical or Christian Principles or Perspectives") and recoded them into either existing codes or new subcodes. We then identified common categories that described groups of similar codes within these subsets and among the large set of codes. After identifying five large initial categories through this process, the research team engaged in several rounds of inter-coder review to confirm and challenge this list. Although several of the original thematic categories remained, others were broken up or reconfigured in ways that better reflected the patterns of meaning found across the entire data set.

Respondents

Regarding the short form answers, 57 percent came from male faculty and 43 percent from female faculty (see table A.1).

Most (58 percent) held a PhD as their highest degree, while 10 percent held an EdD. Another 22 percent held some form of master's degree (MA, MS, MBA, or MFA) (see table A.2).

Those with a doctoral degree most often had received it from a public institution (45 percent), with another 17 percent receiving a terminal degree from a private secular institution of some kind. Only 17 percent received their terminal degree from a religious institution (including 7 percent "Other Protestant," 6 percent CCCU member, and 3 percent Catholic; see table A.3).

Respondents tended to be those more firmly rooted in the profession: 84 percent were employed full-time (with 15 percent part-time or other) (see table A.4), and 38 percent had achieved full professor rank, followed by associate (27 percent), assistant (19 percent), and non-tenure-system faculty (15 percent, through a combination of various titles) (see table A.5).

By discipline, 37 percent taught in a professional program or a four-year degree program with a professional-oriented outcome (e.g., communications, computer science). Another 30 percent taught in the humanities (e.g., philosophy, religion, or theology). Another 14 percent taught in the social sciences, and 9 percent in the sciences (see table A.6).

Table A.1 Gender of Qualitative Respondents

Qualitative Question	Total Responses	Male	Female	No Response
Objectives	523	319	192	12
Objectives %		61%	37%	
Worldview	732	421	292	19
Worldview %		58%	40%	
Motivations	714	371	325	18
Motivations %		52%	46%	
Ethics	329	172	150	7
Ethics %		52%	46%	
Methods	460	243	206	11
Methods %		53%	45%	
Totals	2,758	1,526	1,165	67
		57%	43%	

Table A.2 Highest Degrees of Qualitative Respondents*

Qualitative Question	PhD	EdD	MA/MS	MBA	JD/MD	"Other"	MFA	NS
Objectives	306	45	77	11	5	13	52	6
Objectives %	59%	9%	15%	2%	1%	2%	10%	1%
Worldview	426	66	112	10	11	66	19	12
Worldview %	58%	9%	15%	1%	2%	9%	3%	2%
Motivations	398	68	126	12	8	63	18	12
Motivations %	56%	10%	18%	2%	1%	9%	2%	2%
Ethics	173	33	56	5	2	33	10	5
Ethics %	55%	10%	17%	2%	1%	10%	3%	2%
Methods	260	46	76	8	3	44	8	7
Methods %	57%	10%	17%	2%	1%	10%	2%	1%
Totals	1,563	258	447	46	29	219	107	42
	58%	10%	16%	2%	1%	8%	4%	1%

* Some percentages do not add up to 100% due to rounding.

Table A.3 Terminal Degree Grantor of Respondents*

Qualitative Question	Public	Religious	Secular	Other	Not Stated	Not Received	Total
Objectives	234	97	70	6	84	32	523
Objectives %	45%	19%	13%	1%	16%	6%	
Worldview	327	127	101	5	123	49	732
Worldview %	44%	17%	14%	1%	17%	7%	
Motivations	321	107	94	4	142	46	714
Motivations %	45%	15%	13%	1%	20%	6%	
Ethics	156	52	39	1	65	19	332
Ethics %	47%	16%	12%	0%	19.5%	5.5%	
Methods	207	76	59	4	85	28	459
Methods %	45%	16.5%	13%	1%	18.5%	6%	
Totals	1,245	459	363	20	499	174	2,760
	45%	15%	13%	1%	20%	6%	

* Some percentages do not add up to 100% due to rounding.

For perspective on this cohort, data for all faculty at 45 of the 48 institutions (not all institutions reported data to IPEDS) that participated in the phase II faculty survey show that a higher percentage (61 percent compared to 57 percent of respondents) were male, fewer (61 percent compared to 85 percent of respondents) were employed full-time, and

Table A.4 Employment Terms of Qualitative Respondents*

Qualitative Question	Full-Time	Part-Time	Other	Not Stated	Total
Objectives	444	57	17	5	523
Objectives %	85%	11%	3%	1%	
Worldview	620	77	23	11	731
Worldview %	85%	11%	3%	1%	
Motivations	592	81	27	12	713
Motivations %	83%	11%	4%	2%	
Ethics	271	40	13	4	329
Ethics %	82%	12%	4%	1%	
Methods	376	60	18	5	460
Methods %	82%	13%	4%	1%	
Totals	2,303	315	98	37	2,756
	84%	11%	4%	1%	

* Some percentages do not add up to 100% due to rounding.

Table A.5 Rank of Qualitative Responses

Qualitative Question	Assistant	Associate	Full	Other	Not Stated	Total
Objectives	94	142	206	76	5	518
Objectives %	18%	27%	39.5%	14.5%	1%	
Worldview	147	211	265	99	9	731
Worldview %	20%	29%	35%	14%	1%	
Motivations	140	189	271	102	11	714
Motivations %	20%	26%	38%	14%	1%	
Ethics	65	87	123	50	4	329
Ethics %	20%	26%	38%	14%	2%	
Methods	89	115	176	75	5	460
Methods %	19%	25%	38%	16%	1%	
Totals	535	744	1,041	402	34	2,752
	19%	27%	38%	15%	1%	

* Some percentages do not add up to 100% due to rounding.

Table A.6 Responses by Disciplinary Area

Qualitative Question	Humanities	Social Sciences	Professions	Sciences	Other	Total
Objectives	181	66	175	52	49	523
Objectives %	35%	13%	33%	10%	10%	
Worldview	209	107	263	67	86	732
Worldview %	29%	15%	36%	9%	12%	
Motivations	193	98	269	66	88	714
Motivations %	27%	14%	38%	9%	12%	
Ethics	102	39	133	23	32	329
Ethics %	31%	12%	40%	7%	10%	
Methods	137	65	170	43	45	460
Methods %	30%	14%	37%	9%	10%	
Totals	822	375	1,010	251	300	2,758
	30%	14%	37%	9%	11%	

* Some percentages do not add up to 100% due to rounding.

fewer (32 percent compared to 38 percent of respondents) had achieved professor status. The biggest gap was among assistant professors (33 percent compared to only 19 percent of respondents).[7] This variance might be indicative of a generational difference in faith-integration thinking between veteran and early career faculty members, or it may simply be a reflection of the time pressures associated with pre-tenure status.

Quantitative Responses in Chapter 7

Data collection for the quantitative part of the study was accomplished via an online survey created using Qualtrics software. Invitation messages detailing the purposes of the study were sent via email to the director of institutional research at each of the 79 CCCU member institutions that had participated in an earlier phase of this study. Recipients were provided a separate invitation message that included a link to the online survey and were asked to send this message via email to all faculty who served in their respective institutions.[8] Most participating institutions distributed this initial invitation message to faculty at the beginning of the summer. Near the end of the summer, the research team placed follow-up phone calls to invited institutions whose faculty had not yet completed the online survey in order to confirm whether or not they wished to participate in this phase of the study. Finally, to increase faculty response rates, participating institutions were asked to send out a reminder message several weeks into the fall semester notifying faculty of the upcoming closing date for the online survey. Of the 79 institutions that had participated in phase I of the CCCU Denominational Study, 48 distributed the online survey to their faculty, for a phase II retention rate of 61 percent. A total of 2,255 faculty respondents from these 48 participating institutions completed the entire online survey.

Sample

The sample for this particular study was limited to completed responses from full-time instructional faculty currently serving in denominationally affiliated institutions, resulting in a final sample size of 1,557 faculty members from 37 CCCU member institutions.[9] Response rates for all 37 institutions met a minimum threshold of 20 percent, with an average institutional response rate of 44 percent. As with the sample drawn for the first article in this series,[10] this subset of institutions generally resembled the overall population of denominationally affiliated CCCU member institutions (n = 89) on a number of dimensions. A wide swath of Protestant faith traditions was present in this sample (see table A.7).

Moreover, sample statistics were comparable to population parameters for a number of institutional variables (see table A.8).

Limitations

Two factors posed potential limitations to the external validity of the quantitative results. Because access to faculty participants was dependent on institutional willingness to participate in the CCCU Denominational Study, only the 79 institutions that participated in the first phase of the study (i.e., the institutional survey) were eligible for inclusion in the second phase. Although this subsample closely approximated the wider CCCU sector as a whole on a number of key institutional variables,[11] its construction resulted from the voluntary assemblage of willing participants rather than an intentional selection by the research team for the purpose of achieving representativeness. The second factor related to the faculty participants whose responses comprised the phase II data set. The faculty populations for each of the institutions eligible to participate in phase II of the study were relatively small, with the full-time faculty at these schools numbering only 111 on average. This reality, combined with the voluntary nature of participation in the online survey, suggested a census approach rather than a simple random sample. In short, the

Table A.7 Frequency of Denominationally Affiliated CCCU Member Institutions by Protestant Faith*

	Sample (n = 37)	Population (n = 89)
Wesleyan/Holiness	41%	25%
Baptist	30%	30%
Brethren/Mennonite	11%	9%
Pentecostal	8%	7%
Reformed/Presbyterian	5%	15%
Restoration Movement	3%	8%
Other	3%	6%

* Some percentages do not add up to 100% due to rounding.

Table A.8 Sample Statistics vs. Population Parameters: Key Institutional Factors

	Sample (n = 37)	Population (n = 89)
Total FTE enrollment, fall 2011		
Mean	2,386	2,118
Range	14,142	14,525
Standard deviation	2,361	1,708
Total employees, fall 2011		
Mean	501	448
Range	2,140	2,212
Standard deviation	377	292
Operating budget, FY 2011		
Mean	$42.3M	$40.3M
Range	$134.5M	$139.0M
Standard deviation	$28.2M	$26.3M
Total cost of attendance, AY 2010–2011		
Mean	$32,947	$32,273
Range	$15,475	$20,493
Standard deviation	$4,395	$4,503
Endowment value, end of FY 2011		
Mean	$22.0M	$35.1M
Range	$123.7M	$328.1M
Standard deviation	$24.9M	$51.8M

data collection methodology employed for this study was susceptible to selection effects at both the institutional and individual levels.

To reduce potential bias resulting from selection effects at the individual level, the research team developed a series of data weights. First, demographic variables of academic rank and gender were used to calculate a within-institution weight designed to increase the sample size to the total number of full-time instructional faculty at each institution. Then, a between-institution weight was created to correct for differential response rates across the institutions within the sample, so that institutions with higher survey participation rates would not disproportionately affect the study results. The final weight applied to each case was the product of the within-institution weight and the between-institution weight. Last, to reduce the effects of non-response bias, the issue of missing data was addressed by conducting multiple imputation through the use of SPSS 20 software.

Notes

Foreword

1. Perry L. Glanzer, Nathan F. Alleman, and Todd Ream, *Restoring the Soul of the University: Unifying Higher Education in a Fragmented Age* (Downers Grove, IL: InterVarsity Press, 2017); and William Egginton, *The Splintering of the American Mind: Identity Politics, Inequality, and Community on Today's College Campuses* (New York: Bloomsbury Publishing, 2018).
2. Glanzer, Alleman, and Ream, *Restoring the Soul of the University*, 322.

Introduction

1. Charles Taylor, *The Sources of the Self: The Making of Modern Identity* (Cambridge, MA: Harvard University Press, 1989), 28.
2. Perry L. Glanzer, "Building the Good Life: Using Identities to Frame Moral Education in Higher Education," *Journal of College and Character* 14, no. 2 (May 2013): 177–84. doi:10.1515/jcc-2013-0023.
3. "1915 Declaration of Principles on Academic Freedom and Academic Tenure," American Association of University Professors, https://www.aaup.org/NR/rdonlyres/A6520A9D-0A9A-47B3-B550-C006B5B224E7/0/1915Declaration.pdf, accessed March 6, 2019, 296.
4. Stephen Cahn, *Saints and Scamps: Ethics in Academia* (Totowa, NJ: Rowman and Littlefield, 2010), 34.
5. "Statement on Professional Ethics," American Association of University Professors, last updated and approved by Association's Council in 2009, https://www.aaup.org/report/statement-professional-ethics.
6. Stanley Fish, *Save the World on Your Own Time* (New York: Oxford University Press, 2008), 68.
7. Ibid., 18.
8. Ibid.
9. Ibid., 18–19.
10. Ibid., 19.
11. Ibid., 23.
12. Ibid., 24.
13. Ibid., 26.

14. Ibid., 27 (italics in original).
15. Ibid., 53.
16. Parker J. Palmer, *The Courage to Teach* (San Francisco: Jossey-Bass, 2007), 13.
17. Ibid., 12.
18. Ibid., 10 (italics in original).
19. Parker Palmer, *To Know as We Are Known* (New York: HarperOne, 1983), 35.
20. Palmer, *The Courage to Teach*, 10–11.
21. Ibid., 14.
22. Ibid., 15.
23. Ibid., 16.
24. Palmer, *To Know as We Are Known*, 8.
25. William G. Perry Jr., *Forms of Intellectual and Ethical Development in the College Years: A Scheme* (San Francisco: Jossey-Bass, [1968] 1999).
26. Chris Anderson, *Teaching as Believing: Faith in the University* (Waco, TX: Baylor University Press, 2004), 9.
27. Ibid., 14.
28. Bruce Kuklick, Review of *The Soul of the American University: From Protestant Establishment to Established Nonbelief*, by George M. Marsden, *Method and Theory in the Study of Religion* 8, no. 1 (1996): 82.
29. George M. Marsden, *The Outrageous Idea of Christian Teaching* (New York: Oxford University Press, 1997), 60.
30. We should note that Marsden does touch upon teaching at times, although he largely focuses on scholarship.
31. David I. Smith and James K. A. Smith, eds., *Teaching and Christian Practices: Reshaping Faith and Learning* (Grand Rapids, MI: William B. Eerdmans Publishing Company, 2011), 4.
32. Ibid., 5.
33. Elizabeth J. Tisdell, "Spirituality, Diversity, and Learner Centered Teaching: A Generative Paradox," in *The American University in a Postsecular Age*, ed. Douglas Jacobsen and Rhonda Hurstedt Jacobsen (New York: Oxford University Press, 2008), 153.
34. In addition to Smith and Smith's *Teaching and Christian Practices*, two other works are noteworthy: Karen E. Eifler and Thomas M. Landy, eds., *Becoming Beholders: Cultivating Sacramental Imagination and Actions in College Classrooms* (Collegeville, MN: Liturgical Press, 2014); and David I. Smith, *On Christian Teaching* (Grand Rapids, MI: William B. Eerdmans Publishing Company, 2017).
35. These two volumes take this more focused approach: Smith and Smith, *Teaching and Christian Practices*; and Smith, *On Christian Teaching*.

Chapter 1

1. Warren Nord, *Does God Make a Difference? Taking Religion Seriously in Our Schools and Universities* (New York: Oxford University Press, 2010), 64.
2. See Charles Taylor, *A Secular Age* (Cambridge, MA: Harvard University Press, 2007) for an answer to this question: "[W]hy was it virtually impossible not to believe in

God in, say, 1500 in our Western society, while in 2000 many of us find this not only easy, even inescapable?" (p. 25).
3. For a discussion of the reasons for this, see Perry L. Glanzer and Konstantin Petrenko, "Resurrecting the Russian University's Soul: The Emergence of Eastern Orthodox Universities and Their Distinctive Approaches to Keeping Faith with Their Religious Tradition," *Christian Scholar's Review* 36 (Spring 2007): 263-84, http://www.csreview.org/XXXVI3/glanzer.
4. Willem Frijhoff, "Patterns," in *A History of the University in Europe*, vol. II, *Universities in Early Modern Europe, 1500-1800*, ed. Hilde De Ridder-Symoens (Cambridge, UK: Cambridge University Press, 1996).
5. Peter A. Vandermeersch, "Teachers," in *A History of the University in Europe*, vol. II, *Universities in Early Modern Europe, 1500-1800*, ed. De Ridder-Symoens (Cambridge, UK: Cambridge University Press, 1996).
6. Part of this assumption was based on the fact that the difference between teachers and students was not as great as it is today. Bachelor's and master's students were often expected to give lectures. See Vandermeersch, "Teachers," 211.
7. Jacques Verger, "Teachers," in *A History of the University in Europe*, vol. I, *Universities in the Middle Ages*, ed. Hilde De Ridder-Symoens (Cambridge, UK: Cambridge University Press, 1992), 162-63.
8. Ibid., 163.
9. Michael Higton, *A Theology of Higher Education* (New York: Oxford University Press, 2013).
10. Frijhoff, "Patterns."
11. Ibid., 224.
12. Vandermeersch, "Teachers," 226.
13. Ibid., 226-27.
14. John W. O'Malley, S.J., *The Jesuits: A History from Ignatius to the Present* (Lanham, MD: Rowman and Littlefield, 2014).
15. Robert D. Anderson, *European Universities from the Enlightenment to 1914* (New York: Oxford, 2004), 23-34.
16. Ibid.
17. John T. McGreevey, *American Jesuits and the World: How an Embattled Religious Order Made Modern Catholicism Global* (Princeton, NJ: Princeton University Press, 2016).
18. Walter Rüegg, "Themes," in *A History of the University in Europe*, vol. III, *Universities in the Nineteenth and Early Twentieth Centuries, 1800-1945*, ed. Walter Rüegg (Cambridge, UK: Cambridge University Press, 1996), 3.
19. Vandermeersch, "Teachers."
20. Frijhoff, "Patterns."
21. George M. Marsden, *The Soul of the American University: From Protestant Establishment to Established Nonbelief* (New York: Oxford University Press, 1994).
22. Donald G. Tewksbury, *The Founding of American Colleges and Universities before the Civil War* (New York: Teacher College Press, 1932), 136-42.
23. Ibid., 141.
24. John R. Thelin, *The History of Higher Education in America*, 2nd ed. (Baltimore, MD: Johns Hopkins University Press, 2013).
25. Ibid., 136-42.

26. "Charter of Rhode Island College (Brown University), 1764," in *American Higher Education: A Documentary History*, vol. 1, ed. Richard Hofstadter and Wilson Smith (Chicago: University of Chicago Press, 1961), 135–36.
27. Richard Hofstadter and Wilson Smith, "The Collegiate System in the Eighteenth Century," in *American Higher Education*, vol. 1, ed. Hofstadter and Smith (Chicago: University of Chicago Press, 1961), 97.
28. William Livingston, "William Livingston Opposes a Sectarian College for New York, 1753," in *American Higher Education*, vol. 1, ed. Hofstadter and Smith (Chicago: University of Chicago Press, 1961), 101.
29. Ibid.
30. "Samuel Johnson Advertises the Opening of King's College (Columbia), 1754," in *American Higher Education*, vol. 1, ed. Hofstadter and Smith (Chicago: University of Chicago Press, 1961), 110.
31. There would at times be some overlap. For example, at Yale the Prudential Committee, which chose faculty, consisted of the president and three other men, one of whom was commonly the governor or lieutenant governor of the state of Connecticut. See "Benjamin Silliman on the Government of Yale, 1830," in *American Higher Education*, vol. 1, ed. Hofstadter and Smith (Chicago: University of Chicago Press, 1961), 306. Regarding the end of state establishments, see Steven K. Green, *The Second Disestablishment: Church and State in Nineteenth Century America* (New York: Oxford University Press, 2010), 119–47.
32. Edgar B. Wesley, *Proposed: The University of the United States* (Minneapolis: University of Minnesota Press, 1936), 5–12.
33. John C. Fitzpatrick, ed., *Writings of George Washington, 1745–1799*, vol. XXXV (Washington, DC: Government Printing Office, 1940), 316–17
34. James Madison to Edward Everett, March 19, 1823, in *The Writings of James Madison, 1819–1836*, vol. 9, ed. Gaillard Hunt (1910), 124.
35. Anderson, *European Universities from the Enlightenment to 1914*, 91.
36. "Report of the Rockfish Gap Commission on the Proposed University of Virginia, 1818," in *American Higher Education*, vol. 1, ed. Hofstadter and Smith (Chicago: University of Chicago Press, 1961), 198.
37. Marsden, *The Soul of the American University*, 73.
38. Charles L. Glenn, *The Myth of the Common School* (Amherst: University of Massachusetts Press, 1988).
39. "The Michigan Regents Warn against Sectarianism," in *American Higher Education*, vol. 1, ed. Hofstadter and Smith (Chicago: University of Chicago Press, 1961), 438.
40. Ibid., 437.
41. Ibid., 438.
42. Marsden, *The Soul of the American University*.
43. Tewksbury, *The Founding of American Colleges and Universities before the Civil War*, 55–132.
44. William C. Ringenberg, *The Christian College: A History of Protestant Higher Education in America*, 2nd ed. (Grand Rapids, MI: Baker Academic Press, 2006), 59.

45. Tewksbury, *The Founding of American Colleges and Universities before the Civil War*, 33.
46. Daniel Coit Gilman, "Gilman's Inaugural Address," Johns Hopkins University, https://www.jhu.edu/about/history/gilman-address, accessed July 18, 2018.
47. Hugh Hawkins, *Pioneer: A History of the Johns Hopkins University, 1874–1889* (Ithaca, NY: Cornell University Press, 1960), 41.
48. D. G. Hart, *The University Gets Religion: Religious Studies in American Higher Education* (Baltimore, MD: Johns Hopkins University Press, 1999), 44.
49. Ibid., 36.
50. Julie Reuben, *The Making of the Modern University: Intellectual Transformation and the Marginalization of Morality* (Chicago: University of Chicago Press, 1996).
51. Thomas L. Haskell, *The Emergence of Professional Social Science: The American Social Science Association and the Nineteenth-Century Crisis of Authority* (Urbana, IL: University of Chicago Press, 1977), 68.
52. Ibid., 89.
53. Matti Klinge, "Teachers," in *A History of the University in Europe*, vol. III, ed. Walter Rüegg (Cambridge, UK: Cambridge University Press, 2004), 123–62.
54. Haskell, *The Emergence of Professional Social Science*.
55. Julie Robin Solomon, *Objectivity in the Making: Francis Bacon and the Politics of Inquiry* (Baltimore, MD: Johns Hopkins University Press, 1998).
56. Marsden, *The Soul of the American University*, 150–66.
57. Anderson, *European Universities from the Enlightenment to 1914*, 102.
58. Max Weber, "The 'Objectivity' of Knowledge in Social Science and Social Policy," in Max Weber, *The Essential Weber: A Reader*, ed. Sam Whimster (New York: Routledge, 2004), 359–404. See also Peter Novick, *That Noble Dream: The "Objectivity Question" and the American Historical Profession* (New York: Cambridge University Press, 1988).
59. Sven Ove Hansson, "Science and Pseudo-Science," in *The Stanford Encyclopedia of Philosophy*, ed. Edward N. Zalta (Palo Alto, CA: The Metaphysics Research Lab, 2017), https://plato.stanford.edu/archives/sum2017/about.html.
60. Max Weber, "Science as a Vocation," in *From Max Weber: Essays in Sociology*, trans. and ed. H. H. Gerth and C. Wright Mills (New York: Oxford University Press, 1946), 133.
61. Max Weber, "The Vocation of Science," in Max Weber, *The Essential Weber: A Reader*, ed. Sam Whimster (New York: Routledge, 2004), 277.
62. Ibid., 279.
63. Ibid.
64. Ibid.
65. Ibid.
66. Ibid., 282.
67. Ibid., 283.
68. Ibid., 285.
69. Ibid., 280.

70. Ibid., 279.
71. Walter Moberly. *The Crisis of the University* (London: SCM, 1949), 54.
72. Parker J. Palmer, *The Courage to Teach* (San Francisco: Jossey-Bass, 2007), 18.
73. Berenice Malka Fisher, *No Angel in the Classroom: Teaching Through Feminist Discourse* (Lanham, MD: Rowman and Littlefield Publishers, 2001), 14.
74. George M. Marsden, *The Outrageous Idea of Christian Scholarship* (New York: Oxford University Press, 1997), 13.
75. Nord, *Does God Make a Difference?*, 95.
76. Chris Anderson, *Teaching as Believing: Faith in the University* (Waco, TX: Baylor University Press, 2004), 5. Italics added.
77. bell hooks, *Teaching to Transgress: Education as the Practice of Freedom* (New York: Routledge, 1994), 2
78. Ibid., 3.
79. Ibid.
80. Ibid.
81. Ibid., 16.
82. Ibid., 16–17.
83. For some examples, see Penny Light, Tracy Nichalas, and Renée Bondy, *Feminist Pedagogy in Higher Education* (Waterloo, ON: Wilfrid Laurier University Press, 2015); and Fisher, *No Angel in the Classroom*.
84. Parker Palmer, *To Know as We Are Known* (New York: HarperOne, 1993), 68.
85. Palmer, *The Courage to Teach*, 18.
86. Stanley Fish, *Save the World on Your Own Time* (New York: Oxford University Press, 2008), 139.
87. Ibid., 140.
88. Stanley Hauerwas, *Sanctify Them in the Truth: Holiness Exemplified* (New York: Bloomsbury Publishing, 2016), 235.
89. Fish, *Save the World on Your Own Time*, 140.
90. Ibid.
91. The nature of this conflict can be seen in a short example shared by Berenice Malka Fisher, a scholar of feminist pedagogy, who wrote appreciatively about one of her teachers, the well-known sociologist Anselm Strauss. She described how he cared for her differently and more holistically. "In contrast to my philosophy teachers, he nurtured me as an individual. He paid attention to the social context in which I was studying and gave me advice about how to handle the problems I faced as a doctoral student." Here Fisher provides evidence to support hooks's and Palmer's vision for connecting all of one's self and many of one's nonacademic identities to teaching. Yet later in her book, Fisher shares that Strauss was her cousin. Here, we might find a possible identity coherence or conflict. Being a cousin may have merely amplified certain virtues Strauss would also show to other students. Yet Fish may argue that this additional identity role and family connection could corrupt Strauss's teaching practice, perhaps coloring it with favoritism. Both identity coherence and identity conflict can make a crucial difference in our teaching practices and may bring possible good or ill upon our students. Although scholars from various underrepresented groups

have begun to examine these uniquenesses from the perspective of race, gender, and sexuality, the matter of religious identity has been different. See Fisher, *No Angel in the Classroom*, 12.

92. For example, see James T. Burtchaell, *The Dying of the Light: The Disengagement of Colleges and Universities from Their Christian Churches* (Grand Rapids, MI: Eerdmans, 1998); Marsden, *The Soul of the American University*; and Douglas Sloan, *Faith and Knowledge: Mainline Protestantism and American Higher Education* (Louisville, KY: Westminster/John Knox, 1994).

93. Robert Benne, *Quality with Soul: How Six Premier Colleges and Universities Keep Their Faith with Their Religious Tradition* (Grand Rapids, MI: Eerdmans, 2002); Paul J. Dovre, ed., *The Future of Religious Colleges* (Grand Rapids, MI: Eerdmans, 2002); Alice Gallin, *Negotiating Identity: Catholic Higher Education since 1960* (Notre Dame, IN: University of Notre Dame Press, 2000); Richard T. Hughes and William B. Adrian, *Models for Christian Higher Education: Strategies for Success in the Twenty-First Century* (Grand Rapids, MI: Eerdmans, 1997); and John Wilcox and Irene King, *Enhancing Religious Identity: Best Practices from Catholic Campuses* (Washington, DC: Georgetown University Press, 2000).

94. For one example, see Cynthia B. Dillard, Daa'lyah Ab-dur-Rashid, and Cynthia Tyson, "My Soul Is a Witness: Affirming Pedagogies of the Spirit," *International Journal of Qualitative Studies in Education* 13, no. 5 (2000): 447–62.

95. Joel C. Carpenter, Perry L. Glanzer, and Nick Lantinga, eds., *Christian Higher Education: A Global Reconnaissance* (Grand Rapids, MI: Eerdmans, 2014).

96. Ringenberg, *The Christian College*; and Perry L. Glanzer, Nathan F. Alleman, and Todd C. Ream, *Restoring the Soul of the University: Unifying Christian Higher Education in a Fragmented Age* (Downers Grove, IL: InterVarsity, 2017).

Chapter 2

1. George Marsden, *The Outrageous Idea of Christian Scholarship* (New York: Oxford University Press, 1997), 61.
2. K. Anders Ericsson, Ralf Th. Krampe, and Clemens Tesch-Romer, "The Role of Deliberate Practice in the Acquisition of Expert Performance," *Psychological Review* 100, no. 3 (1993): 363–406.
3. There are a few more works that address Christian teaching at the K–12 level. See, for example, John Van Dyk, *The Craft of Christian Teaching* (Sioux City, IA: Dordt Press, 2000).
4. David I. Smith and James K. A. Smith, eds. *Teaching and Christian Practices: Reshaping Faith and Learning* (Grand Rapids, MI: Eerdmans, 2011), 2.
5. One review of literature found "only a tiny percentage of the scholarly writing that emerges from Christian higher education is devoted to the development of . . . nuanced accounts of how teaching and learning are supposed to work in a Christian setting." Smith and Smith, eds. *Teaching and Christian* Practices, 3.

6. Ibid.; Karen E. Eifler and Thomas M. Landy, eds., *Becoming Beholders: Cultivating Sacramental Imagination and Actions in College Classrooms* (Collegeville, MN: Liturgical Press, 2014); David I. Smith, *On Christian Teaching* (Grand Rapids, MI: William B. Eerdmans Publishing Company, 2017); Chris Anderson, *Teaching as Believing: Faith in the University* (Waco, TX: Baylor University Press, 2004); Jean B. Elshtain, "Does, or Should, Teaching Reflect the Religious Perspective of the Teacher?," in *Religion, Scholarship, and Higher Education: Perspectives, Models, and Future Prospects*, ed. Andrea Sterk (Notre Dame, IN: University of Notre Dame, 2002), 193–201; Richard T. Hughes, "What Might It Mean to Teach from a Christian Perspective," in Richard T. Hughes' *How Christian Faith Can Sustain the Life of the Mind* (Grand Rapids, MI: Eerdmans, 2001), chapter 5; various essays in Stephen R. Haynes, ed., *Professing in the Postmodern Academy: Faculty and the Future of Church-Related Colleges* (Waco, TX: Baylor University Press, 2002); and John Van Dyk, *The Craft of Christian Teaching* (Sioux City, IA: Dordt Press, 2000).
7. For more about the methodology of the study, see the appendix.
8. The CCCU states, "We are committed to supporting, protecting and promoting the value of integrating the Bible—divinely inspired, true, and authoritative—throughout all curricular and co-curricular aspects of the educational experience on our campuses, including teaching and research." "About," www.cccu.org/about.
9. For articles describing and drawing upon this survey, see Phil Davignon, Perry L. Glanzer, and Jesse Rine, "Assessing the Denominational Identity of American Evangelical Colleges and Universities, Part III: The Student Experience," *Christian Higher Education* 12, 5 (2013): 315–30; and Phil Davignon, "Factors Influencing College Choice and Satisfaction for Christian College Students," *Religion and Education* 43, no. 1 (2016): 77–94.
10. This list of faith traditions reflects those used in other national religion surveys, such as the Baylor Religion Survey. We do not suppose that we know all that each respondent assumes about the selected tradition. Nevertheless, most traditions do include important points of convergence, each requiring more explanation than is possible here. We recommend that readers interested in better understanding the implications of these faith traditions consult the following resources: Hughes, *How Christian Faith Can Sustain the Life of the Mind*; Richard T. Hughes and William B. Adrian, *Models for Christian Higher Education: Strategies for Success in the Twenty-First Century* (Grand Rapids, MI: Eerdmans, 1997); Richard J. Foster, *Streams of Living Water: Celebrating the Great Traditions of Christian Faith* (San Francisco: HarperCollins, 2001); and Douglas Jacobsen and Rhonda Hustedt Jacobsen, *Scholarship and Christian Faith: Enlarging the Conversation* (New York: Oxford, 2004).
11. Lincoln A. Mullen, *The Chance of Salvation: A History of Conversion in America* (Cambridge, MA: Harvard University Press, 2017), 5.
12. Robert Barro, Jason Hwang, and Rachel McCleary, "Religious Conversion in 40 Countries," *Journal for the Scientific Study of Religion* 49, no. 1 (2010): 15–36.
13. Pew Research Center, "Faith in Flux" (April 2009), http://www.pewforum.org/2009/04/27/faith-in-flux.

14. Although one might be critical of the fact that professors often only mentioned one part of a learning taxonomy instead of the full range of objectives that would entail understanding and applying a theological tradition in a critical manner, we should note that professors were only asked to give one example.
15. For more about our coding method as well as our overall method, see the appendix.
16. For a summary, see Todd C. Ream and Perry L. Glanzer, *Christian Faith and Scholarship: An Exploration of Contemporary Developments*, ASHE-ERIC Higher Education Report (San Francisco: Jossey-Bass, 2007), 47–57.
17. Charles Taylor, *The Sources of the Self: The Making of Modern Identity* (Cambridge, MA: Harvard University Press, 1989), 30.
18. Nicholas Wolterstorff, *Reason within the Bounds of Religion* (Grand Rapids, MI: Eerdmans, 1987).
19. Thomas Kuhn, *The Structure of Scientific Revolutions* (Chicago: University of Chicago Press, 1962); and David K. Naugle, *Worldview: The History of a Concept* (Grand Rapids, MI: Eerdmans, 2002).
20. Neal Postman, *The End of Education* (New York: Vintage Books, 1995).
21. Todd C. Ream and Perry L. Glanzer, *Christian Faith and Scholarship: An Exploration of Contemporary Developments*, ASHE-ERIC Higher Education Report (San Francisco: Jossey-Bass, 2007).
22. Warren Nord, *Does God Make a Difference? Taking Religion Seriously in Our Schools and Universities* (New York: Oxford University Press, 2010).
23. G. I. Williamson, *The Westminster Shorter Catechism: For Study Classes* (Phillipsburg: P and R Publishing Company, 2003), 1.
24. One finds this kind of appeal from some of the teachers interviewed in Jennifer Lindholm, *The Quest for Meaning and Wholeness: Spiritual and Religious Connections in the Lives of College Faculty* (San Francisco: Jossey-Bass, 2014), 104–5.
25. This aspect of being placed as stewards of creation is aptly captured in Psalm 8, where David asks a poignant question. "What is man that you are mindful of him, the son of man that you care for him? You have made him a little lower than the heavenly beings and crowned him with glory and honor. You made him ruler over the works of your hands; you put everything under his feet: all the flocks and herds, and the beasts of the field, the birds of the air, and the fish of the sea, all that swim the paths of the seas" (Psalm 8:4, NIV).
26. For similar writing on this theme, see Chris M. Golde, "Preparing Stewards of the Discipline," in Chris M. Golde, George E. Walker, and Associates, *Envisioning the Future of Doctoral Education: Preparing Stewards of the Discipline—Carnegie Essays on the Doctorate* (San Francisco: Jossey-Bass, 2006), 10–12.
27. This theme, of course, reflects the themes of stewardship found in Jesus's parables and other New Testament teachings. See Matthew 25:14–30; Luke 16:1–15; and I Peter 4:10.
28. Mike Higton, *A Theology of Higher Education* (New York: Oxford University Press, 2013), 154.
29. American Association of University Professors, "Statement on Professional Ethics," last updated and approved by Association's Council in 2009, https://www.aaup.org/report/statement-professional-ethics.

30. Ibid., 34.
31. Some may argue that our own theological categorizations of the data lean towards the Reformed and evangelical perspectives. For example, organization around the concept of "narrative" and "story" might suggest to some triumphalist assumptions at the cost of identification with the lived struggle for justice that others might emphasize. Although we would describe our categories as broadly inclusive, they may not appear so for these and other reasons.
32. Carolyn Call, "The Rough Trail to Authentic Pedagogy: Incorporating Hospitality, Fellowship, and Testimony into the Classroom," in *Teaching and Christian Practices: Reshaping Faith and* Learning, ed. David I. Smith and James K. A. Smith (Grand Rapids, MI: Eermans Publishing Company, 2011), 61–79. All of the following quotes are taken from this chapter.

Chapter 3

1. Eric Cunningham, "Beholding the Eschaton: Transforming Self and World through the Study of World History," in *Becoming Beholders: Cultivating Sacramental Imagination and Actions in College Classrooms*, ed. Karen E Eifler and Thomas M. Landy (Collegeville, MN: Liturgical Press, 2014), 206.
2. Ibid., 205.
3. Ibid., 206.
4. Ibid.
5. Ibid., 207.
6. Ibid., 213.
7. Ibid., 212.
8. Ibid., 218.
9. Ibid.
10. Ibid., 219.
11. Ibid.
12. One also finds this characteristic in the scholarly conversation. See, for example, Elizabeth J. Tisdell, "Spirituality, Diversity, and Learner Centered Teaching: A Generative Paradox," in *The American University in a Postsecular Age*, ed. Douglas Jacobsen and Rhonda Hurstedt Jacobsen (New York: Oxford University Press, 2008), 151–65.
13. See George Marsden, *The Outrageous Idea of Christian Scholarship* (New York: Oxford University Press, 72–77).
14. James Sweeney, "Theology and Sociology," in *Christianity and the Disciplines: The Transformation of the University*, ed. Oliver D. Crisp, Gavin D'Costa, Mervyn Davies, and Peter Hampson (New York: T & T Clark, 2012), 107.
15. Ibid., 109.
16. William Purcell and William Lies, CSC, "Solidarity through 'Poverty and Politics,'" in *Becoming Beholders*, ed. Eifler and Landy (Collegeville, MN: Liturgical Press, 2014), 163.

17. For the origins of this use, see David K. Naugle, *Worldview: The History of a Concept* (Grand Rapids, MI: Eerdmans, 2002).
18. Marsden, *The Outrageous Idea of Christian Scholarship*, 84–90.
19. Perry L. Glanzer, *The Quest for Russia's Soul* (Waco, TX: Baylor University Press, 2002).
20. David Smith, interview with author, October 13, 2004. The interview has been edited for readability.
21. We should note that we are not necessarily arguing that this spiritual addition approach is ideal or represents faith and learning. Indeed, as Rick Ostrander argues, "professors who insert religious material into their classes are not necessarily integrating faith and learning." Rick Ostrander, *Why College Matters to God: An Introduction to the Christian College*, rev. ed. (Abilene, TX: Abilene Christian University Press, 2012), 109.
22. Anne Colby, Thomas Ehrlich, Elizabeth Beaumont, and Jason Stephens, *Educating Citizens: Preparing America's Undergraduates for Lives of Moral and Civic Responsibility* (San Francisco: Jossey-Bass, 2003).
23. John Howard Yoder, *The Politics of Jesus* (Grand Rapids, MI: Eerdmans, 1972).
24. Aristotle, *Nicomachean Ethics* 4.3.
25. Perry L. Glanzer and Andrew J. Milson, "Legislating the Good: A Survey and Evaluation of Contemporary Character Education Legislation," *Educational Policy* 20, no. 3 (2006): 525–50.
26. Ibid.
27. This also proved true with several references to the golden rule, an ethical concept that is not exclusively Christian (e.g., "The concept of the Golden Rule can be found in everything I teach, including principles, scenarios, examples, etc."). For an overview of how the three strands mentioned are applied in higher education, see Anne Colby et al., *Educating Citizens*.
28. Extended details about this story can be found in David I. Smith, Sarah L. De Young, A. Uyaguari, and Kate Avila, "Of Log Cabins, Fallen Bishops, and Tenacious Parents: (Auto)biographical Narrative and the Spirituality of Language Learning," in *Spirituality, Social Justice, and Language Learning*, ed. David. I. Smith and Terry A. Osborn (Charlotte, NC: Information Age Press, 2007), 107–29.
29. Doug G. Jacobsen and Rhonda H. Jacobsen, eds., *Scholarship and Christian Faith: Enlarging the Conversation* (New York: Oxford University Press, 2004), 90–94.

Chapter 4

1. David I. Smith, *On Christian Teaching* (Grand Rapids, MI: Eerdmans Publishing Company, 2017), 130.
2. Warren Nord, *Religion and American Education: Rethinking a National Dilemma* (Chapel Hill: University of North Carolina Press, 1995), 155.

3. Warren Nord, *Does God Make a Difference? Taking Religion Seriously in Our Schools and Universities* (New York: Oxford University Press, 2010), 48.
4. Peter Alonzi, "Pauses," in *Becoming Beholders: Cultivating Sacramental Imagination and Actions in College Classrooms*, ed. Karen E. Eifler and Thomas M. Landy (Collegeville, MN: Liturgical Press, 2014), 86.
5. Ibid., 88.
6. Ibid., 89.
7. Ibid., 90.
8. Ibid., 92.
9. Ibid.
10. Ibid., 93.
11. Ibid., 98–99.
12. David I. Smith and James K. A. Smith, eds., *Teaching and Christian Practices: Reshaping Faith and Learning* (Grand Rapids, MI: Eerdmans, 2011), 5.
13. David I. Smith, Joonyong Um, and Claudia D. Beversluis, "The Scholarship of Teaching and Learning in a Christian Context," *Christian Higher Education* 13, no. 1 (2014): 74–87.
14. Smith, *On Christian Teaching*, 146–53.
15. Smith and Smith, *Teaching and Christian Practices*.
16. Jennifer A. Lindholm, *The Quest for Meaning and Wholeness: Spiritual and Religious Connections in the Lives of College Faculty* (San Francisco: Jossey-Bass, 2014), 210.
17. One finds a similar approach in John Van Dyk, *The Craft of Christian Teaching* (Sioux City, IA: Dordt Press, 2000).
18. Smith, *On Christian Teaching*, 15.
19. David Bridges, *Fiction Written Under Oath? Essays in Philosophy and Educational Research* (Dordrecht: Kluwer, 2003), 1, quoted in Smith, *On Christian Teaching*, 35.
20. Ibid., 36.
21. Ibid., 37.
22. Parker J. Palmer, *To Know as We Are Known: A Spirituality of Education* (San Francisco: Harper & Row, 1983), 30.
23. Christopher Peterson and Martin Seligman, *Character Strengths and Virtues: A Handbook and Classification* (New York: Oxford University Press, 2004); and Perry L. Glanzer and Andrew J. Milson, "Legislating the Good: A Survey and Evaluation of Contemporary Character Education Legislation," *Educational Policy* 20, no. 3 (2006): 525–50.
24. We should note that we do not believe this chart summarizes every type of integration that occurs.
25. Carolyn Call, "The Rough Trail to Authentic Pedagogy: Incorporating Hospitality, Fellowship, and Testimony into the Classroom," in *Teaching and Christian Practices: Reshaping Faith and Learning*, ed. David I. Smith and James K. A. Smith (Grand Rapids, MI: Eermans Publishing Company, 2011), 61–79. All of the following quotes are taken from this chapter.
26. Ann Green, "Stumbling Towards Grace: Meditations on Communion and Community in the Writing Classroom," in *Becoming Beholders*, ed. Eifler and Landy

(Collegeville, MN: Liturgical Press, 2014), 118–28. All of the following quotes are taken from this chapter.

Chapter 5

1. Doug G. Jacobsen and Rhonda Hustedt Jacobsen, eds., *Scholarship and Christian Faith: Enlarging the Conversation* (New York: Oxford University Press, 2004), 78.
2. "The Michigan Regents Warn against Sectarianism," in *American Higher Education: A Documentary History*, vol. 1, ed. Richard Hofstadter and Wilson Smith (Chicago: University of Chicago Press, 1961), 438.
3. George M. Marsden, *The Soul of the American University: From Protestant Establishment to Established Nonbelief* (New York: Oxford University Press, 1994); Philip Gleason, *Contending with Modernity: Catholic Higher Education in the Twentieth Century* (New York: Oxford University Press, 1995); and James T. Burtchaell, *The Dying of the Light: The Disengagement of the Colleges and Universities from Their Christian Churches* (Grand Rapids, MI: Eerdmans, 1998).
4. Kevin D. Dougherty, Byron R. Johnson, and Edward C. Polson, "Recovering the Lost: Remeasuring U.S. Religious Affiliation," *Journal for the Scientific Study of Religion* 46, no. 4 (2007): 483–499, doi:10.1111/j.1468-5906.2007.00373.x
5. Ibid.
6. Arthur Holmes, *The Idea of a Christian College*, rev. ed. (Grand Rapids, MI: William B. Eerdmans Publishing Company, 1987); George Marsden, *The Outrageous Idea of Christian Scholarship* (New York: Oxford, 1996); and Nicholas Wolterstorff, *Educating for Shalom: Essays on Christian Higher Education*, ed. Clarence Joldersma and Gloria Stronks (Grand Rapids, MI: William B. Eerdmans Publishing Company, 2004).
7. Jacobsen and Jacobsen, eds., *Scholarship and Christian Faith*, 80–90.
8. William R. Estep, Jr., "Voluntarism is a Flagship of the Baptist Tradition," in *Defining Baptist Convictions: Guidelines for the Twenty-First Century*, ed. Charles W. Deweese (Franklin, TN: Providence House Publishers, 1996).
9. William Purcell and Rev. William Lies, CSC, "Solidarity through 'Poverty and Politics,'" in *Becoming Beholders: Cultivating Sacramental Imagination and Actions in College Classrooms*, ed. Karen E. Eifler and Thomas M. Landy (Collegeville, MN: Liturgical Press, 2014), 166.
10. Richard Mouw, *The God Who Commands: A Study in Divine Command Ethics* (South Bend, IN: University of Notre Dame Press, 1990), 150.
11. Karen E. Eifler and Thomas M. Landy, eds., *Becoming Beholders: Cultivating Sacramental Imagination and Actions in College Classrooms* (Collegeville, MN: Liturgical Press, 2014).
12. Michael J. Himes, "Finding God in All Things: A Sacramental Worldview and Its Effects," in *Becoming Beholders*, ed. Eifler and Landy (Collegeville, MN: Liturgical Press, 2014), 10.
13. Ibid., 13.

14. Ibid., 15.
15. Ibid., 14.
16. See, for example, Neil Postman, *The End of Education* (New York: Random House Publishers, 1995); Derek Bok, *Our Underachieving Colleges: A Candid Look at How Much Students Learn and Why They Should Be Learning More* (Princeton, NJ: Princeton University Press, 2006); and Andrew Delbanco, *College: What It Was, Is and Should Be* (Princeton, NJ: Princeton University Press, 2012).
17. Himes, "Finding God in All Things," ix.
18. Ibid., x.
19. Stephen W. Angell and Ben Pink Dandelion, eds., *The Oxford Handbook of Quaker Studies* (New York: Oxford University Press, 2013).
20. See, for example, Eifler and Landy, *Becoming Beholders*.
21. For Benjamin S. Bloom's original taxonomy, see Benjamin S. Bloom, ed., *Taxonomy of Educational Objectives: The Classification of Educational Goals by a Committee of College and University Examiners* (New York: Longmans, Green, 1956).
22. Warren Nord, *Does God Make a Difference? Taking Religion Seriously in Our Schools and Universities* (New York: Oxford University Press, 2010), 111.
23. H. Richard Niebuhr, *Christ and Culture*, exp. 50th anniv. ed. (San Francisco: Harper One Publishers, 1975).
24. For example, see Rick Ostrander, *Why College Matters to God: An Introduction to the Christian College*, rev. ed. (Abilene, TX: Abilene Christian University Press, 2012); Marsden, *The Outrageous Idea of Christian Scholarship*; and Al Wolters, *Creation Regained: Biblical Basics for a Reformational Worldview*, rev. ed. (Grand Rapids, MI: William B. Eerdmans Publishing Company, 2005).
25. Eifler and Landy, *Becoming Beholders*.
26. Stanley Fish, *Save the World on Your Own Time* (New York: Oxford University Press, 2008), 68.

Chapter 6

1. Mark Edwards Jr., "Why Faculty Find It Difficult to Talk about Religion," in *The American University in a Postsecular Age*, ed. Douglas Jacobsen and Rhonda Hurstedt Jacobsen (New York: Oxford University Press, 2008), 81.
2. Matt Pearce, "Who Was Responsible for the Violence? Here's What Witnesses Say," *Los Angeles Times*, August 15, 2017, http://www.latimes.com/nation/la-na-charlottesville-witnesses-20170815-story.html.
3. Rosie Gray, "Alt-Right Leaders Won't Condemn Ramming Suspect," *The Atlantic Monthly*, August 14, 2017, https://www.theatlantic.com/politics/archive/2017/08/alt-right-leaders-wont-condemn-ramming-suspect/536880.
4. Chad Wellman, "For Moral Clarity Don't Look to Universities," *The Chronicle of Higher Education*, August 15, 2017, http://www.chronicle.com/article/For-Moral-Clarity-Dont-Look/240921?cid=wcontentgrid_hp_1b/.

5. Ibid.
6. Ibid.
7. Ibid.
8. In reality, even at universities that claim to be pluralistic, identity-based prejudices still play a role in hiring and student admissions. For instance, George Yancey found that faculty at colleges still saw various identity markers as damaging or enhancing a candidate's job changes. Indeed, two of the identities that academics saw as most problematic were religious: fundamentalist and evangelical. For more on this, see George Yancey, *Compromising Scholarship: Religious and Political Bias in American Higher Education* (Waco, TX: Baylor University Press, 2011), 123.
9. For instance, the following is one key academic reason for promoting diversity in general:

    There is a strong consensus in the academic world that diversity is important because bringing diverse viewpoints to bear on social, intellectual, philosophical, legal, and moral problems is likely to enhance the quality of the scholarship that bears on those issues. We enthusiastically embrace this view. The academic world must have viewpoint diversity if it is to function properly and produce reliable research.

    Heterodox Academy, "The Problem," https://heterodoxacademy.org/the-problem.
10. Thomas A. Howard, *Protestant Theology and the Making of the Modern German University* (New York: Oxford University Press, 2006).
11. See Warren Nord, *Does God Make a Difference? Taking Religion Seriously in Our Schools and Universities* (New York: Oxford University Press, 2010), 202.
12. Heterodox Academy, "The Problem."
13. Ibid.; Nord, *Does God Make a Difference?*; and Yancey, *Compromising Scholarship*.
14. Nord, *Does God Make a Difference?*
15. Ibid., 85, 94.
16. Jennifer A. Lindholm, *The Quest for Meaning and Wholeness: Spiritual and Religious Connections in the Lives of College Faculty* (San Francisco: Jossey-Bass, 2014), 25.
17. Parker J. Palmer, *The Courage to Teach* (San Francisco: Jossey-Bass, 2007), 31.
18. American Association of University Professors, "Statement on Teaching Evaluation," *AAUP Bulletin* 61, no. 2 (August 1975): 201.
19. Stanley Fish, *Save the World on Your Own Time* (New York: Oxford University Press, 2008), 18.
20. Ibid., 81.
21. Chris Anderson, *Teaching as Believing: Faith in the University* (Waco, TX: Baylor University Press, 2004), 133. Italics in original.
22. Steven Glazer, *The Heart of Learning: Spirituality in Education* (New York: Putnam Press, 1999), 2 (italics in original).
23. Perry L. Glanzer, Jonathan P. Hill, and Byron R. Johnson, *The Quest for Purpose: The Collegiate Search for a Meaningful Life* (Albany: State University of New York Press, 2017).
24. John Rawls, *Political Liberalism* (New York: Columbia University Press, 1996), xviii.
25. Alexander W. Astin, Helen S. Astin, and Jennifer Lindholm, *Cultivating the Spirit: How College Can Enhance Students' Inner Lives* (San Francisco: Jossey-Bass, 2011).

26. Anderson, *Teaching as Believing*, 151–52.
27. The pluralistic academy appears the most confused about these matters when it comes to "studies" majors. We are thinking particularly of religious studies and gender studies. When universities were Christian, they offered education in theology in the hopes of making students theologians. Religious studies emerged as a field as a way to accommodate pluralism, because universities and their students were increasingly less Christian. Oddly, instead of following the example of religious studies in seeking to be less focused on one identity, gender studies departments today often become feminist seminaries, in which only true believers gather or it is hoped the nonbelievers will be converted to a particular identity (e.g., feminism).
28. Palmer, *The Courage to Teach*, 10. Italics in original.
29. Nord, *Does God Make a Difference?*, 164.
30. Ibid., 172.
31. *Abingdon School District v. Schempp*, 374 U.S.203 (1963).
32. *Abington Township v. Schemp*, 374 U.S. 203, 225 (1963).
33. Ibid., 306.
34. Warren Nord and Charles Haynes, *Taking Religion Seriously Across the Curriculum* (Alexandria, VA: Association for Supervision and Curriculum Development, 1998), 18.
35. Mark U. Edwards Jr., *Religion on Our Campuses: A Professor's Guide to Communities, Conflicts and Promising Conversations* (New York: Palgrave Macmillan, 2006), 148.
36. See, for example, "Religion in the Public Schools: A Joint Statement of Current Law," https://www.aclu.org/other/joint-statement-current-law-religion-public-schools.
37. Douglas Jacobsen and Rhonda Hustedt Jacobsen, *No Longer Invisible: Religion in University Education* (New York: Oxford University Press, 2012), 40–41.
38. Ibid., 40.
39. Mike Higton, *A Theology of Higher Education* (New York: Oxford University Press, 2013), 174.
40. Ibid., 178.
41. Ibid., 196.
42. Anderson, *Teaching as Believing*, 186.
43. Of course, the important question is how a belief in God's love is expressed by Christian professors. Christian teachers who fail to meet the purposes Fish identifies but believe they are showing God's love to their students or who emphasize loving relationships may be mistaken in their understanding of what it means to care for their students. Teaching that neglects the acquisition of certain skills but spends inordinate time exploring the needs and views of students may not actually be loving.
44. Fish, *Save the World on Your Own Time*, 68.
45. Ibid., 18–19.
46. Perry L. Glanzer and Andrew J. Milson, "Legislating the Good: A Survey and Evaluation of Contemporary Character Education Legislation," *Educational Policy* 20, no. 3 (2006): 525–50.
47. George Marsden, *The Outrageous Idea of Christian Scholarship* (New York: Oxford University Press, 1997), 48.

48. Christopher Peterson and Martin Seligman, *Character Strengths and Virtues: A Handbook and Classification* (New York: Oxford University Press, 2004); and Glanzer and Milson, "Legislating the Good," 525–50.
49. We should note that one concept mentioned by some of the surveyed Christian professors and used quite often in the academy might fit into the category of controversial moral teaching due to its frequent association with a particular political agenda. We are referring to the concept of "social justice." Proponents fit many things under the banner of social justice, and whether those things are controversial or not will depend on the degree of acceptance in the culture. We think that this may be one of the controversial moral views Fish has in mind.
50. Fish, *Save the World on Your Own Time*, 38.
51. Stanley Hauerwas, *Sanctify Them in the Truth: Holiness Exemplified* (Nashville, TN: Abingdon, 1998), 234–35.
52. Ibid., 235.
53. Fish, *Save the World on Your Own Time*, 40.
54. Nord, *Does God Make a Difference?*, 113–14.
55. Neil Postman, *The End of Education* (New York: Random House Publishers, 1995), 57.
56. Ibid.
57. Heterodox Academy, "The Problem."
58. The Gospel Coalition, "An Open Letter from Christian Scholars on Racism in America Today," August 25, 2017, https://blogs.thegospelcoalition.org/evangelical-history/2017/08/25/an-open-letter-from-christian-scholars-on-racism-in-america-today.

Chapter 7

1. Warren Nord, *Does God Make a Difference? Taking Religion Seriously in Our Schools and Universities* (New York: Oxford University Press, 2010), 214–15.
2. Not surprisingly, some studies also show that forming one's professional identity as a teacher proves vital to becoming a good teacher. See Janet Alsup, *Teacher Identity Discourses: Negotiating Personal and Professional Spaces* (Urbana, IL: National Council of Teachers of English, 2006); and Patrick M. Jenlick, ed., *Teacher Identity and the Struggle for Recognition: Meeting the Challenges of a Diverse Society* (Lanham, MD: Rowman and Littlefield, 2014).
3. Ludwig Heinrich Jacob, *Uber die Universitäten in Deutschland, Besonders in Den Königl. Preussischen Staaten* (Berlin, 1798), 26, cited in R. Steven Turner, "University Reformers and Professorial Scholarship in Germany, 1760–1806," in *The University in Society*, vol. II, ed. Lawrence Stone (Princeton, NJ: Princeton University Press, 1974), 516–17.
4. Stephen Cahn, *Saints and Scamps: Ethics in Academia* (Totowa, NJ: Rowman and Littlefield, 2010), 1.
5. We recognize that in the era of the faculty of scholars the normative ideal of researcher, if sufficiently pursued, provides an implicit excuse for those who cut

corners in the classroom. That is not to say that what they are doing does not come with some disapproval, but in the research university context it also comes with recognition by others that teaching may pay the price for the kind of academic notoriety worth striving for. In other words, different academic environments may look differently on the sacrificing of teaching at the altar of scholarship.

6. Cahn, *Saints and Scamps*, 15.
7. Alasdair MacIntyre, *After Virtue*, 3rd ed. (South Bend, IN: University of Notre Dame Press, 2007).
8. bell hooks, *Teaching Community: A Pedagogy of Hope* (New York: Routledge, 2003), 181.
9. Ibid.
10. Kathleen deMarrais and Stephen D. Lapan, *Foundations for Research: Methods of Inquiry in Education and the Social Sciences* (Mahwah, NJ: Erlbaum Associates, 2004).
11. George Marsden, *The Outrageous Idea of Christian Scholarship* (New York: Oxford University Press, 1997), 42.
12. R. Eugene Rice, "Faculty Priorities: Where Does Faith Fit?," in *The American University in a Postsecular Age*, ed. Douglas Jacobsen and Rhonda Hurstedt Jacobsen (New York: Oxford University Press, 2008), 111.
13. Chris Anderson, *Teaching as Believing: Faith in the University* (Waco, TX: Baylor University Press, 2004), 143.
14. Nord, *Does God Make a Difference?*, 171.
15. Mark Edwards Jr., "Why Faculty Find It Difficult to Talk about Religion," in *The American University in a Postsecular Age*, ed. Jacobsen and Jacobsen (New York: Oxford University Press, 2008), 91.
16. Cahn, *Saints and Scamps*, 30–31.
17. Ibid., 31.
18. See, for example, Alexander George Theodoridis, "The Hyper-Polarization of America," *Scientific American*, November 7, 2016, https://blogs.scientificamerican.com/guest-blog/the-hyper-polarization-of-america.
19. Parker J. Palmer, *To Know as We Are Known: A Spirituality of Education* (San Francisco: Harper & Row, 1983), 26.
20. Student response found in Anderson, *Teaching as Believing*, 6.
21. hooks, *Teaching Community*, 128.
22. Ibid., 6.
23. Parker J. Palmer, *The Courage to Teach* (San Francisco: Jossey-Bass, 2007).
24. Nord, *Does God Make a Difference?*, 110.
25. Ibid.
26. Palmer, *The Courage to Teach*, 31.
27. Stanley Hauerwas, *After Christendom?* (Nashville, TN: Abingdon Press, 1991), 68.
28. For more about this argument see Perry L. Glanzer, "Taking the Tournament of Worldviews Seriously in Education: Why Teaching about Religion Is Not Enough," in *Education and Religion: Major Themes in Education*, ed. Philip Barnes and James Arthur (New York: Routledge Taylor Francis, 2016).

29. Alasdair C. MacIntyre, *Three Rival Versions of Moral Enquiry: Encyclopedia, Genealogy, and Tradition* (Notre Dame, IN: University of Notre Dame Press, 1990), 231.
30. Ibid.
31. bell hooks, *Teaching to Transgress: Education as the Practice of Freedom* (New York: Routledge, 1994), 21.
32. Warren Nord, *Religion and American Education* (Chapel Hill: University of North Carolina Press, 1995), 123.
33. Ibid., 221.
34. Oliver D. Crisp, Gavin D'Costa, Mervyn Davies, and Peter Hampson, *Christianity and the Disciplines: The Transformation of the University* (New York: T & T Clark, 2012); Todd C. Ream and Perry L. Glanzer, *Christian Faith and Scholarship: An Exploration of Contemporary Developments*, ASHE-ERIC Higher Education Report (San Francisco: Jossey-Bass, 2007).
35. Nord, *Does God Make a Difference?*, 115–16
36. Palmer, *The Courage to Teach*.
37. Carolyn Call, "The Rough Trail to Authentic Pedagogy: Incorporating Hospitality, Fellowship, and Testimony into the Classroom," in *Teaching and Christian Practices: Reshaping Faith and Learning*, ed. David I. Smith and James K.A. Smith (Grand Rapids, MI: Eerdmans, 2011), 61–79.
38. Danica Savonick, "Timekeeping as Feminist Pedagogy," *Insider Higher Ed*, June 27, 2017, https://www.insidehighered.com/advice/2017/06/27/how-social-hierarchies-influence-who-gets-most-time-speak-classrooms-essay.
39. Ibid.
40. Anderson, *Teaching as Believing*, 133.
41. We should note that we do not always agree about what these virtues look like in practice. See Perry L. Glanzer, "Finding the Gods in Public School: A Christian Deconstruction of Character Education," *Journal of Education and Christian Belief* 4, no. 2 (Autumn 2000): 115–30; and Perry L. Glanzer, "Exit Interviews: Learning about Character Education from Post-Soviet Educators," *Phi Delta Kappan* 82 (May 2001): 691–93.
42. Marsden, *The Outrageous Idea of Christian Scholarship*, 91.
43. Timothy Larsen, "No Christianity Please, We're Academics," *Inside Higher Education*, July 30, 2010, https://www.insidehighered.com/views/2010/07/30/no-christianity-please-were-academics.
44. Ibid.
45. Ibid.
46. Robert N. Bellah, Richard Madsen, William M. Sullivan, Ann Swidler, and Steven M. Tipton, *Habits of the Heart: Individualism and Commitment in American Life* (San Francisco: Harper & Row, 1985), 221.
47. Perry L. Glanzer, Jonathan P. Hill, and Byron R. Johnson, *The Quest for Purpose: The Collegiate Search for a Meaningful Life* (Albany: State University of New York Press, 2017).

Chapter 8

1. George Marsden, *The Outrageous Idea of Christian Scholarship* (New York: Oxford University Press, 1997), 19.
2. This line of argument is set forth in Elmer Thiessen, *In Defense of Religious Schools and Colleges* (Montreal: McGill-Queen's University Press, 2002); and Elmer Thiessen, *Teaching for Commitment: Liberal Education, Indoctrination and Christian Nurture* (Montreal: McGill-Queen's University Press, 1993).
3. Peter Conn, "The Great Accreditation Farce," *The Chronical of Higher Education* June 30, 2014, 11..
4. Alasdair C. MacIntyre, *Three Rival Versions of Moral Enquiry: Encyclopedia, Genealogy, and Tradition* (Notre Dame, IN: University of Notre Dame Press, 1990), 234.
5. For example, see Perry L. Glanzer, "Giving Christian Universities a Scarlet Letter: Examining the Canadian Association of University Teachers' Opposition to Faith-Based Hiring," *Religious Education* 108, no. 2 (2013): 148–63.
6. Anthony J. Diekema, *Academic Freedom and Christian Scholarship* (Grand Rapids, MI: William B. Eerdmans Publishing Company, 2000).
7. Ibid., 77.
8. Ibid., 85.
9. American Association of University Professors, "1940 Statement of Principles on Academic Freedom and Tenure," http://www.aaup.org/AAUP/pubsres/policydocs/contents/1940statement.htm, 3.
10. Thiessen, *In Defense of Religious Schools and Colleges*, 90–91.
11. Anthony J. Diekema, *Academic Freedom and Christian Scholarship* (Grand Rapids, MI: William B. Eerdmans Publishing Company, 2000); George M. Marsden, "Liberating Academic Freedom," *First Things* 88 (December 1998): 11–14; Michael M. McConnell, "Academic Freedom in Religious Colleges and Universities," in *Freedom and Tenure in the Academy*, ed. W. W. Van Alstyne (Durham, NC: Duke University Press, 1993), 303–24; Thiessen, *In Defense of Religious Schools and Colleges*; and Nicholas Wolterstorff, "Ivory Tower or Holy Mountain?: Faith and Academic Freedom," *Academe* 87, no. 1 (2001): 17–21.
12. George M. Marsden, *The Soul of the American University: From Protestant Establishment to Established Nonbelief* (New York: Oxford University Press, 1994), 435.
13. Douglas Jacobsen and Rhonda Hustedt Jacobsen, *No Longer Invisible: Religion in University Education* (New York: Oxford University Press, 2012), 96.
14. Thiessen, *In Defense of Religious Schools and Colleges*, 92–93.
15. For example, see the various essays in David I. Smith and James K. A. Smith, eds. *Teaching and Christian Practices: Reshaping Faith and Learning* (Grand Rapids, MI: Eerdmans, 2011).
16. Perry L. Glanzer, P. Jesse Rine, and Phil Davignon, "Assessing the Denominational Identity of American Evangelical Colleges and Universities, Part I: Denominational Patronage and Institutional Policy," *Christian Higher Education* 12, no. 3 (2013): 181–202.

17. Jesse Rine, Perry L. Glanzer, and Phil Davignon, "Assessing the Denominational Identity of American Evangelical Colleges and Universities, Part II: Faculty Perspectives and Practices," *Christian Higher Education* 12, no. 4 (2013): 243–65.
18. Melanie Morey and John Piderit, *Catholic Higher Education: A Culture in Crisis* (New York: Oxford University Press, 2006); and Jason King, *Faith with Benefits: Hookup Culture on Catholic Campuses* (New York: Oxford University Press, 2016).
19. Glanzer, Rine, and Davignon, "Assessing the Denominational Identity of American Evangelical Colleges and Universities, Part I."
20. Morey and Piderit, *Catholic Higher Education*.
21. Ibid.
22. Perry L. Glanzer, Theodore Cockle, Britney Graber, Elijah Jeong, and Jessica Robinson, "Are Nondenominational Colleges More Liberal than Denominational Colleges? A Comparison of Faculty Beliefs," *Christian Higher Education* (forthcoming).
23. David Bebbington, *Evangelicalism in Modern Britain: A History from the 1730s to the 1980s* (London: Unwin Hyman, 1989).
24. Glanzer, Rine, and Davignon, "Assessing the Denominational Identity of American Evangelical Colleges and Universities, Part I."
25. Ibid.
26. Samuel Schuman, *Seeing the Light: Religious Colleges in Twenty-First Century America* (Baltimore, MD: Johns Hopkins University Press, 2010), 145.
27. Rine, Glanzer, and Davignon, "Assessing the Denominational Identity of American Evangelical Colleges and Universities, Part II," 243–65.
28. Phil Davignon, Perry L. Glanzer, and Jesse Rine, "Assessing the Denominational Identity of American Evangelical Colleges and Universities, Part III: The Student Experience," *Christian Higher Education* 12, no. 5 (2013): 315–30.
29. American Association of University Professors, "1915 Declaration of Principles on Academic Freedom and Academic Tenure," http://www.aaup.org/AAUP/pubsres/policydocs/contents/1915.htm.
30. John G. Stackhouse, "CAUT versus Trinity Western," *University Affairs* 51, no. 1 (2010): 37, http://www.universityaffairs.ca/caut-versus-trinity-western.aspx.
31. James Hunter, *The Death of Character: Moral Education in an Age Without Good or Evil* (New York: Basic Books, 2000), 155.
32. Ibid.
33. Ibid., 276.
34. For a more extended review of this evidence, see Perry L. Glanzer and Todd C. Ream, *Christianity and Moral Identity in Higher Education* (New York: Palgrave Macmillan, 2009).
35. John Templeton Foundation, ed., *Colleges That Encourage Character Development* (Radnor, PA: Templeton Foundation Press, 1999).
36. Kevin M. Eagan, Ellen B. Stolzenberg, Jennifer Berdan Lozano, Melissa C. Aragon, Maria R. Suchard, and Sylvia Hurtado, *The American College Teacher: National Norms for the 2013–2014 HERI Faculty Survey* (Los Angeles: Higher Education Research Institute, UCLA, 2014), 32.

37. Allen Fisher, "Religious and Moral Education at Three Kinds of Liberal Arts Colleges: A Comparison of Curricula in Presbyterian, Evangelical, and Religiously Unaffiliated Liberal Arts Colleges," *Religious Education* 90, no. 1 (Winter 1995): 30–49.
38. George Kuh, "Do Environments Matter? A Comparative Analysis of the Impress of Different Types of Colleges and Universities on Character," *Journal of College and Character* 1, no. 4 (2002). doi:10.2202/1940-1639.1277. https://naspa.tandfonline.com/doi/pdf/10.2202/1940-1639.1277?needAccess=true; and Donna Freitas, *Sex and the Soul: Juggling Sexuality, Spirituality, Romance, and Religion on America's College Campuses* (New York: Oxford University Press, 2008).
39. Previous studies of student moral reasoning using Kohlbergian developmental classifications have found that private liberal arts colleges, most of which were religious, demonstrated the greatest gains in moral reasoning. Most of the liberal arts colleges in the study by McNeel (and reanalyzed by Pascarella and Terenzini) were Christian colleges with strong commitments to developing students' Christian faith and moral lives (e.g., Alverno College, Bethel College, Houghton College, Messiah College, Wheaton College). Steven P. McNeel, "College Teaching and Student Moral Development," in *Moral Development in the Professions: Psychology and Applied Ethics*, ed. James R. Rest and Darcia Narvaez (Hillsdale, NJ: Lawrence Erlbaum Associates Publishers, 1994), 26–47; and Ernest T. Pascarella and Patrick T. Terenzini, *How College Affects Students: A Third Decade of Research* (San Francisco: Jossey-Bass, 2005), 2:351–52.
40. Hardwick-Day, *Brand Archeology: Excavating for Position, Persona, and Attitude* (Minneapolis, MN: Hardwick-Day Publishers, 2003).
41. For a more extended review of this evidence, see Glanzer and Ream, *Christianity and Moral Identity in Higher Education*, chs. 6 and 7.
42. Farran Powell and Briana Boyington, "Why Enrollment Is Rising at Large Christian Colleges," *US News & World Report*, December 6, 2017, https://www.usnews.com/education/best-colleges/articles/2017-12-06/why-enrollment-is-rising-at-large-christian-colleges.
43. Alec MacGillis, "How Liberty University Built a Billion-dollar Empire Online," *New York Times*, April 17, 2018, https://www.nytimes.com/2018/04/17/magazine/how-liberty-university-built-a-billion-dollar-empire-online.html.
44. Ashley A. Smith, "Religious University and 2-Year College," *Inside Higher Ed*, August 23, 2017, www.insidehighered.com/news/2017/08/23/growing-number-religious-universities-offer-two-year-degrees.
45. Based on IPEDS institutional self-report data on degree-granting, religiously-affiliated institutions in the United States. Excluded from this comparison group were Roman Catholic, Mormon, Seventh Day Adventist, Unitarian, and Universalist institutions.
46. See, for example, Glanzer, "Giving Christian Universities a Scarlet Letter."
47. See Perry L. Glanzer, "Searching for the Soul of English Universities: An Analysis of Christian Higher Education in England," *British Journal of Educational Studies* 56 (June 2008): 163–83; and Joel C. Carpenter, Perry L. Glanzer, and Nick Lantinga, eds.,

Christian Higher Education: A Global Reconnaissance (Grand Rapids, MI: William B. Eerdmans Publishing Company, 2014).
48. Carpenter, Glanzer, and Lantinga, *Christian Higher Education*.
49. Ken Bain, *What the Best College Teachers Do* (Cambridge, MA: Harvard University Press, 2004).
50. Jacobsen and Jacobsen, *No Longer Invisible*.
51. Alexander W. Astin, Helen S. Astin, and Jennifer Lindholm *Cultivating the Spirit: How College Can Enhance Students' Inner Lives* (San Francisco: Jossey-Bass, 2011), 6.
52. "Best Colleges," *U.S. News and World Report*, https://www.usnews.com/best-colleges. Indeed, professors at evangelical institutions lament the state of evangelical thinking in their colleges. See, for example, Mark A. Noll, *The Scandal of the Evangelical Mind* (Grand Rapids, MI: William B. Eerdmans Publishing Company, 1994).
53. We recognize that many would be quite resistant to this characterization, since their academic freedom protections are strong enough that their mentality would be very different than, say, that of K–12 teachers.
54. Glanzer and Ream. *Christianity and Moral Identity in Higher Education*.
55. Ibid. See also Perry L. Glanzer, review of *Educating Citizens: Preparing America's Undergraduates for Lives of Moral Responsibility*, by Anne Colby, Thomas Ehrlich, Elizabeth Beaumont, and Jason Stephens, *Journal of Research in Character Education* 1, no. 1 (2003): 57–60.
56. George Yancey, *Compromising Scholarship: Religious and Political Bias in American Higher Education* (Waco, TX: Baylor University Press, 2011). Yancey's study of faculty attitudes toward different Christian groups finds that the two groups faculty despise most are evangelicals and Christian fundamentalists (p. 123).
57. Matthew Burchett, "Religion, Spirituality, and Identity: A Study on the Experience of Graduate Student Identity Development" (PhD diss., University of Texas, Austin, 2017), 68.
58. C. John Sommerville, *The Decline of the Secular University* (New York: Oxford University Press, 2006); and Warren Nord, *Does God Make a Difference: Taking Religion Seriously in Our Schools and Universities* (New York: Oxford University Press, 2010).
59. bell hooks, *Teaching Community: A Pedagogy of Hope* (New York: Routledge, 2003), 176.
60. Burchett, "Religion, Spirituality, and Identity."
61. Marsden, *The Soul of the American University*, 412.
62. Heterodox Academy, "The Problem," https://heterodoxacademy.org/the-problem/.
63. Ibid.
64. Burchett, "Religion, Spirituality, and Identity."
65. MacIntyre, *Three Rival Versions of Moral Enquiry*, 234.
66. We take this phrase from James McClendon, *Ethics* (Nashville, TN: Abingdon Press, 1986), 143.
67. Augustine, *Confessions*, trans. John Ryan (New York: Image Books, 1960).

68. Parker J. Palmer, *To Know as We Are Known: A Spirituality of Education* (San Francisco: Harper and Row Publishers, 1983), 1.

When Christian Teaching Is Really Outrageous

1. Joel C. Carpenter, Perry L. Glanzer, and Nick Lantinga, eds., *Christian Higher Education: A Global Reconnaissance* (Grand Rapids, MI: William B. Eerdmans Publishing Company, 2014).
2. The John Paul II Catholic University of Lublin, "History of the University," http://www.kul.pl/university-history,249.html, accessed November 15, 2018.
3. The John Paul II Catholic University of Lublin, "Catholic University of Lublin Mission Statement," 2009, www.kul.lublin.pl/uk/statement.html, accessed May 1, 2010 (no longer active).
4. S. Slantcheva and D. C. Levy, *Private Higher Education in Post-Communist Europe: In Search of Legitimacy* (New York: Palgrave Macmillan Publishers, 2007). KUL received financial support from the Polish episcopate, Polish churches, a private foundation called the Potulicka Foundation, and the western Friends of the Catholic University of Lublin society. John Paul II Catholic University of Lublin, "History of University," 2018. See, for example, http://www.tpkul.com/culhome.htm, accessed November 15, 2018.
5. John Paul II Catholic University of Lublin, "History of the University."
6. The phrase, of course, comes from Paulo Friere's well-known work, *Pedagogy of the Oppressed*, trans. Myra Bergman Ramos (New York: Continuum, 1993).
7. John Connelly, *Captive University: The Sovietisation of East German, Czech, and Polish Higher Education, 1945–56* (Chapel Hill: University of North Carolina Press, 2000), 220.
8. John Paul II Catholic University of Lublin, "History of the University."
9. The John Paul II Catholic University of Lublin, "The Period of the People's Republic of Poland," http://www.kul.pl/the-period-of-people-s-republic-of-poland,art_40709.html, accessed November 15, 2018.
10. George Wiegel, *Witness to Hope: The Biography of John Paul II* (New York: Cliff Street Books, 1999).
11. Yu Jie, "China's Christian Culture," *First Things* (August 2016), www.firstthings.com/article/2016/08/chinas-christian-future.
12. Ibid.
13. Ibid.
14. Ibid.
15. Ibid.
16. Ibid.
17. Ibid.
18. Ibid.

Appendix

1. For a report based on some findings from this survey, see Perry L. Glanzer, Jesse Rine, and Phil Davignon, "Assessing the Denominational Identity of American Evangelical Colleges and Universities, Part I: Denominational Patronage and Institutional Policy," *Christian Higher Education* 12, no. 3 (2013): 182–202.
2. For a summary of the method for this portion of the study, see Jesse Rine, Perry L. Glanzer, and Phil Davignon, "Assessing the Denominational Identity of American Evangelical Colleges and Universities, Part II: Faculty Perspectives and Practices," *Christian Higher Education* 12, no. 4 (2013): 243–65. It should be noted that the results reported in this article pertain only to the faculty respondents working with denominational institutions.
3. Sharlene J. Hesse-Biber, *The Practice of Qualitative Research: Engaging Students in the Research Process*, 3rd ed. (Los Angeles: Sage Publications, 2017).
4. Johnny Saldaña, *The Coding Manual for Qualitative Researchers*, 2nd ed. (Los Angeles: SAGE Publications, 2016).
5. Ibid.
6. Hennie Boeije, *Analysis in Qualitative Research* (Los Angeles: Sage Publications, 2010), 109.
7. National Center for Education Statistics, *Integrated Postsecondary Education Data System* (Washington, DC: US Department of Education, Office of Educational Research and Improvement, National Center for Education Statistics, 2013).
8. Institutional researchers who did not wish to contact all faculty were given the option of sending the invitation letter to a random sample. However, to our knowledge, none of the participating institutions chose to exercise this option.
9. An additional 45 eligible respondents were excluded from the sample because they failed to correctly identify the denominational status of their current institution, which prevented them from receiving a significant number of survey questions relating to denominational identity due to skip logics. Moreover, this phenomenon was not limited to faculty at church-related colleges. Among the full sample of participants in the faculty survey (n = 2,255), 5.7 percent misidentified the denominational status of their current institution. Although beyond the scope of this particular article, the apparent presence of "denominational confusion" among Christian college faculty (i.e., believing that one's employer is denominationally affiliated when it is not, and vice versa) invites further investigation.
10. Glanzer, Rine, and Davignon, "Assessing the Denominational Identity of American Evangelical Colleges and Universities, Part I."
11. Ibid.

Select Bibliography

American Association of University Professors. "1915 Declaration of Principles on Academic Freedom and Academic Tenure." https://www.aaup.org/ NR/rdonlyres/ A6520A9D-0A9A-47B3-B550-C006B5B224E7/0/1915Declaration.pdf.
American Association of University Professors. "1940 Statement of Principles on Academic Freedom and Tenure." http://www.aaup.org/AAUP/pubsres/ policydocs/ contents/1940statement.htm.
American Association of University Professors. "Statement on Professional Ethics." Last updated 2009. https://www.aaup.org/report/statement-professional-ethics.
American Association of University Professors. "Statement on Teaching Evaluation." *AAUP Bulletin* 61, no. 2 (August 1975): 200–202.
Anderson, Chris. *Teaching as Believing: Faith in the University*. Waco, TX: Baylor University Press, 2004.
Anderson, Robert D. *European Universities from the Enlightenment to 1914*. New York: Oxford University Press, 2004.
Angell, Stephen W., and Ben Pink Dandelion, eds. *The Oxford Handbook of Quaker Studies*. New York: Oxford University Press, 2013.
Apple, Michael. *Ideology and Curriculum*. 2nd ed. New York: Routledge, 1990.
Astin, Alexander W., Helen S. Astin, and Jennifer Lindholm. *Cultivating the Spirit: How College Can Enhance Students' Inner Lives*. San Francisco: Jossey-Bass, 2011.
Bain, Ken. *What the Best College Teachers Do*. Cambridge, MA: Harvard University Press, 2004.
Bebbington, David. *Evangelicalism in Modern Britain: A History from the 1730s to the 1980s*. London: Unwin Hyman,1989.
Bloom, Benjamin S., ed. *Taxonomy of Educational Objectives: The Classification of Educational Goals by a Committee of College and University Examiners*. New York: Longmans, 1956.
Bok, Derek. *Beyond the Ivory Tower: Social Responsibilities of the Modern University*. Boston: Harvard University Press, 1984.
Cahn, Stephen. *Saints and Scamps: Ethics in Academia*. Totowa, NJ: Rowman and Littlefield, 2010.
Carpenter, Joel C., Perry L. Glanzer, and Nick Lantinga, eds. *Christian Higher Education: A Global Reconnaissance*. Grand Rapids, MI: William B. Eerdmans Publishing Company, 2014.
Colby, Anne, Thomas Ehrlich, Elizabeth Beaumont, and Jason Stephens. *Educating Citizens: Preparing America's Undergraduates for Lives of Moral Responsibility*. San Francisco: Jossey-Bass, 2003.
Crisp, Oliver D., Gavin D'Costa, Mervyn Davies, and Peter Hampson. *Christianity and the Disciplines: The Transformation of the University*. New York: T. & T. Clark Publishers, 2012.

De Ridder-Symoens, Hilde, ed. *A History of the University in Europe*. Vol. 1, *Universities in the Middle Ages*. Cambridge, UK: Cambridge University Press, 1992.

De Ridder-Symoens, Hilde, ed. *A History of the University in Europe*. Vol. 2, *Universities in Early Modern Europe, 1500–1800*. Cambridge, UK: Cambridge University Press, 1996.

deMarrais, Kathleen, and Stephen D. Lapan. *Foundations for Research: Methods of Inquiry in Education and the Social Sciences*. Mahwah, NJ: Erbarum Associates, 2004.

Dewey, John, and James Tufts. *Ethics*. New York: Holt, Rinehart, and Winston, 1908.

Dougherty, Kevin D., Byron R. Johnson, and Edward C. Polson. "Recovering the Lost: Remeasuring U.S. Religious Affiliation." *Journal for the Scientific Study of Religion* 46, no. 4 (2007): 483–99. doi:10.1111/j.1468-5906.2007.00373.x.

Edwards, Mark U., Jr. *Religion on Our Campuses: A Professor's Guide to Communities, Conflicts and Promising Conversations*. New York: Palgrave Macmillan, 2006.

Elshtain, Jean B. "Does, or Should, Teaching Reflect the Religious Perspective of the Teacher?" In *Religion, Scholarship, and Higher Education: Perspectives, Models, and Future Prospects*, edited by Andrea Sterk, 193–201. South Bend, IN: University of Notre Dame Press, 2002.

Fish, Stanley. *Save the World on Your Own Time*. New York: Oxford University Press, 2008.

Fisher, Allen. "Religious and Moral Education at Three Kinds of Liberal Arts Colleges: A Comparison of Curricula in Presbyterian, Evangelical, and Religiously Unaffiliated Liberal Arts Colleges." *Religious Education* 90, no. 1 (Winter 1995): 30–49.

Fisher, Berenice M. *No Angel in the Classroom: Teaching Through Feminist Discourse*. Lanham, MD: Rowman and Littlefield Publishers, 2001.

Fitzpatrick, John C., ed. *Writings of George Washington, 1745–1799*. Vol. 35. Washington, DC: Government Printing Office, 1940.

Foster, Richard J. *Streams of Living Water: Celebrating the Great Traditions of Christian Faith*. San Francisco: HarperCollins, 2001.

Glanzer, Perry L. "Building the Good Life: Using Identities to Frame Moral Education in Higher Education." *Journal of College and Character* 14, no. 2 (2013): 177–84. doi:10.1515/jcc-2013-0023.

Glanzer, Perry L. "Giving Christian Universities a Scarlet Letter: Examining the Canadian Association of University Teachers' Opposition to Faith-Based Hiring." *Religious Education* 108, no. 2 (2013): 148–63.

Glanzer, Perry L. *The Quest for Russia's Soul*. Waco, TX: Baylor University Press, 2002.

Glanzer, Perry L. "Searching for the Soul of English Universities: An Analysis of Christian Higher Education in England." *British Journal of Educational Studies* 56 (June 2008): 163–83.

Glanzer, Perry L., Jonathan P. Hill, and Byron R. Johnson. *The Quest for Purpose: The Collegiate Search for a Meaningful Life*. Albany: State University of New York Press, 2017.

Glanzer, Perry L., and Andrew J. Milson. "Legislating the Good: A Survey and Evaluation of Contemporary Character Education Legislation." *Educational Policy* 20, no. 3 (2006): 525–50. doi:10.1177/0895904805284115.

Glanzer, Perry L., and Konstantin Petrenko. "Resurrecting the Russian University's Soul: The Emergence of Eastern Orthodox Universities and Their Distinctive Approaches to Keeping Faith with Their Religious Tradition." *Christian Scholar's Review* 36 (Spring 2007): 263–84. doi:http://www.csreview.org/XXXVI3/glanzer.

Glanzer, Perry L., and Todd C. Ream. *Christianity and Moral Identity in Higher Education.* New York: Palgrave Macmillan, 2009.
Glanzer, Perry L., Jesse Rine, and Phil Davignon. "Assessing the Denominational Identity of American Evangelical Colleges and Universities, Part I: Denominational Patronage and Institutional Policy." *Christian Higher Education* 12, no. 3 (2013): 182–202. doi:10.1080/15363759.2013.785871.
Glazer, Steven. *The Heart of Learning: Spirituality in Education.* New York: Putnam Press, 1999.
Glenn, Charles L. *The Myth of the Common School.* Amherst: University of Massachusetts Press, 1988.
Hart, D. G. *The University Gets Religion: Religious Studies in American Higher Education.* Baltimore, MD: Johns Hopkins University Press, 1994.
Haskell, Thomas L. *The Emergence of Professional Social Science: The American Social Science Association and the Nineteenth-Century Crisis of Authority.* Urbana: University of Chicago Press, 1977.
Hauerwas, Stanley. *After Christendom.* Nashville, TN: Abingdon Press, 1991.
Hauerwas, Stanley. *Sanctify Them in the Truth: Holiness Exemplified.* Nashville, TN: Abingdon University Press, 1998.
Hawkins, Hugh. *Pioneer: A History of the Johns Hopkins University, 1874–1889.* Ithaca, NY: Cornell University Press, 1960.
Haynes, Stephen R. ed. *Professing in the Postmodern Academy: Faculty and the Future of Church-Related Colleges.* Waco, TX: Baylor University Press, 2002.
Higton, Michael. *A Theology of Higher Education.* New York: Oxford University Press, 2013.
Hofstadter, Richard, and Wilson Smith, eds. *American Higher Education: A Documentary History.* Vol. 1. Chicago: University of Chicago Press, 1961.
Holmes, Arthur. *The Idea of a Christian College.* Rev. ed. Grand Rapids, MI: William B. Eerdmans Publishing Company, 1987.
hooks, bell. *Teaching Community: A Pedagogy of Hope.* New York: Routledge, 2003.
hooks, bell. *Teaching to Transgress: Education as the Practice of Freedom.* New York: Routledge, 1994.
Hughes, Richard T. *How Christian Faith Can Sustain the Life of the Mind.* Grand Rapids, MI: William B. Eerdmans Publishing Company, 2001.
Hughes, Richard T., and William B. Adrian. *Models for Christian Higher Education: Strategies for Success in the Twenty-First Century.* Grand Rapids, MI: William B. Eerdmans Publishing Company, 1997.
Hunter, James. *The Death of Character: Moral Education in an Age Without Good or Evil.* New York: Basic Books, 2000.
The Incredibles. Directed by Brad Bird, 2004. Emeryville, CA: Pixar Animation Studios, 2005. DVD.
Jacobsen, Douglas, and Rhonda Hustedt Jacobsen, eds. *The American University in a Postsecular Age.* New York: Oxford University Press, 2008.
Jacobsen, Douglas, and Rhonda Hustedt Jacobsen. *No Longer Invisible: Religion in University Education.* New York: Oxford University Press, 2012.
Jacobsen, Douglas, and Rhonda Hustedt Jacobsen. *Scholarship and Christian Faith: Enlarging the Conversation.* New York: Oxford University Press, 2004.
Jenlick, Patrick M. ed. *Teacher Identity and the Struggle for Recognition: Meeting the Challenges of a Diverse Society.* Lanham, MD: Rowman and Littlefield, 2014.

Jie, Yu. "China's Christian Culture." Trans. H. C. Hsu. *First Things* (August 2016). www.firstthings.com/article/2016/08/chinas-christian-future.

King, Jason. *Faith with Benefits: Hookup Culture on Catholic Campuses*. New York: Oxford University Press, 2016.

Klinge, Matti. "Teachers." In *A History of the University in Europe*. Vol. 3, *Universities in the Nineteenth and Early Twentieth Centuries*, edited by Walter Rüegg, 123–62. Cambridge, UK: Cambridge University Press, 2004.

Kuhn, Thomas. *The Structure of Scientific Revolutions*. Chicago: University of Chicago Press, 1962.

Kuklick, Bruce. Review of *The Soul of the American University: From Protestant Establishment to Established Nonbelief*, by George M. Mardsen. *Method and Theory in the Study of Religion* 8, no. 1 (1996): 79–84. doi:10.1163/157006896X00107.

Larsen, Timothy. "No Christianity Please, We're Academics." *Inside Higher Education*, July 30, 2010. https://www.insidehighered.com/views/2010/07/30/no-christianity-please-were-academics.

Light, Penny, Tracy Nichalas, and Renée Bondy. *Feminist Pedagogy in Higher Education*. Waterloo, ON: Wilfrid Laurier University Press, 2015.

Lindholm, Jennifer A. *The Quest for Meaning and Wholeness: Spiritual and Religious Connections in the Lives of College Faculty*. San Francisco: Jossey-Bass, 2014.

MacIntyre, Alasdair. *After Virtue*. 3rd ed. South Bend, IN: University of Notre Dame Press, 2007.

MacIntyre, Alasdair C. *Three Rival Versions of Moral Enquiry: Encyclopaedia, Genealogy, and Tradition*. Notre Dame, IN: University of Notre Dame Press, 1990.

Marsden, George M. "Liberating Academic Freedom." *First Things* 88 (December 1998): 11–14.

Marsden, George M. *The Outrageous Idea of Christian Scholarship*. New York: Oxford University Press, 1997.

McConnell, Michael M. "Academic Freedom in Religious Colleges and Universities." In *Freedom and Tenure in the Academy*, edited by W. W. Van Alstyne, 303–24. Durham, NC: Duke University Press, 1993.

McGreevey, John T. *American Jesuits and the World: How an Embattled Religious Order Made Modern Catholicism Global*. Princeton, NJ: Princeton University Press, 2016.

McNeel, Steven P. "College Teaching and Student Moral Development." In *Moral Development in the Professions: Psychology and Applied Ethics*, edited by James R. Rest and Darcia Narvaez, 26–47. Hillsdale, NJ: Lawrence Erlbaum Associates Publishers, 1994.

Moberly, Walter. *The Crisis of the University*. London: SCM, 1949.

Morey, Melanie, and John Piderit. *Catholic Higher Education: A Culture in Crisis*. New York: Oxford University Press, 2006.

Mouw, Richard. *The God Who Commands: A Study in Divine Command Ethics*. South Bend, IN: University of Notre Dame Press, 1990.

Naugle, David K. *Worldview: The History of a Concept*. Grand Rapids, MI: William B. Eerdmans Publishing Company, 2002.

Niebuhr, H. Richard. *Christ and Culture*. Exp. 50th anniv. ed. San Francisco: Harper One Publishers, 1975.

Noddings, Nel. *Educating for Intelligent Belief or Unbelief*. New York: Teachers College Press, 1993.

Noll, Mark. *The Scandal of the Evangelical Mind*. Grand Rapids, MI: William B. Eerdmans Publishing Company, 1995.

Nord, Warren. *Does God Make a Difference? Taking Religion Seriously in Our Schools and Universities*. New York: Oxford University Press, 2010.
Nord, Warren, and Charles Haynes. *Taking Religion Seriously Across the Curriculum*. Alexandria, VA: Association for Supervision and Curriculum Development, 1998.
Novick, Peter. *That Noble Dream: The "Objectivity Question" and the American Historical Profession*. New York: Cambridge University Press, 1988.
O'Malley, John W., S.J. *The Jesuits: A History from Ignatius to the Present*. Lanham, MD: Rowman and Littlefield, 2014.
Ostrander, Rick. *Why College Matters to God: An Introduction to the Christian College*. Rev. ed. Abilene, TX: Abilene Christian University Press, 2012.
Palmer, Parker J. *The Courage to Teach*. San Francisco: Jossey-Bass, 2007.
Palmer, Parker J. *To Know as We Are Known: A Spirituality of Education*. San Francisco: Harper and Row, 1986.
Pascarella, Ernest T., and Patrick T. Terenzini. *How College Affects Students: A Third Decade of Research*. Vol. 2. San Francisco: Jossey-Bass, 2005.
Perry, William G., Jr. *Forms of Intellectual and Ethical Development in the College Years: A Scheme*. San Francisco: Jossey-Bass, (1968) 1999.
Peterson, Christopher, and Martin Seligman. *Character Strengths and Virtues: A Handbook and Classification*. New York: Oxford University Press, 2004.
Postman, Neil. *The End of Education*. New York: Vintage Books, 1995.
Rawls, John. *Political Liberalism*. New York: Columbia University Press, 1996.
Ream, Todd C., and Perry L. Glanzer. *Christian Faith and Scholarship: An Exploration of Contemporary Developments*. ASHE-ERIC Higher Education Report. San Francisco: Jossey-Bass, 2007.
Reuben, Julie. *The Making of the Modern University: Intellectual Transformation and the Marginalization of Morality*. Chicago: University of Chicago Press, 1996.
Rine, Jesse, Perry L. Glanzer, and Phil Davignon. "Assessing the Denominational Identity of American Evangelical Colleges and Universities, Part II: Faculty Perspectives and Practices." *Christian Higher Education* 12, no. 4 (2013): 243–65.
Ringenberg, William C. *The Christian College: A History of Protestant Higher Education in America*. 2nd ed. Grand Rapids, MI: Baker Academic Press, 2006.
Rüegg, Walter, ed. *A History of the University in Europe*. Vol. 3, *Universities in the Nineteenth and Early Twentieth Centuries, 1800–1945*. Cambridge: Cambridge University Press, 1996.
Savonick, Danica. "Timekeeping as Feminist Pedagogy." *Inside Higher Ed*, June 27, 2017. https://www.insidehighered.com/advice/2017/06/27/how-social-hierarchies-influence-who-gets-most-time-speak-classrooms-essay.
Schuman, Samuel. *Seeing the Light: Religious Colleges in Twenty-First Century America*. Baltimore, MD: Johns Hopkins University Press, 2010.
Sloan, Douglas. "The Teaching of Ethics in the American Undergraduate Curriculum, 1876–1976." In *Ethics Teaching in Higher Education*, edited by Daniel Callahan and Sissela Bok, 1–57. New York: Plenum Press, 1980.
Smith, David I. *On Christian Teaching*. Grand Rapids, MI: William B. Eerdmans Publishing Company, 2017.
Smith, David I., and James K. A. Smith, eds. *Teaching and Christian Practices: Reshaping Faith and Learning*. Grand Rapids, MI: William B. Eerdmans Publishing Company, 2011.
Solomon, Julie R. *Objectivity in the Making: Francis Bacon and the Politics of Inquiry*. Baltimore, MD: Johns Hopkins University Press, 1998.

Sommerville, C. John. *The Decline of the Secular University*. New York: Oxford University Press, 2006.
Taylor, Charles. *A Secular Age*. Cambridge, MA: Harvard University Press, 2007.
Taylor, Charles. *The Sources of the Self: The Making of Modern Identity*. Cambridge, MA: Harvard University Press, 1989.
Tewksbury, Donald G. *The Founding of American Colleges and Universities before the Civil War*. New York: Teacher College Press, 1932.
Thiessen, Elmer. *In Defense of Religious Schools and Colleges*. Montreal: McGill-Queen's University Press, 2002.
Thiessen, Elmer. *Teaching for Commitment: Liberal Education, Indoctrination and Christian Nurture*. Montreal: McGill-Queen's University Press, 1993.
Van Dyk, John. *The Craft of Christian Teaching*. Sioux City, IA: Dordt Press, 2000.
Weber, Max. "The 'Objectivity' of Knowledge in Social Science and Social Policy." In *From Max Weber: Essays in Sociology*, edited and translated by H. H. Gerth and C. Wright Mills, 359–404. New York: Oxford University Press, 1946.
Weber, Max. "Science as a Vocation." In *From Max Weber: Essays in Sociology*, edited and translated by H. H. Gerth and C. Wright Mills, 129–56. New York: Oxford University Press, 1946.
Wellman, Chad. "For Moral Clarity Don't Look to Universities." *The Chronicle of Higher Education*, August 15, 2017. http://www.chronicle.com/article/For-Moral-Clarity-Dont-Look/240921?cid=wcontentgrid_hp_1b/.
Wesley, Edgar B. *Proposed: The University of the United States*. Minneapolis: University of Minnesota Press, 1936.
Wiegel, George. *Witness to Hope: The Biography of John Paul II*. New York: Cliff Street Books, 1999.
Williamson, G. I. *The Westminster Shorter Catechism: For Study Classes*. Phillipburg, NJ: P. & R. Publishing Company, 2003.
Wolters, Al. *Creation Regained: Biblical Basics for a Reformational Worldview*. Rev. ed. Grand Rapids, MI: William B. Eerdmans Publishing Company, 2005.
Wolterstorff, Nicholas. *Educating for Shalom: Essays on Christian Higher Education*. Edited by Clarence Joldersma and Gloria Stronks. Grand Rapids, MI: William B. Eerdmans Publishing Company, 2004.
Wolterstorff, Nicholas. *Reason within the Bounds of Religion*. Grand Rapids, MI: William B. Eerdmans Publishing Company, 1987.
Yancey, George. *Compromising Scholarship: Religious and Political Bias in American Higher Education*. Waco, TX: Baylor University Press, 2011.
Yoder, John Howard. *The Politics of Jesus*. Grand Rapids, MI: William B. Eerdmans Publishing Company, 1972.

Index

Abington Township v. Schemp, 139
Abraham Kuyper, 93*b*
academic disciplines
   African American studies, 131
   arts, 3, 21–22, 49, 53, 56–57, 64, 156
   gender studies, 131
   humanities, x, 35, 148, 201, 208
   SCIENCES, 21–22, 27, 35, 45, 49–50, 64, 133, 148, 156
   social sciences, 156, 208
academic freedom, 4–5, 19, 22, 39, 135–36, 138, 157, 176–78, 192, 195
academic honesty, 156
academic integrity, 73, 90–91, 156
academic standards, 73, 165
"academicize," 7–8
accreditation, 174–75, 194–95
Adam and Eve, 159
administrators and leaders, university, 6–7, 18–19, 22–23, 25–30, 104, 128, 130, 134–35, 156, 178–79, 180–81, 194
"All Truth is God's Truth," 51, 87, 116, 177
Alonzi, Peter, 81–82, 83–84
Alumni, 127, 192, 201
American Association of University Professors, the (AAUP), 4–5, 57, 134, 176–77, 190
   on Academic Freedom, 4–5, 176–77, 190
   on Professional Ethics, 5, 57
   on Teacher Evaluation, 134
Anderson, Chris, 10–11, 32, 143, 156–57, 169
Anderson, Robert, 27–28
"Arena of Theological Gladiators," 23–24, 198
Aristotle, 72, 154
Asbury University, 187
Augustine, St., 198
Azusa Pacific University, 186–87

Bacon, Francis, 27–28
Baylor University, 187, 192
behavior
   Christ-like, 169
   professional, 73
   unprofessional, 7
beliefs
   formative, 7
   religious, 23–24, 117, 196–97
Bellah, Robert, 172–73
bell hooks, 32–34, 155, 160–61, 164, 196–97
Bible, the, 32, 43–44, 46–48, 68–71, 83–84, 108–9, 114–17, 125, 139, 146, 159–62, 167, 170, 189–90, 192, 199, 204–5
Bible colleges, 187
Bill of Rights, The, 23–24
Biola University, 187
Bloom's taxonomy, 117
Bonhoeffer, Dietrich, 203
Brown University (also College of Rhode Island), 21, 22–23, 198
Burtchaell, James, 104

Cahn, Steven, 5, 10, 57, 153–54, 158–59
Call, Carolyn, 54–55*b*, 85–86*b*
calling, 49–50, 51–52, 57–58, 106–7, 113–14, 121, 124, 133, 142, 199–200
Calvin College, 12–13, 68, 93*b*, 192
Canadian higher education, 20–21, 40, 194–95
Catholicism, 17–18, 107–8, 109, 186–87
China, 176, 202–5
Christ, as model, 72, 94–95, 96, 97*b*, 124, 137, 204–5
"Christianese," 58
Christian scriptures, 46, 47–48, 58, 66–67, 71, 72, 83, 84, 86, 92, 109, 114–16, 121–22

Christian transformation professors, 62, 63–65, 68, 71–74, 78–79, 83, 84–86, 99–101, 119–24, 125–26, 165–66, 167, 168–69, 202
Chronicle of Higher Education, The, 127, 174–75
Church of the Brethren, 108, 120, 124
Church, the (corporate), 17–21, 22, 24–25, 47–48, 77, 78, 84, 86, 98*b*, 108, 115, 125, 128, 136, 149, 179–80, 202, 203–4
citizenship, as goal of education, 3, 129
Clark, Tom C., 139
classroom
  content, 18, 71
  practices, 1, 4–5, 6–7, 10, 13–14, 18, 22, 32, 33–34, 37, 40, 46–47, 48, 49, 53, 54*b*, 55–57, 62, 71, 73, 85–93*b*, 88–95, 100, 106, 111–12, 117, 121, 123, 125–26, 129–30, 135, 138, 140, 143, 145, 147, 149–51, 153–56, 158, 167, 169, 172, 178–79, 183, 185, 194, 196–97, 198, 199, 207
  meditation, 54*b*, 83, 141
co-curricular, 178
coding, 207–8
  axial, 207–8
  holistic, 207
  meta-code, 207–8
  qualitative, 101
Colorado Christian University, 187
Columbia University (King's College), 20–21, 22
communism, 201–2
community
  academic, xi, 51–52, 178–79
  Christian, 87, 115, 161
"common teacher" myth, 24
"comprehensive moral culture," 191–92
confession, 22, 23–24, 31, 99–100, 150, 154, 186–87, 202–3
Congress, 138–39
Conn, Peter, 174–75
constrained disagreement, 163, 174, 180–81, 190
Council of Christian Colleges and Universities, The (CCCU), 11–12, 14–15, 39, 207, 208, 211–12
course content (academic), 71, 121
course objectives (academic), 40, 41*t*, 62–63, 64, 66–67, 68, 74, 84, 94, 101–2, 114, 120, 124, 179
creation, doctrine of, 18, 23, 44, 45, 49–50, 51, 52, 55–56, 66–67, 74–75, 99, 113, 116, 121, 187, 197
creativity, 46–47, 52, 53, 199–200
critical thinking
  Christian, 42–43, 66, 119, 152
  general, 1–2, 4–5, 134–35, 148–49
Cunningham, Eric, 60–61, 62, 63
cura personalis, 98*b*
curriculum, 14–15, 24, 25, 36, 52, 56, 62, 64, 66–67, 70, 71, 74, 75, 77–79, 81, 82, 100–1, 116, 119–20, 121, 125, 130, 132, 154, 164, 165–66, 178, 180–81, 192, 199, 204

Danticat, Edwidge, 98*b*
Dartmouth University, 20–21, 22–23
deism, 24, 25
democratic education, 122
Department of Education, 193
devotional reading, 83, 84, 121–22, 139, 167
Diekema, Anthony, 176
dignity, of human's, 64–65, 107, 137, 138, 150–51, 168, 199–200, 203
discipleship, 10–11, 56–57, 114, 117, 142–43
disputatio, 18
diversity, x, 22, 23, 25–26, 45, 57, 68–69, 104, 105–6, 117, 128, 129, 131–32, 137, 144, 171, 174, 180–82, 197
  ideological, 131–32
Divinity degree, 24, 136
Dominican University, 80
Duke University, 178

economy, 129, 192–93
educational psychology, 66–67, 136
Edwards, Jr., Mark, U., 127, 139–40, 157–58
Ellsworth, Elizabeth, 97*b*

"empathetic understanding," 118, 144
engagement, students', xiii, 95, 98–99b, 122
epistemological humility, 103–4
Establishment Clause, 140
ethical thinking, 65, 91–92, 100–1
ethics, 5, 14–15, 18, 24, 36, 42, 47, 57, 64, 67, 72–73, 82, 84, 89, 94–95, 96–99, 97b, 120, 123, 145, 146, 153, 159, 162, 164–65, 171, 192
European Higher Education, 17, 27–28, 76, 200–1
evolution, 181
external validity, 212–13

faculty
  attitudes, 26, 94, 192
  development programs, 101, 131–32, 194
  ethics, 4–5, 18, 57, 67, 73, 83–84, 94–95, 153, 158, 164–65, 192
  faith animating learning, 13, 37
  German, 28, 68, 75, 88–89, 93b, 127
  informed teaching, 5–6, 114, 131, 175, 184, 196
  as voluntary, 109
fall, doctrine of, 44, 56, 58, 113, 114, 116–17, 121
favoritism, 120, 139, 141–42, 159, 178
fellowship, 54–55b, 84, 85–86b, 97b
First Amendment, 138–39, 140, 141–42, 157
Fish, Stanley, 6–10, 11, 12–13, 34–36, 125–26, 128, 135, 142–45, 146–48, 150–51, 159, 199–200
flat Earth perspective, 166
flourishing, human, 26, 100, 129, 143–44
formation, of students', 36, 40, 57, 70, 100–1, 190
freedom, 5–6, 18–19, 20, 23, 25–26, 27, 64, 80, 174, 176, 177, 178–80, 183, 190, 199–200, 203

George Fox University, 181–82
Georgetown University, 20–21, 178, 191
Gilman, Daniel Coit, 26–27
Glazer, Steven, 136

Gleason, Philip, 104
Goldberg, Arthur J., 139
"good life, The," 3, 29–30, 115, 128, 136, 144, 159
Gordon College, 187
grading, 87, 91, 92, 95–96, 100, 153, 170, 171
graduate education, xi, 97b, 130–32, 170–71, 189, 193, 196–97
"green chemistry," 157–58
grounded theory (as Method), 207

habituation, 132
"hanging out," 85b
Hart, D.G., 26–27
Harvard University, 26–27
Haskell, Robert, 27, 89
Hauerwas, Stanley, 35, 147–48, 163
Hegel, Georg Wilhelm Friedrich, 129
Herberg, Will, 196–97
"hermeneutics of suspicion," 158
Heterodox Academy, 149, 197
higher education
  types of
    denominational, 12, 22, 25–26, 109, 174, 180, 183, 185, 186–89, 190–91, 192, 207–8, 211–12
    faith-based, 6, 13, 38–39, 125–26, 131, 176, 177, 178, 188, 189–91
    pluralistic, ix, 5–8, 10–11, 12–13, 15–16, 23–24, 39, 100, 125–26, 128, 129–30, 131–34, 135, 136–39, 141, 142, 146, 148, 149, 150–51, 153–54, 156–60, 164–65, 166–67, 169, 171, 172, 174, 175, 176–77, 178–79, 180–83, 189, 190–92, 194, 198, 199–200, 202
    private, 125–26, 129, 137, 138–39, 175, 191–92, 195–96
    public, 1, 17, 24–27, 33, 72–73, 124, 125–26, 129, 132, 139, 141, 149, 175, 193, 204, 208
    state-funded, 1, 139
Higton, Mike, 56–57, 142–43
Himes, Michael, 111–12
hiring practices, 26, 176, 180–81, 187–88, 192, 193–94, 196

historical movements
  Civil War, 26, 187
  Cold War, 62
  Colonial Higher Education, 21–22, 198
  Early European, 17, 19–20
  Enlightenment, 19, 34, 157, 175
  French Revolution, 19
  governmental control, 18–19, 20, 23
  Holocaust, 166
  Protestant Reformation, 12–13, 18, 20–21
  Revolutionary War, 25–26
  World War I, 76
  World War II, 76, 201
Holy Spirit, 90, 94, 110–11
Hunter, James Davison, 191
Hus, Jon, 18

identity
  boundaries, 4, 8, 9–10, 11, 36, 103–4, 130, 139, 144, 153–54, 187–88
  commitment, 6–7, 10, 149, 150, 157–58, 159, 163–65, 167–68, 176, 194
  conflict, 2, 3, 34, 119, 163–64, 196–97
  congruence, 3, 11
  conversion, 136, 137–38, 139, 140, 141–45, 149–50, 155, 162, 169, 186–87, 196
  development, 36, 53, 55, 58, 65, 73–74, 78–79, 100–1, 137, 155, 192
  excellence, 2, 3, 6–7, 8, 35, 38, 39, 48–49, 95, 134, 136, 148, 197
  integration, 5–6, 12, 13, 114, 123, 129–30, 177
  intersection, 12
  prioritization, 19–20, 114, 116, 125, 154
  separation of, 33, 104, 105–6, 112
  types of
    academic, 36, 147, 164–65
    common, 103–4, 178
    economic, 154
      capitalist, 149
    ethnic
      American, 1–2, 10, 23, 26, 27
      German, 28, 70
      Hispanic, 27–28
      Islamic, 36
      Russian, 1–2, 67, 76, 103
      Southern, 42, 103
    extraprofessional, 128, 129–30, 133–34, 153–54, 167
    gender, 31–32, 52, 58, 132, 154, 157, 196–97, 213
      male, 32, 34, 58, 94, 208, 213
      female, 3, 12–13, 152
    national, 15, 19–20, 23, 26–27, 129, 154
    non-religious, 40, 104, 138–40, 141, 172–73
      agnostic, 137–38, 141, 160–61, 172–73, 189–90, 191
      atheist, 4–5, 25, 137–38, 141, 157, 160–61, 172–73, 189–91
      "nones," 104
    personal, 172
      golfer, 38
      musician, 38
    philosophical
      environmentalist, 2, 3, 4–5, 6–7, 11, 15, 113, 154–55, 157
      feminist, 2, 3, 4–5, 6–7, 11, 15, 36, 97b, 141, 149, 154–55, 164–65, 167–68, 175
      Marxist, 2, 3, 4–5, 6–7, 11, 15, 36, 141, 149
      materialist, 133, 149
      utilitarianist, 68–69, 80, 120, 149
    political
      citizen, 3, 20, 23, 36, 57, 100, 103–4, 129
      communist, 1, 67, 72, 166, 194–95, 201–4
      conservative, 157, 191, 196
      democrat, 2, 4–5
      liberal, 23–24, 131–32, 157, 191, 197
      libertarian, 6–7
      Marxist, 15, 36, 141, 149, 201–2
      republican, 2, 3, 4–5
    professional, 9, 27–29, 138, 142, 144, 149, 152, 159, 164, 199–200
      accountant, 131, 137, 197
      anthropologist, 161
      biologist, 27–28, 36, 129, 136, 194–95
      chemist, 12–13, 62–63, 75, 144, 157–58

dentist, 3, 154–55
educational psychologist, 66–67, 136
historian, 12–13, 36, 136, 137, 147
nurse, 61, 169
physicist, 149
psychologist, 27–28, 95, 136, 137, 149, 197
scholar, 13, 14, 27, 33–34, 38–39, 53, 57, 60, 139–40, 150–51, 155–56, 159, 165, 166, 169, 195
social worker, 136
sociologist, 36, 129, 144, 149
teacher, 3, 117
racial, 2, 154
　African American, 17, 32–33, 63, 131, 135
relational
　parent, 2–3, 7–8, 32–33, 53–55, 58, 77, 172–73
　sibling, 53, 57, 58, 59, 98b
　spouse, 2–3, 75–76, 128, 204–5
religious
　Anabaptist, 39, 105–6, 107, 109, 110–11, 114–15, 117–18, 120, 121–22, 123, 179–80
　Anglican, 15, 22–23, 105–6, 180
　Assemblies of God, 180–81
　Augustinian, 103, 121
　Baptist, 15, 25–27, 39, 41, 42, 104, 105–6, 109, 110–11, 114, 118, 119, 125, 170, 187–88, 191
　Buddhist, 141–42, 189–90
　Catholic, xi, 12–13, 15, 17–20, 27–28, 41, 101–2, 103, 105–6, 136, 178–79, 181, 186–87
　Christian, ix, 1–2, 5–6, 10, 12–13, 14–15, 26–27, 36–37, 38, 40–41, 42, 44, 59, 60, 62, 71, 74, 84–86, 87, 89, 96–99, 103–4, 105–6, 117, 119, 125–26, 142, 162, 167, 178, 180, 181–82, 186–87, 188–89, 202
　Church of Christ, 103, 105–6, 180–81
　Evangelical, 41–42, 107, 120, 123–24, 125, 187, 188
　Hindu, 116, 138, 141, 164–65
　Jewish, 2, 138, 175
　Lutheran, 104, 105–6
　Mennonite, 76, 77, 191
　Methodist, 25–27, 103
　Muslim, 2, 3, 138
　Nazarene, 107
　Orthodox, Eastern, 39, 103, 112, 186–87
　Pentecostal, 103, 105–6, 179
　Presbyterian, 12–13, 26–27, 103
　Quaker, 15, 107, 123–24, 125
　Reformed, 15, 105–6, 125, 180
　Unitarian, 25
　Wesleyan, 15, 105–6, 108, 125, 180
secular, ix–x, 19, 60, 71, 74, 141–42, 161–62, 166, 179, 189, 195, 196, 200–1
sexual, 52, 104, 132, 154, 196–97
social class, 58, 196
　working, 27–28
social identity, 196
spiritual, 133
ideological unity, 149
imagination, 77, 111–13, 128, 141
incarnation, 44, 78–79, 96, 110–11
inclusivity, 123
indoctrination, 10–11, 132, 139–40, 145, 158–59, 174
Institute of Education, London, 88
integration of faith and learning, 5–6, 12–13, 39, 82–83, 86, 100–1, 177, 193
integrity, x–xii, 4, 8, 11, 73, 87, 92, 130, 134, 138, 150–51, 162, 196, 199–200
interpretation, 58, 61–62, 67, 92, 113–14, 140, 156, 159, 160–62, 164–65, 168, 178–79, 207

Jacob, Ludwig Heinrich, 152
Jacobsen, Douglas, and Jacobsen, Rhonda, 78, 103, 105–6, 140, 178
Jefferson, Thomas, 23–25, 53, 198
Jie, Yu, 202–5
Johns Hopkins University, 26–27
journaling, 86, 122

K–12 education, 139, 167
Kelbert, Adaline, 75–78, 93b

Kingdom of God, 179–80
knowledge, sources of, 114, 116–17, 125
Kuklick, Bruce, 12–13
Kuyer's Institute for Christian Teaching and Learning, the, 68

Larsen, Timothy, 170–71
Last Supper, the, 108, 124
Latin American Universities, 20–21
learning, ix–x, 4–5, 8–9, 10, 11–12, 13, 32, 33–34, 37, 38, 45, 46, 56–57, 59, 63, 65, 67, 68–69, 70, 73, 75–76, 77–78, 83–84, 86, 88–89, 91–92, 93*b*, 98*b*, 103, 112–13, 114, 115, 117, 119, 122, 123–24, 129, 134–35, 143–44, 147, 158, 162, 177, 193–94
   goals, objectives, or outcomes, 44, 46, 69, 72, 84, 101, 114, 124, 125, 133, 134–35, 143, 158
lectio divina, 121–22
Lewis, C.S., 171, 181
liberal arts, 160–61
liberal democracy, 1, 137, 194–95, 203
liberal education, 119, 130, 148–49, 158, 160–61, 166
liberal university, 163–64
Liberty University, 192–93
Lindholm, Jennifer, 87, 132–33
Livingston, William, 22
Luther, Martin, 18
Lyotard, Jean Francois, 61–62

MacIntyre, Alasdair, 154, 163–64, 175, 198
Madison, James, 23–24, 198
Marsden, George, xii, 12–13, 24, 27–28, 31, 38, 104, 146, 155–56, 169–70, 174, 177, 196–97
melting pot, metaphor, 25
"mere Christianity," 181
"methodological atheism," 169–70
"methodological secularization," 27–28, 169–70
Moberly, Walter, 30
modeling
   of economics, 81
   of the objective teacher, x–xi, 34
   of the good professor, 3, 9, 20–21, 36, 82, 92, 97*b*, 100–1, 122, 144, 150, 154, 169, 194–95, 199, 200, 202–5
moral
   argument or reasoning, 10, 28–29, 34, 84, 125–26, 141, 144, 149–50, 153–54, 157
   commitments, 6–7, 11, 149, 150, 157, 163
   ends or purposes, 3, 128
   guidance, 130
   imagination, 77, 128, 141
   orientation, 47–48, 74, 90, 121
   principles, 73–74, 145–46
   standards, 4
   tradition, 2, 14, 18, 80, 129, 130, 150, 152, 166
   virtue, 142–43, 146
moralism, as philosophy, 123
motivations, of the teacher, 14, 40, 47, 58, 59, 68–69, 80, 85–86, 90, 106, 108, 115, 130, 133–34, 140, 142, 143, 199
Mouw, Richard, 110–12
Mullen, Lincoln A., 40

narratives
   Christian, 45–46, 88–89, 96–101, 121, 125, 162–63, 178–79, 199
   economic, x, 32–33, 35, 52, 56, 67, 68–69, 75–76, 80–82, 83–84, 112–13, 192–93
   political, 18–19, 113, 131, 136, 137, 202
neutrality, 30, 139
Nobel Peace Prize, 204
nonbeliever, 137
Nord, Warren, 17, 31–32, 80–81, 119, 130–31, 132, 148–49, 152, 157, 161–62, 165–67

objectivity, 31
   "empathetic objectivity," 161
   of the professor, x–xi, 26–28, 158–61, 163–64
online
   degrees, 192
   education, 131–32
oppression, 34, 200
Oral Roberts University, 187, 191
ordination of women, 181

orientation, religious, 47–48, 74, 90, 121
outrageous, ix–x, 12–13, 199, 200–2, 204–5

pacifism, 120, 179–80, 181–83
Palmer, Parker
  Courage to Teach, 8
  divided self, 134, 189, 196, 200
  on academic culture, 30–31
  on identity and selfhood, 9–10, 11, 33–35, 36, 150–51, 159, 161, 199–200
  on the professor as model, 92–94
  on teaching, 14, 33, 134, 138, 145, 150–51, 153–54, 162, 164, 171, 196, 198
  undivided self, 9, 145, 178–79
peace, 17, 45, 72, 135–36, 182, 204
pedagogy
  course content and, 100, 121
  course objectives or outcomes and, 82, 100
  ethics and, 18, 78 79, 82, 89, 93*b*, 122, 145
  fellowship and, 54*b*, 97*b*
  guiding foundation as, 14, 91, 201
  hospitality and, 54*b*, 97*b*
  practices and, 1, 4–5, 6–7, 10, 13–14, 18, 22, 32, 33–34, 37, 46–47, 48, 49, 53, 54*b*, 55–57, 62, 71, 73, 82, 85–93*b*, 88–95, 100, 106, 111–12, 117, 121, 123, 125–26, 129–30, 135, 138, 140, 143, 145, 147, 149–51, 153–56, 158, 167, 169, 172, 178–79, 183, 185, 194, 196–97, 198, 199, 207
  "pauses" as a pedagogical practice, 82
  scripture as a pedagogical practice, 83, 122
  testimony and, 54*b*, 97*b*
  theology and, 203
Penn University, 174–75
Perry, William, 10–11
personal convictions, 14–15, 28–29, 91, 127, 158–59, 162
philosophy of religion course, 138, 139–40, 208
plagiarism, 87, 99–100, 172
Plato, 154

pluralism, 21–25, 104, 130, 137, 150, 176–77, 179, 185, 196–98
Poland, 201
Pope Clement XIV, 19
Pope John Paul II, 199–200
positionality statement, 155–56
Postman, Neil, 128
postmodernism, 15, 31–34, 61, 62, 144–45, 158
power, 12, 18–19, 20, 23, 29, 200
  abuse of, 58, 138, 140, 146, 162–63, 168, 200
  of god, 45, 72, 78, 85*b*, 86, 110–11, 115, 155
  of language, 69
  of the professor, 53, 91–92, 95, 96, 129–30, 139, 144–45, 153–54
prayer, 78, 81, 83–84, 94, 132, 167, 182, 199
Princeton University, 20–21, 22, 37
professional degrees, 193, 208
professional dress, 3
professor
  as mentor, 41–42, 53, 92–94, 148
  as researcher, 28–29
  as scholar, xi, 5, 12–13, 17–18, 19–20, 27, 33–34, 36–37, 38, 42–44, 47, 53–55, 57, 66–67, 68, 71, 78–79, 82–83, 91–92, 105–6, 121, 127, 133, 137, 139–40, 142–43, 148–49, 150–51, 152–53, 155, 157, 159, 165–66, 169, 171, 176–78, 197, 201–2
  as servant, 20, 27, 49, 72, 73, 90, 92, 94–95, 107, 108, 121, 123–24, 169, 197
  Christian transformationist, 62, 63–65, 68, 71–74, 78–79, 83, 84–86, 99–101, 119–24, 125–26, 165–66, 167, 168–69, 202
  spiritual additionist, 62, 63–64, 65, 71, 74, 78–79, 81, 83–84, 100, 119, 125, 165–66, 167
proselytization, 21–22, 139–40
Protestantism, 25, 109
purpose
  of education, x, 36, 130, 136–37, 147, 158, 175, 199–200
  of life, x, 52, 130, 142

qualitative research, 41, 68, 96–99, 101, 104, 155–56, 207
quantitative research, 82–83, 188, 207, 211
Qualtrics, 211

Rawls, John, 1, 137
Regent University, 187
Religion Clause, First Amendment, 138–40
religious orders
   Augustinian, 17–18
   Benedictine, 17–18
   Dominican, 17–18
   Franciscan, 17–18
resistance, 97b, 204
restoration, 44, 121
revelation, 17, 115–16
   general, 125
   special, 46, 116–17, 146
Rice, R. Eugene, 156
Rice University, 89
rituals, 167
rules, 3, 134, 153–54, 162–63, 199–200
   "do not inculcate controversial moral views," 24–25, 144, 146, 147
   general, ix–x, 3, 134–35, 153, 158, 162–63
   "no unwanted identity conversion," 138, 140, 141–42, 144–45, 155, 162, 169, 186–87, 196, 199–200
Rutgers University, 20–21, 22–23

sacraments, 109, 111–13
salvation, 45, 46, 117, 187
same-sex marriage, 181
Savonick, Danica, 167–68
scholarship
   Christian, ix, 12–13, 38, 42–43
   secular, ix, 12–13, 27–28, 127
science, 21–22, 27, 28–29, 30, 35, 44, 45, 47–48, 49–50, 56, 64, 66, 133, 148, 156, 169–70, 177, 179–80, 208
   as profession, 28–29
   as vocation, 28–29
scientist, 24–27, 43–44, 49–50, 56
scripture, 32, 43–44, 46–48, 68–71, 83–84, 108–9, 114–17, 125, 139, 146, 159–62, 167, 170, 189–90, 192, 199, 204–5
Sectarianism, 23, 25
self-disclosure, 156
self-expression, 199–200
selfhood, 9–10, 11, 33–35, 36, 150–51, 159, 161, 199–200
September 11th, 2001, 1
service-learning, 73, 86, 122, 169
Smith, David, 13, 38, 68, 75, 80, 82–83, 88, 93b
Smith, David and Smith, James, K.A., 13, 38, 82–83
social activism, 181–82
social contract (Theory), 137
social justice, 71, 73–74, 78–79, 98–99b, 137, 162–63, 172–73, 174, 182, 192
Sola Scriptura, 109, 116
spirituality, 13, 63, 67, 87, 132–33, 136, 137, 155, 196–97
spiritual additionist professors, 62, 63–64, 65, 71, 74, 78–79, 81, 83–84, 100, 119, 125, 165–66, 167
spiritual practices
   Bible reading, 68–69, 83, 114, 115, 139, 159–61, 162, 167, 185
   communion (or Eucharist), 97b, 98b
   devotional reading, 83, 84, 121–22, 139, 167
   fellowship, 54–55b, 84, 85–86b, 97b
   hospitality, 54b, 67, 68–70, 75–76, 77, 84, 85b, 89, 123, 167, 169
   prayer, 78, 81, 83–84, 94, 132, 167, 182, 199
   testimony, 54b, 97b
St. Joseph's University, 97b
Stackhouse, Jon, 190, 195
Stanford University, 27
stewardship, 47, 51–52, 55–56, 57, 60, 67, 75, 81–82, 83, 95–96, 129–30
students
   academic integrity, 73, 90–91, 156
   as children of God, 53, 55b, 56, 57, 106
   and development or ethical growth, 11, 63, 65, 67, 80, 89, 90–92, 93b, 107, 123–24, 137, 139, 140, 144, 148–49, 150, 153, 169, 199

INDEX 255

as God's gift, 54b, 56, 57, 58, 68, 83,
    91, 98–99b
and God's image, ix–x, 20, 44, 46–47,
    52–53, 54b, 55–56, 57, 59, 65, 67,
    88–89, 90, 91, 99, 106, 107, 128,
    133–34, 142, 143–44, 150–51,
    168, 178, 197, 199
  student life or student affairs,
    189, 196–97
  and moral reasoning, 10, 192
  and participation, 122, 163
  pedagogy, student-focused, 204
  and well-being, 92
Sullivan, Theresa, 128–29
Supreme Court, 139, 140
Sweeney, James, 63

Taylor, Charles, 2, 43
Taylor University, 187, 192
Teacher
  as activist, 7–8, 154–55
  attitude of, 28–29, 40, 45, 48, 53, 89–90,
    92 94, 123, 196
  care of students, 50–51, 53–56, 63, 64–
    65, 67, 72–73, 92, 98b, 145–46,
    147, 149, 197
  definition, 9
  emotions of, 2, 10, 54–55, 89, 122, 160
  ethics of, 5, 14–15, 18, 24, 36, 42, 47, 57,
    64, 67, 72–73, 82, 84, 89, 94–95,
    96–99, 97b, 120, 123, 145, 146,
    153, 159, 162, 164–65, 171, 192
  faith-informed, 196
  integrity, xi–xii, 4–5, 8–9, 11, 73, 87, 92,
    129–30, 134, 138–39, 150–51,
    162, 196, 199–200
  interpretation of, 92, 113–14, 140, 156,
    159, 161–62, 164–65
  language of, 31, 45–47, 55–56, 58, 63,
    69–70, 87, 89, 104, 118, 137,
    150, 171
  as model, 3, 9, 20–21, 36, 82, 92, 97b,
    100–1, 122, 144, 150, 154, 169,
    194–95, 199, 200, 202–5
  motivation of, 14, 40, 47, 58, 59, 68–69,
    80, 85–86, 90, 106, 108, 115, 130,
    133–34, 140, 142, 143, 199,

  as servant, 20, 27, 49, 72, 73, 90, 92,
    94–95, 107, 108, 121, 123–24,
    169, 197
  myth of the "common teacher," 24
  relationship with God, 47, 48–49, 50,
    53, 58, 64, 98–99b, 100, 143–44,
    199–200, 203
  worldview, 31, 40, 43, 46, 52, 61–62,
    64, 65, 66–67, 68, 70, 88–89,
    99, 100–1, 109, 114, 118–19,
    128, 129–30, 131, 139, 148–49,
    161–63, 166–67, 169, 185,
    190, 194–95
teaching
  as calling, 49–50, 51–52, 58, 107, 114,
    124, 133–34, 142–43, 199–200
  as craft, 8, 9, 96
  definition of, 9, 13–14, 36
  ends of, 64, 117, 125, 134
  excellence in, 6–7, 35–36, 38, 48–49
  identity-informed, 16, 131, 143, 172–73,
    174, 175, 184, 195
  as inspiring learning, 33
  intimate approach, 9–10, 32
  methods, 1, 4–5, 6–7, 10, 13–14, 18, 22,
    32, 33–34, 37, 46–47, 48, 49, 53,
    54b, 55–57, 62, 71, 73, 85–93b,
    88–95, 100, 106, 111–12, 117,
    121, 123, 125–26, 129–30, 135,
    138, 140, 143, 145, 147, 149–51,
    153–56, 158, 167, 169, 172, 178–
    79, 183, 185, 194, 196–97, 198,
    199, 207
  as modeling, 3, 9, 20–21, 36, 82, 92, 97b,
    100–1, 122, 144, 150, 154, 169,
    194–95, 199, 200, 202–5
  as sacred responsibility, 48–49
  as worship, 47–48, 49–50, 51–52, 112,
    118, 120, 134
tenure, 190, 193–94, 208
terminological vagueness, 134–35
theological convictions, 91, 107, 159
Thiessen, Elmer, 176–77, 178–79
Tisdell, Elizabeth, 13
Totalitarianism, x, 202–3
Tournament of Narratives and Identities,
    148, 153–54, 198

256 INDEX

tradition
- democratic, 1, 27, 28–29, 112–13, 137, 194–95, 202
- denominational, 107
- disciplinary, xi, 13–14, 18, 27, 30, 35, 42–43, 44, 45, 46, 49, 52, 55–57, 59, 60, 63, 67–68, 74–75, 87, 90–91, 92, 95–96, 109, 112–13, 118, 119, 121–22, 131, 141, 142–43, 144, 145, 148–49, 161, 169, 178–79, 207–8
- ecclesial, 124–25
- feminism, 186–87
- high-church, 110–11
- intellectual, 1–2, 41, 112–13, 118, 125, 144, 148–49, 161, 163, 175, 181–83, 191
- Jesuit, 60, 103, 109, 110–12, 122
- low-church, 115, 117–18
- moral, 2, 14, 18, 80, 129, 130, 150, 152, 166
- Muslim ethics, 164–65
- religious, ix–xii, 12–13, 14, 25, 27–28, 39–40, 57, 67, 105–6, 107, 112–13, 141, 158, 161, 165–67, 171, 175, 178–79, 180, 186–87, 188, 191
  - charismatic, 39, 78, 110–11, 191
  - contemplative, 78
  - evangelical, 78
  - holiness, 78
  - incarnational, 78
  - social justice, 78
- scientific (or empirical), 35
- theological, 39, 40–41, 67, 72–73, 82–83, 86, 87, 101–2, 114, 120, 121–22, 145–46, 171
Trinity, the (or Triune God), 60, 90, 110–12, 114, 181, 197
truth, sources of, 86, 114, 125, 169
trustees or regents, University, 22, 25, 103–4, 183, 187–88

Ukraine, 67, 76
Universities
- ethos of, 92, 115, 182, 186–87, 191
- types of
  - Baptist, 15, 20–21, 25–27, 117, 187–88, 190
  - Catholic, 10–11, 12–13, 15, 18–21, 97*b*, 104, 132, 136, 178–79, 181, 186–87, 191, 200–2
  - church-related, 19, 178
  - denominational (or sectarian), 12, 22, 25–26, 109, 174, 180, 183, 185, 186–89, 190–91, 192, 207–8, 211–12
    - Anglican, 15, 18, 20–21, 22–23, 39, 118, 179–80, 190
    - Anabaptist, 39, 76, 117, 123, 179–80
    - Assemblies of God, 180–81
    - Baptist, 15, 20–21, 25–27, 104, 117, 187–88, 191
    - Calvinist, 18, 93*b*, 121
    - Catholic, 12–13, 17–21, 37, 39, 61, 97*b*, 101, 104, 132, 178–79, 181, 185, 200–2
    - Congregationalist, 20–21
    - Dutch Reformed, 20–21
    - Jesuit, 19, 60, 103, 109, 110–12, 122
    - Lutheran, 18, 20–21, 104, 105–6, 120
    - Methodist, 20–21, 25–27, 103
    - Nazarene, 107
    - Presbyterian, 12–13, 20–21, 22, 26–27, 103, 191
    - Quaker, 15, 20–21, 25–26, 107, 109, 112, 113–14, 115, 123, 125, 181–83
    - reformed, 12–13, 15, 18, 39, 41, 44, 105–6, 109, 110–11, 112–14, 116, 118, 121–22, 125, 178–79, 180
  - ecclesial Christian, 103–4, 178
  - Evangelical, 15, 181–82, 187, 188
  - faith-based, 6, 13, 38–39, 125–26, 131, 176, 177, 178, 188, 189–91
  - female, 131, 175
  - German research, 23–24, 129, 176
  - historically-black colleges and universities, 131, 175

interdenominational, 174, 177, 178, 180–83, 187
Ivy League, 138–39
Jewish, 175, 190–91
liberal, 163–64
male, 131
military, 131
Protestant (mainline), ix–x, 12–13, 18–20, 22–23, 25–27, 101–2, 104, 132, 186–87, 188
pluralistic (or, secular)
  private, 125–26, 129, 137, 138–39, 175, 195
  public, 1, 16, 23–24, 125–26, 129, 131–32, 139, 175, 193
post-liberal, 163, 175, 198
tribal, 131, 175
University of California at Berkeley, 155–56
University of Chicago, 27
University of Lublin, 200–1
University of Michigan, 25–26, 103–4
University of North Carolina, 80
University of Notre Dame, 192
University of Virginia, 23–24, 25–26, 127, 129–30, 150, 198
U.S. News and World Report, 192–93, 195
utilitarian individualism (as philosophy), 80

Vandermeersch, Peter, 19–20
Vatican II, 108
vices, 1–2, 72
violence, 127, 129, 146
  to the self, 162
virtues
  common virtues, 72–73, 91, 145, 165
    care, 55, 63, 64–65, 66, 67, 72–73, 85*b*, 86, 87, 92, 107, 109, 145–46, 147, 149, 169, 197
    dignity, 64–65, 107, 137, 138, 150–51, 168, 199–200, 203
    empathy, 2, 51–52, 67, 92, 145
    fairness, 91–92, 139, 149–50, 157, 158–59, 165
    golden rule, 145, 158
    honesty, 1–2, 64–65, 72–73, 90, 92–94, 96, 142–43, 145, 154, 165, 169

hospitality, 54*b*, 67, 68–70, 75–76, 77, 84, 85*b*, 89, 123, 167, 169
integrity, x–xii, 4, 8, 11, 73, 87, 92, 130, 134, 138, 150–51, 162, 196, 199–200
kindness, 165
patience, 165
respect, 4, 5, 12–13, 16, 21–22, 52, 54*b*, 55–56, 57, 64–65, 67, 72–73, 87, 88–89, 90, 91, 95–96, 99, 107, 122, 129, 137, 138–39, 145–46, 150–51, 155, 156, 157, 159, 169, 171, 176–77, 187–88, 196, 199–200, 202
service to others, 8–9, 30, 71, 72, 73, 86, 89, 107, 122, 135–36, 169, 192, 193
civic virtues, 154
  courage, 4, 11, 94–95, 138, 153–55, 156, 169, 196
  fairness, 91–92, 139, 149–50, 157, 158–59, 165
  integrity, x–xii, 4, 8, 11, 73, 87, 92, 130, 134, 138, 150–51, 162, 196, 199–200
  justice, 1–2, 10, 28, 58, 73, 90, 91–92, 137–39, 154, 157–58, 164–66, 168–73, 197, 199–200, 202–3
  self-control, 154
  service, 8–9, 30, 71, 72, 73, 86, 89, 107, 122, 135–36, 169, 192, 193
  social justice, 71, 73–74, 78–79, 98–99*b*, 137, 162–63, 172–73, 174, 182, 192
intellectual virtues (or academic virtues)
  honesty, 1–2, 64–65, 72–73, 90, 92–94, 96, 142–43, 145, 154, 165, 169
moral virtues, 142–43, 146
personal virtues, 64–65, 94–95
redemptive virtues, 72, 73–74, 91–92, 95, 123, 146, 165
  forgiveness, 50, 53, 67, 72, 90–92, 99–100, 146, 165, 169–70, 197
  grace, 30, 45, 50, 51–52, 58, 63, 67, 72, 90, 91–92, 95, 97*b*

virtues (*cont.*)
    humility, xi–xii, 64–65, 72, 91–92, 94, 95, 116, 124, 146, 150, 156, 165, 169, 197
    imitation of Christ, 72
    justice, 1–2, 10, 28, 58, 73, 90, 91–92, 137–39, 154, 157–58, 164–66, 168–73, 197, 199–200, 202–3
    kindness, xi–xii, 72–73
    love of enemies, 72
    mercy, 52, 53, 90, 91–92, 95, 98*b*, 169, 172, 197
    non-violence, 146
    patience, xi–xii, 41–42, 92, 169
    peace, 17, 45, 72, 135–36, 182, 204
    sacrificial love, 72, 143, 165, 197
    servanthood, 72, 73, 95, 108, 124, 169
    servant leadership, 94–95, 146
    service, 107, 108, 120, 141–42
    stewardship, 47, 51–52, 55–56, 57, 60, 67, 75, 81–82, 83, 95–96, 129–30
  transcendental virtues
    beauty, 147, 148
    goodness, 58, 147, 148
    truth, 51, 73, 91–92, 94–95, 147, 168
vocation, x, 27–28, 30, 32, 58, 74–75, 129, 143, 152

Washington, D.C., 204–5
Washington, George, 23
wars
  Civil War, 26, 187
  Cold War, 62
  Revolutionary War, 25–26
  World War I, 76
  World War II, 76, 201
Weber, Max, 28–36, 128, 134, 144, 158–59
Wellman, Chad, 127, 150
Wesley, John, 116
Wesleyan Quadrilateral, 116
Westminster Shorter Catechism, 47–48
Westmont College, 187
Wheaton College, 187, 192
white nationalism (or supremacy), 128, 129, 150
wisdom
  divine, 20, 125, 203
  human, 53, 116–17
  intellectual, x–xi, 94, 125
  sources of, 114
Wissenschaft, 28
Wojtyla, Karol, 201–2
worldview, 31, 40, 43, 46, 52, 61–62, 64, 65, 66–67, 68, 70, 88–89, 99, 100–1, 109, 114, 118–19, 128, 129–30, 131, 139, 148–49, 161–63, 166–67, 169, 185, 190, 194–95
worship, 47, 48, 49–50, 51–52, 72, 112, 116, 118, 120, 123, 141
Wycliffe, John, 18

Xiaobo, Liu, 199–200

Yale University, 20–21, 37, 129–30
Yongkang, Zhou, 202, 204–5

www.ingramcontent.com/pod-product-compliance
Ingram Content Group UK Ltd.
Pitfield, Milton Keynes, MK11 3LW, UK
UKHW021250180426
11946UKWH00003B/64